Online &
Engaged ▶

NASPA.
Student Affairs Administrators
in Higher Education

Online & Engaged▶

Innovative Student Affairs Practices
for Online Learner Success

STEPHANIE SMITH BUDHAI
AND ASSOCIATES

Foreword by **SUSAN R. KOMIVES**

NASPA.
Student Affairs Administrators
in Higher Education

Published by
NASPA–Student Affairs Administrators in Higher Education
111 K Street, NE
10th Floor
Washington, DC 20002
www.naspa.org

Library of Congress Cataloging-in-Publication Data
(Prepared by The Donohue Group, Inc.)

Names: Budhai, Stephanie Smith, author. | NASPA-Student Affairs
    Administrators in Higher Education, issuing body.
Title: Online and engaged : innovative student affairs practices for online learner
    success / Stephanie Smith Budhai and associates.
Description: First edition. | Washington, DC : NASPA-Student Affairs
    Administrators in Higher Education, [2020] | Includes bibliographical
    references and index.
Identifiers: ISBN 9781948213257 (paperback) | ISBN 9781948213264 (mobi)
    | ISBN 9781948213271 (ePub)
Subjects: LCSH: Student affairs services. | Web-based instruction.
    | Educational innovations. | Education, Higher--Computer-
    assisted instruction--Administration.
Classification: LCC LB2342.9 .B94 2020 (print) | LCC LB2342.9 (ebook) |
    DDC 378.197--dc23

Printed and bound in the United States of America

FIRST EDITION

CONTENTS

SECTION 2
Toward a Paradigm Shift:
Bringing Traditional Student Affairs Online

SECTION 3
Leveraging Ubiquitous Technologies:
Advancing the Work of Student Affairs
Practitioners for Online Learners

FOREWORD

All Students Matter

IN THE EARLY days of the National Clearinghouse for Commuter Programs, I loved that Director Barbara Jacoby had blue buttons made for national conferences and to wear around campus that said, "All Students Matter." Her emphasis was to challenge student affairs to include commuter students in their implicit definitions of students for whom they were responsible through their services and programs. It was a brilliant slogan; it said it all. It still does!

"All Students Matter" challenges our assumptions about the students for whom we design programs, the student needs that get professional attention, and how every group of students deserves to thrive and succeed in postsecondary education. Over the history of higher education, student affairs professionals had to stand back and ponder these questions as they modified, enhanced, or created programs and services for women students, students of color, transfer students, first-generation students, low-income students, LGBTQIA students, and students with disabilities, to name a few. When I was a new professional in the late 1960s and early 1970s at the University of Tennessee, the division of student affairs had programs addressing "displaced homemakers" for adult women who were returning or starting college.

Online learners matter. This population faces challenges in persistence, motivation, sense of belonging, and technological support. This is not a surprise. For over 20 years, student affairs educators know they "should" attend to these students' needs to ensure success, yet "building student support infrastructure for these students is still a nascent field" (Kruger & Jarrat, 2018, para. 4) needing focused attention in every college and university that offers even one distance learning experience. Blogger and technological observer Eric Stoller (2019) has long advocated for student affairs professionals to focus attention on online learners. Baffled the field seems to still act surprised about the numbers of online learners on any given campus, Stoller believes student affairs is clearly past due in accepting responsibility for designing programs and services appropriate for this population of students.

Technology Continually Redefines Modalities for Distance Learning

As evident throughout this book, the history of distance learning in the United States can be traced back to the early 1700s when the advent of postal services meant the technology of letter writing could connect scholars and students (see https://www.worldwidelearn.com/education-articles/history-of-distance-learning.html). Every technological advance—such as typewriters, radio, photo copying, television, film, video, tape recorders, CD players, computers, the Internet, and social media—brought new forms of distance learning that challenged the very notion of "distance" and "learning." Each modality highlighted the changing needs these modalities created for student learners and the educators who engaged them.

Every new technology challenges, even threatens, educators with the imagined impact of that technology. Although I do not remember the source, I was fascinated years ago to read that when the modern public library system was advanced in the late 19th century, commentators forewarned of the demise of free public education; after all, now that every person could get free books from the library, why would schools be needed? Higher education adapted to the technologies of correspondence courses and televised courses, but the advent of the Internet was a sea change. Now with massive open online courses, some commentators even forecast the demise of brick-and-mortar U.S. higher education as we know it ("Are Online Degrees Replacing Brick and Mortar Universities," 2017)!

I saw this change played out vividly at my family dinner table. My son, Jeff, was in ninth grade in 1996 as the World Wide Web opened new avenues for learning. At dinner one night, Jeff described a paper he was writing. He asked his father, Ralph, and me if we knew the gross national product of Costa Rica. Coming from the encyclopedia generation, we would have said, "Look it up." With the Internet as a resource, we thought we were savvy to say, "Go online and find it!" Feeling proud we were advanced parents teaching our son how to use reference tools, I was surprised when he came out of his room fairly quickly and said, "She is going to get back to me." Confused about what he meant, Ralph said, "What do you mean *she* will get back to you?" Jeff replied, "I got onto a teacher help site, and you can post questions and they get you the answers." I said, "Oh no, no, no. You have to go back and find websites about Costa Rica and read them and find the answer yourself!" We all had much to learn. Jeff already knew more about the Web than we did.

All Students Are Online Learners

Distance learners clearly comprise the definition of online learners, but they are not the only ones. It is past time to acknowledge all students are online learners to some degree: they all learn in the digital, cyber environment.

Even those who are physically present in a class in real time are online learners. They seek information from institutional websites, they "Google" assignment topics for resources, they find and download journal articles, they access book chapters through interlibrary loan, they listen to podcasts and watch course-related YouTube videos, they use course management systems like Canvas or Blackboard, and they use online meeting programs like Zoom or Google Hangouts to connect with project teams. Students form friendships online, they form support groups, and they learn.

Attention to good practices in online learning will benefit all students. Read this book with a definition of *online learners* that includes both distance learners and on-campus learners in mind. They will all benefit from your attention to designing meaningful online supports for their learning and development.

Integrated or Separate?

It is not heresy to say "whatever student services are offered for on-campus students should be offered in an equitable fashion for online students" (Westra, 2018, para. 3). The literature on distance learning to guide online student affairs services and programs is growing (see Andrade, 2016; Crawley, 2012), but it appears adaptation of online programs and services lag. The need for this book is critical to any institution's moral obligations to enact the philosophy that all students matter.

This book addresses the needs for online learners and how to ensure their persistence and success. It is critical to do so. After studying 196 institutions with online programs, Blackboard Institute (2011) concluded, "There is growing agreement that student services in predominantly online programs can be as important to student success as course and instructor quality" (p. 6).

At a basic level, colleges and universities should decide if they believe online learners are similar or different from campus-based learners. According to Kumar and Geraci (2011), "Campuses that believe distance and campus-based students have same or similar needs often partner with on-campus services to address distance learners" (p. 9). These partnerships lead to integrated programs and services. "Those that believe distance learners have distinctly different needs typically set up separate distance student services resources" (Kumar & Geraci, 2011, p. 9), often within the division of distance learning. Kumar and Geraci's (2011) study of 12 select institutions found a blended model in which "most institutions integrate administrative services and develop distance-learner specific advising services" (p. 4).

In this book, Stephanie Smith Budhai and the contributing authors explore how student affairs can address the needs of online learners from either an integrated or a separate perspective. Regardless of the model adopted, as Kruger and Jarrat (2018) warned, "Institutions must do more than simply migrate traditional support services online. They must craft new and varied supports that deeply consider the unique challenges of an online education" (para. 13). Kruger and Jarrat (2018) concluded, "Only then can we meet a growing number of students where they are: online" (para. 13). *Because all students matter.*

Susan R. Komives
Professor Emerita
University of Maryland

References

Andrade, M. S. (Ed.). (2016). *Issues in distance education* (New Directions for Higher Education, No. 173). San Francisco, CA: Jossey-Bass.

Are online degrees replacing brick and mortar universities? (2017, September 12). *The Yale Tribune.* Retrieved from https://campuspress.yale.edu/tribune/are-online-degrees-replacing-brick-and-mortar-universities

Blackboard Institute. (2011). *Effective practices snapshot: Student services for online learners* (Higher Education Edition). Retrieved from https://www.blackboard.com/resources/getdocs/536bbc35-3889-4342-acec-ff7b9682ef72_effective-practices-snapshot-student-services-for-online-learners—-higher-ed-edition.pdf

Crawley, A. (2012). *Supporting online students: A practical guide to planning, implementing, and evaluating services.* San Francisco, CA: Jossey-Bass.

Kruger, K., & Jarrat, D. (2018, December 16). Student affairs goes digital: Translating student support to the world of online learning. *Diverse Issues in Higher Education.* Retrieved from https://diverseeducation.com/article/134371

Kumar, P., & Geraci, L. (2011). *Developing services for distance learners.* Washington, DC: The Advisory Board Company.

Stoller, E. (2019, March 28). Online education: The forgotten frontier in student affairs. *Inside Higher Ed.* Retrieved from https://www.insidehighered.com/blogs/student-affairs-and-technology/online-education-forgotten-frontier-studentaffairs

Westra, K. (2018, October 29). Online student services: What, where, who, when, how, and most importantly, why. *EDUCAUSE Review.* Retrieved from https://er.educause.edu/articles/2018/10/online-student-services-what-where-who-when-how-and-most-importantly-why

INTRODUCTION

The Role of Student Affairs in Online Learning:

Challenges, Opportunities, and Next Steps

Stephanie Smith Budhai

NESTLED IN THEORY and carried out astutely with integrative practices, student affairs has led higher education institutions in developing students throughout the entirety of their college experience. Only two decades into the 21st century, the overall landscape of higher education is undergoing a considerable shift in organizational structure, dynamics, and where and how students learn. According to Allen and Seaman (2017), "29.7% of all students are taking at least one distance course" (p. 3), with total distance enrollments "composed of 14.3% of students (2,902,756) taking exclusively distance courses and 15.4% (3,119,349) who are taking a combination of distance and non-distance courses" (p. 3). Additionally, "the vast majority (4,999,112, or 83.0%) of distance students are studying at the undergraduate level" (Allen & Seaman, 2017, p. 3), a level where students typically are supported through key functional areas within student affairs, including, but limited to, new student orientation, advising, multicultural affairs, wellness and mental health services, leadership development, and student activities.

Student affairs must remain at the helm of all things related to college student development and their college experience and cannot be left behind when it comes to supporting all student groups. The history of student affairs is long, and "the beginning of the student affairs field might best be dated to the hiring of administrators who were primarily responsible for the welfare and behavior of students" (Hevel, 2016, p. 857). In the age of distance learning, the question begs, Who is concerned with the health, happiness, and prosperity of online learners? Student affairs practitioners have an opportunity to shape student services within online learning paradigms and can address adherent challenges to doing so to ensure all students in the future flourish and grow as they earn a postsecondary degree, regardless of where they take their courses.

Challenges

While online learning is not new to higher education, developing student affairs supports for online learners can be described as fledgling (Kruger & Jarrat, 2018). There is a clear understanding on-campus students receive "physical and tangible services such as admissions, registrar, accounts payable or receivable, and financial aid offices; library and resource buildings; housing; technology labs;

student union facilities; and the health care center" (Conceicao & Lehman, 2016, p. 438), albeit "many of these services can be accomplished online and serve both face-to-face and online students" (p. 438). As we think of how to provide similar services to online learners, one challenge is the limitations to services requiring physical spaces that will require student affairs to think and reframe how to provide flexible services in a dynamic environment and across multiple time zones and schedules (Conceicao & Lehman, 2016), acknowledging online learners have different needs than traditional on-campus students (MacDonald, 2018).

Another challenge in solidifying the role of student affairs in online learning surrounds academic training programs preparing practitioners for the field of student affairs. Most college student personnel and student affairs graduate programs are taught in a traditional on-campus format. In 2011, a study by Connolly and Diepenbrock (2011) indicated "many mid-level professionals in student affairs are not ready to accept online education as a method for preparing new professionals for the field" (p. 89). There are now several online graduate programs training student affairs practitioners, but the content in which graduate students are being trained is focused on services and supports for on-campus student populations. Moreover, "in terms of content focus, usage, and candidate ability, the delivery of services to online students is not yet seen as an integral component of student affairs preparation programs" (Calhoun, Green, & Burke, 2017, p. 58). Student affairs professionals must find a way to shift their practice to support online learners, an area in which they are not usually trained.

In thinking about these challenges, as we also are preparing students for jobs that do not currently exist, traditional functional areas or positions for student affairs professionals seeking to work specifically with online learners, but not in an academic role (i.e., retention, advising, academic success coaching), are not prevalent. Student engagement and leadership development are often robustly integrated in student unions and activities centers. The creation of positions, such as Coordinator for Online Student Community Engagement and Programming or Online Student Leadership Development Specialist, would precipitate the creation of required roles and responsibilities for student affairs professionals charged with intentionally providing supports to online learners, and the occurrence of similar positions would become more pervasive throughout institutions of higher education.

Opportunities

Identifying, researching, and creating supports for diverse populations of students is the crux of student affairs work (Hevel, 2016). Students who identify as LGBTQIA, women, racial and ethnic minorities, students with disabilities, and commuter students are among the student groups that have all found units, offices, and divisions dedicated to their college experience and success. By focusing on online learners, student affairs practitioners have the opportunity to support different sets of student groups, thus expanding the overarching mission of student services and helping more students grow, learn, and develop throughout their college experience.

While online learners are a student group within themselves, they often have other identities typically lumped within the nontraditional student (MacDonald, 2018) category. These student groups include those who are parents; married; living in rural community areas (Austin, 2010) with limited access to physical infrastructure and immediate resources; first-generation college students (Garza & Fullerton, 2018), whose parents did not obtain a postsecondary degree; and employed while attending college. Student affairs practitioners have always been innovative leaders, moving the field forward, staying abreast of trends and movements, and developing contemporary ways to meet students where they are. This area, online learners, is one to move forward.

Meeting students where they are means bringing student services and supports to online learners by creating innovative ways to carry out traditional student affairs functions. This process has seemed to start with academic student services more posthaste than student activities, for example. Research has been conducted on the needs of supporting online learners though library services (Skarl & Del Bosque, 2019), and, given the electronic nature of online journals and research databases, the transition may be more seamless than in other functional areas.

In the area of mental health and wellness, there are telehealth services (Center for Connected Health Policy, 2019) that can be provided to online learners. Instead of physically visiting a student health center, students can use online video technology to show health professionals areas of concern or speak over the phone to describe pain. For online learners who need counseling services, the same type of technology services can be used to talk through issues. Within career services, mock interviews and résumé critiques can be conducted via video conferencing. For multicultural affairs, social media technology has had an impact on exploring racial identity in online spaces (Chan, 2017). A synchronous virtual student orientation can be created where new students "meet" others and engage in discourse. Shared governance through student government and student organizations would be welcomed by online learners seeking to have a voice and participate in a shared community. Having a representative for online learners as a position on student government would be a start. An institution can mail swag to new students and even have a lunch delivered to each student's home during orientation. The future of student affairs is providing needed student support services to online learners, and this is already beginning to happen on campuses across the United States.

Next Steps

Regardless of the student group, the mission of student affairs work remains unchanged and is guided by professional associations:

Student affairs has a diverse and complicated set of responsibilities. As a partner in the educational enterprise, student affairs enhances and supports the academic mission. In addition student affairs professionals must advocate for the common good and champion the right of the individual; encourage intelligent risk taking and set limits on behavior; encourage independent thought and teach interdependent behavior. The extent to which colleges are successful in creating climates in which these paradoxical goals can coexist will be reflected in how well students are able to recognize and deal with such dilemmas during and after college. (National Association of Student Personnel Administrators, 1989, p. 19)

If "student affairs professionals aim to reach students where they are" (Junco, 2014, p. 1) and remain true to the overarching purpose and mission of student affairs, the online learner must become a critical focus area. It is well established "distance education is not a new phenomenon, and it is quickly becoming a standard method for delivering educational content at higher education institutions" (Skarl & Del Bosque, 2019, p. 169); therefore, the next step for student affairs practitioners is to provide a body of work to guide the role of student affairs in online learning.

Organized in three sections, this book is comprised of chapters from student affairs professionals across the United States in different functional areas who share best practices, case studies, examples, experiences, and strategies for supporting online learners through their college experience. To provide accessible nuggets of information throughout the book readers can immediately use, technology and innovative tools are highlighted in each chapter, as well as cutting edge technology and innovative practices, websites, and mobile apps student affairs practitioners can explore and use to support their work with online learners, along with how and why to use them. This book is research informed but practical, and tips for getting started and taking the first step are provided in each chapter on logical and immediate actions student affairs practitioners can take to prepare and provide online learners with student support services. Change can be difficult, and there are always roadblocks student affairs practitioners face, especially when moving forward with online student services. In each chapter, the authors identify potential challenges and provide practical solutions to help ameliorate those challenges. Finally, reflection questions are provided in each chapter to help readers think more about their current role and how they can use the information in this book to move forward in supporting online learners.

The first section of the book is focused on preparing for the ever-changing higher education landscape and situating student affairs in the 21st century. The authors address how to support learners taking hybrid and fully online courses within virtual learning environments and how to educate and support 21st-century students. The section also includes general conceptual chapters about student affairs and supports in a technology and media-driven world. The following questions are addressed in Section 1:

- What is the role of student affairs in supporting 21st-century students who learn online in a technology and media-driven world?
- What student development frameworks speak best to understanding how online learners grow and develop in college?
- What are some of the challenges student affairs practitioners face when supporting online learners, and what are some ways to ameliorate those challenges?
- How can student affairs practitioners provide services to students in virtual learning environments?

The second section focuses on the paradigm shift needed to bring traditional student affairs work to the online environment. The authors aim to address how individual functional areas within student affairs (e.g., student engagement, student activities, mental health/wellness, advising, multicultural affairs, career services, new student orientation) provide or can provide services and supports to students who take their courses 100% online and to traditional on-campus students who take online courses. Authentic case study examples are provided that demonstrate how the work of student affairs practitioners in online environments can extend beyond transactional relationships. The following questions are addressed in Section 2:

- How can services offered in functional areas within student affairs be offered to online learners?
- How have or can college student personnel programs prepare practitioners for supporting all types of students, particularly online learners?
- What are unique programs and supports student affairs units and higher education institutions have put into place to support online learners?

The third and final section is focused on leveraging technology to advance the work of student affairs for online learners. The authors detail how different technology tools—including learning management systems, virtual conferencing tools, online integrative cocurricular programming, digital badging, and virtual learning communities—have been used in student affairs to support and motivate students by serving as a tool for student engagement and an alternative for face-to-face contact. The following questions are addressed in Section 3:

- How have technology tools been used to connect online learners to the on-campus community, resources, and supports?
- What specific technology tools can be leveraged to support student affairs practitioners in their work?

- What is the potential of virtual learning communities in student engagement efforts?

This work is fertile, interactive, and invigorating. Together, student affairs professionals of all levels can enter the world of distance learning, bringing students closer together and connected to the institutions at which they are earning a college degree. I hope you enjoy the book and find value in it to support your current and future work with online learners.

References

Allen, I. E., & Seaman, J. (2017). *Digital learning compass: Distance education enrollment report 2017.* Babson Survey Research Group, e-Literate, and WCET. Retrieved from https://onlinelearningsurvey.com/reports/digtiallearningcompassenrollment2017.pdf

Austin, G. A. (2010). Administrative challenges and rewards of online learning in a rural community college: Reflections of a distance learning administrator. In R. L. Garza Mitchell (Ed.), *Online education* (New Directions for Community Colleges, No. 150, pp. 27–36). doi:10.1002/cc.402

Calhoun, D. W., Green, L. S., & Burke, P. (2017). Online learners and technology: A gap in higher education and student affairs preparation. *Quarterly Review of Distance Education, 18,* 45–61. Retrieved from https://www.infoagepub.com/quarterly-review-of-distance-education.html

Center for Connected Health Policy. (2019). *About telehealth.* Retrieved from https://www.cchpca.org/about/about-telehealth

Chan, J. (2017). Racial identity in online spaces: Social media's impact on students of color. *Journal of Student Affairs Research and Practice, 54,* 163–174. doi:10.1080/19496591.2017.1284672

Conceicao, S. C. O., & Lehman, R. M. (2016). Students' perceptions about online student supports: Institutional, instructional, and self-care implications. *International Journal on E-Learning, 15,* 433–443. Retrieved from http://www.learntechlib.org/p/130344

Connolly, S., & Diepenbrock, A. (2011). Perspectives of online graduate preparation programs for student affairs professionals. *American Journal of Distance Education, 25,* 79–90. doi:10.1080/08923647.2011.566441

Garza, A. N., & Fullerton, A. S. (2018). Staying close or going away: How distance to college impacts the educational attainment and academic performance of first-generation college students. *Sociological Perspectives, 61,* 164–185. doi:10.1177/0731121417711413

Hevel, M. S. (2016). Toward a history of student affairs: A synthesis of research, 1996-2015. *Journal of College Student Development, 57,* 844–862. doi:10.1353/csd.2016.0082

Junco, R. (2014). *Engaging students through social media.* San Francisco, CA: Jossey-Bass

Kruger, K., & Jarrat, D. (2018). Student affairs goes digital: Translating student support to the world of online learning. *Diverse Higher Education.* Retrieved from https://diverseeducation.com/article/134371

MacDonald, K. (2018). A review of the literature: The needs of nontraditional students in postsecondary education. *Strategic Enrollment Management Quarterly, 5,* 159–164. doi:10.1002/sem3.20115

National Association of Student Personnel Administrators. (1989). *Points of view.* Washington, DC: Author.

Skarl, S., & Del Bosque, D. (2019). Going the distance for grads: What online graduate students want from the library. *Journal of Library & Information Services in Distance Learning, 13,* 167–183. doi:10.1080/1533290X.2018.1499250

SECTION 1

Preparing for the Everchanging Landscape:

Student Affairs in the 21st Century

CHAPTER 1

Student Development Theory and Online Learners

Deborah J. Taub

OVER THE PAST 14 years, enrollment in distance education has increased each year (Seaman, Allen, & Seaman, 2018). Over 6 million students (31.6%) are taking at least one distance course, with a little over 3 million (14.9%) taking distance courses exclusively (Seaman et al., 2018). With the increasing number of students in higher education choosing to take courses online, there have been more calls for student affairs to serve and support online learners (Dungy & Gordon, 2011; Kruger & Jarrat, 2018). Most of the existing literature on supporting online learners is focused on online instruction with little focus on "non-academic supports" (Kruger & Jarrat, 2018, para. 3). Despite the growth of online learning, "In terms of content focus, usage, and candidate ability, the delivery of services to online students is not yet seen as an integral component" (Calhoun, Greene, & Burke, 2017, p. 58) of the graduate preparation curriculum. Student development theory, viewed as an integral component of graduate preparation and a foundation for sound student affairs practice, can be used by student affairs educators to support online learners.

It is helpful to think of theories as tools. Some tools have broad applications, whereas others have very specialized applications. The nature of the task determines which tool or tools are used. No one tool will do every job. And, in our daily lives, we have favorite tools—tools we reach for all the time—and tools we do not ever seem to use but keep in our toolbox, just in case. Student development theories are similar. Some are general and some are more specific. Some will be favorites, and others will not be. But, no one theory will be enough to guide our practice in every situation or with every student.

Student affairs practice and college student development theory have a reciprocal relationship. Often, theory arises in response to a problem or a question raised in practice. For example, Perry (1981) described his theory of cognitive development in college as arising from practice, both in evaluations of his teaching and in the counseling/advising sessions he and his colleagues in the Harvard Bureau of Study Counsel had with students (Perry, 1968). In describing student feedback on one of his courses, Perry (1981) noted students found it both excellent and very bad:

> What can you do with such unaverageable judgements [*sic*] as "This course has changed my whole outlook on education *and life!* Superbly taught! Should be required of all students!" and "This course is falsely advertised and dishonest. You have cheated me of my tuition!" (pp. 76–77)

Similarly, Perry (1968) encountered "the variety of the ways in which students responded to the relativism which permeates the intellectual and social atmosphere of a pluralistic university" (pp. 3–4). These types of observations gave rise to research that ultimately resulted in the Perry scheme, which describes the movement in students' thinking from a dualistic viewpoint to a contextual one.

What we learn from practice has the potential to help us modify how we apply theories to a particular population of students—in this case, online learners. Just as carpenters, plumbers, and others in construction modify their tools to adapt to the job or increase their utility (Wetzel, Haynes, & Holley, 2017), so too can student affairs professionals adapt theories in response to student populations or campus contexts.

Figure 1.1. The Reciprocal Nature of Practice and Theory

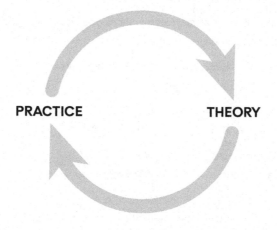

PRACTICE   **THEORY**

Knefelkamp, Golec, and Wells (1985) presented an 11-step model for using theory in student affairs practice—the practice-to-theory-to-practice (PTP) model—which reflects the reciprocity of practice and theory (see Figure 1.1). Student affairs professionals can use the PTP model to practice identifying what concerns or problems of practice need to be addressed. The steps that follow include identifying theories that might be helpful in a particular application, intervention design, implementation, evaluation, and redesign of the intervention, if necessary (see Evans, Forney, Guido, Patton, and Renn [2010] for a helpful description of the model steps).

This chapter presents four theories (or a combination of theories) that can be helpful tools for student affairs professionals working to support online learners. The theories were chosen from many possibilities, either because they address a particular need (e.g., isolation, engagement) or because they are particularly well suited to essential functions in student affairs for online learners.

 Technology and Innovative Tools

These websites and videos are helpful resources for learning more about student development theory:

- **Student Development Theory Resource Guide**
  Association of Fraternity/Sorority Advisors
  https://issuu.com/cliffalexanderoffice/docs/afa_student_development_theory_reso

- **Research on Social Media in Higher Education**
  Josie Ahlquist
  http://www.josieahlquist.com/2013/11/11/socialmediareferences

- **Student Development in College**
  Higher Ed Live
  http://www.youtube.com/watch?v=mocXz-tEQ4M

- **Why Does it Take So Long to Grow Up Today?**
  Jeffrey Jensen Arnett (TEDxPSU)
  http://www.youtube.com/watch?v=fv8KpQY0m6o

- **High-Impact Practices and Student Engagement**
  George Kuh
  http://www.youtube.com/watch?v=4i9xHt5erAc

- **Inalienable Rights: Life, Liberty, and the Pursuit of Belonging**
  Terrell Strayhorn (TEDxColumbus)
  https://www.youtube.com/watch?v=Ak6T9kw0H28

- **Transitions Through Life**
  Nancy Schlossberg, L. Lee Knefelkamp, and Victoria Marsick
  https://www.youtube.com/watch?v=F3WyAnCuxAY

Transition Theory

In Schlossberg's (1981) transition theory, a transition is "any event or nonevent that results in changed relationships, routines, assumptions, and roles" (Anderson, Goodman, & Schlossberg, 2012, p. 39). At the heart of transition theory is the four Ss, an inventory of assets and liabilities that affect a person's ability to cope successfully with transition (Anderson et al., 2012). The four Ss include: (a) situation, (b) self, (c) support, and (d) strategies.

Situation refers to aspects of the transition itself. This S comprises factors including trigger (what precipitated the transition), timing (is the transition "on" time or "off" time and at a "good" time or a "bad" time), control, role change (and whether it is the loss of a role or the gain of a role, such as adding the role of student), duration, previous experience with a similar transition, concurrent stress, and assessment (how the individual in transition views the situation; Anderson et al., 2012). Each of these factors may be an asset or a liability to the person in transition.

Self refers to characteristics about the person in transition. There are two categories of factors related to self. The first is personal and demographic characteristics, which include socioeconomic status, gender, age, race/ethnicity, life stage, and health. The second category is psychological resources, which include aspects of personality, such as outlook (optimism and self-efficacy), ego development, values, spirituality/commitment, and resiliency. Again, each of these can function as an asset or a liability in coping with the transition. Choosing to complete a postsecondary degree online can be such a transition.

Support refers to social support. Types of social support are identified as family, friends, intimate relationships, and organizations/communities. Social support takes a number of forms, and the functions of support are aid, affect, affirmation, and honest feedback. Schlossberg (1981) drew upon the work of Kahn (1975), who conceptualized a "convoy" (p. 1) of social support. The quality and quantity of social support factor into the assessment of how well a person will cope with the transition at hand. Regardless of the type of environment in which a student takes courses, functions of support, such as aid, affect, affirmation, and honest feedback (Anderson et al., 2012), are needed for the student to cope successfully with the transition.

Strategies refers to what people do to try to cope with the transition. Coping responses include those that modify the situation, control the meaning of the situation, and help the person manage stress in the aftermath. There are four modes of coping: (a) information seeking, (b) direct action, (c) inhibition of action, and (d) intrapsychic behavior (e.g., mindsets; Anderson et al., 2012). Those who use multiple strategies are likely to cope most effectively with transition, and student affairs professionals can assist online learners with developing strategies.

Many online learners are in the midst of transition, experiencing changes in "relationships, routines, assumptions, and roles" (Anderson et al., 2012, p. 39). That transition may be from high school to college, from face-to-face to online learning, from working to being a student, or even from working to working and being a student. The greater the changes in those relationships, routines, assumptions, and roles, the more challenging the transition is likely to be. Some students may have more assets than liabilities in their four Ss, and those students may cope more easily with the transition than those who have more liabilities.

There is little student affairs professionals can do related to the first two Ss—situation and self. The elements of the situation and the characteristics of self are things the learner brings with them. However, student affairs professionals can help students with the other two Ss—support and strategies. Student affairs professionals serve as supports to students in their various professional roles and can direct students to other sources of support on and off campus.

They also can advocate for services traditionally housed on campus to be available in alternative formats to support online learners specifically. In addition, student affairs professionals can coach students on coping strategies they may have not considered or tried. With transition theory as a tool, we are guided to examine more and better ways to support and teach strategies to online learners.

As a counseling-based theory, transition theory may be particularly well suited to guide practice in certain areas where we work with students one on one. For example, academic advising, counseling, and career development are three areas where transition theory could be especially helpful. Transition theory is also helpful to specific functions (e.g., orientation) focused on students in transition.

Marginality and Mattering / Sense of Belonging

Schlossberg (1989) noted people in transition often experience feelings of marginality. Marginality is the sense one does not fit in or belong, which is how online learners can feel in terms of their sense of connection to the larger university. Schlossberg observed the larger the difference is between one's role pre- and post-transition, the more marginal one is likely to feel.

The opposite of marginality is mattering. The concept of mattering was introduced by Rosenberg and McCullough (1981), who described it as "the individual's feeling that he or she counts, makes a difference" (p. 163). They identified four dimensions of mattering— attention, importance, ego extension, and dependence—to which Schlossberg (1989) added a fifth: appreciation. Attention is the sense one feels noticed rather than invisible. Importance is the sense someone "cares about what we want, think, and do, or is concerned with our fate" (Rosenberg & McCullough, 1981, p. 164). Ego extension is the feeling someone else will be proud of one's accomplishments and will sympathize with one's failures. Dependence is the sense of being needed by someone else. Appreciation, the dimension added by Schlossberg based on her research, is the feeling one's efforts are appreciated.

Hart (2018) explored the relationship between online learners' use of student support services and their feelings of mattering. Approximately two thirds of online learners who participated in the study indicated they did not feel they mattered to the institution. Hart found mattering to be correlated positively with the use of certain student support services. Hart (2018) observed the services correlated with mattering were relationship based, "suggesting that relationships formed between the student and staff or faculty contribute to students' feelings of mattering" (p. 129). Hart found online learner respondents felt they mattered when campus professionals communicated care and concern, were responsive, and offered personal attention. Interestingly, Hart also found online learners who participated in the study did not distinguish between support services and instructional services, viewing their experience in a more holistic way.

Because feeling isolated has been identified as a challenge faced by online learners (Kruger & Jarrat, 2018), marginality and mattering hold particular promise as a theoretical tool for supporting online learners. Focusing on the dimensions of mattering—attention, importance, ego extension, dependence, and appreciation—can guide student affairs professionals on specific ways they can help online learners feel they matter. In providing services to online learners, such as academic advising, career counseling, and orientation, student affairs professionals should focus on communicating to students they are noticed, important, and appreciated; we care about their successes and their challenges; and we appreciate their efforts.

The tool of marginality and mattering can also be used as a guide for considering the importance of the degree of role change the online learner is experiencing. The greater the difference between roles pre- and post-transition, the more likely a student is to feel marginal. In addition, Schlossberg (1989) pointed to the important role rituals can play in minimizing students' feelings of marginalization. Rituals can bring students into their new roles and new places. As a theoretical tool, marginality and mattering prompts those working with online learners to consider and create rituals to bring online learners into the community as things like Welcome Week do for on-campus students.

Mattering has been found to be closely related to sense of belonging (Cole, Newman, Park, & Hypolite, 2018). According to Strayhorn (2019):

> In terms of college, sense of belonging refers to students' perceived social support on campus, a feeling or sensation of connectedness, and the experience of mattering or feeling cared about, accepted, respected, valued by, and important to the group (e.g., campus community) or others on campus (e.g., faculty, peers). (p. 28)

Strayhorn (2019) described the relationship between mattering and sense of belonging: "Sense of belonging is related to, and seemingly a consequence of, mattering" (p. 36); and mattering "turns our attention to the relational aspects of belonging" (p. 36). Sense of belonging can change as a student's "circumstances, conditions, and contexts change" (Strayhorn, 2019, p. 39). As Strayhorn (2019) observed, "Just because a student feels a sense of belonging today doesn't mean that they'll feel it tomorrow" (p. 39).

There is considerable literature on how instructors can create a sense of belonging for online learners in their classes. Examining the techniques online instructors use can inform how student affairs professionals can create a sense of belonging beyond the classroom.

Tips for Getting Started

Creating a sense of belonging for online learners can be particularly challenging. Take a cue from the literature on mattering. Consider steps that can be taken to help online learners:

* Feel NOTICED
* Feel CARED ABOUT
* Feel someone will be PROUD of their successes
* Feel they are NEEDED
* Feel APPRECIATED

These are important first steps in helping online learners feel a sense of belonging to the institution. Remember, relationships play a vital role in helping online learners feel they matter.

Involvement Theory and Engagement

Astin's (1984) involvement theory is frequently misinterpreted as referring to student involvement on campus in activities and organizations specifically. In fact, Astin (1984) defined *student involvement* as "the quantity and quality of the physical and psychological energy that students invest in the college experience" (p. 307). Involvement is closely related to time on task. As Astin (1984) noted, involvement theory focuses on students' behavior: "It is not so much what the individual thinks or feels, but what the individual does, how he or she behaves, that defines and identifies involvement. . . . The theory of student involvement is more concerned with the behavioral mechanisms or processes that facilitate student development" (pp. 298–301). Astin (1984) focused not only on individual growth and development but also on factors that facilitate development (Patton, Renn, Guido, & Quaye, 2016). Astin (1984) presented five postulates of involvement theory:

1. "Involvement refers to the investment of physical and psychological energy in various objects. The objects may be highly generalized (the student experience) or highly specific (preparing for a chemistry examination" (p. 298).

2. "Involvement occurs along a continuum" (p. 298). A particular student may be more or less involved in a variety of what Astin calls "objects" at various times. Different students may be more or less involved with the same object.

3. Involvement "has both quantitative and qualitative features" (p. 298). The quantitative aspect of involvement would be time on task; the qualitative aspect would be the depth of attention given to the object.

4. "The amount of student learning and personal development associated with any educational program is directly proportional to the quality and quantity of student involvement in that program" (p. 298). The greater the investment, the greater the gain.

5. "The effectiveness of any educational policy or practice is directly related to the capacity of that policy or practice to increase student involvement" (p. 298).

In short, the more students are involved—both quantitatively and qualitatively—the more they will gain in learning and development. The effectiveness of a program or policy can be gauged by how well student involvement increases as a result. The challenge to student development educators then is to find ways to increase students' involvement with all aspects of the college experience. Astin (1984) identified the challenge in that as finding "a 'hook' that will stimulate students to get more involved in the college experience" (p. 305). Even if student affairs professionals have made tremendous strides in encouraging students to get involved in campus life, the challenge remains to create similar efforts for online learners.

More recently, the student affairs and higher education literature has focused on the related concept of engagement. Kuh (2009) defined engagement as "the time and effort that students devote to activities that are empirically linked to desired outcomes of college *and* what institutions do to induce students to participate in these activities" (p. 683). Thus, the concept of engagement encompasses both the role and actions of students and of institutions of higher education. In an interview described by Wolf-Wendel, Ward, and Kinzie (2009), Kuh distinguished engagement from involvement: "Engagement differs from involvement in that it links more directly to desired educational processes and outcomes and emphasizes action that the institution can take to increase student engagement" (p. 414). Wolf-Wendel et al. (2009) provided a very good comparison of the terms, derived from interviews with Astin, Kuh, and Tinto.

Using the theoretical tools of involvement and engagement, we ask: How can we increase online learners' involvement and engagement? What are the "hook[s]" (Astin, 1984, p. 527) we might use to encourage students to get more involved in their college experience? Involvement theory reminds us involvement goes beyond joining a club and is, in fact, the investment of time and energy in the college experience. The more recent research on engagement directs our focus to both students and institutional practices. Appreciative inquiry (AI; Cooperrider, Stavros, & Whitney, 2008) can be used to focus on what the institution is doing well already to engage online learners. Successes can then be used to inform new strategies.

Limitations of Theoretical Tools

Student development theories can be extremely valuable tools. Theories also have limitations. This section outlines just a few limitations that are particularly relevant.

No Universal Theoretical Tool

There is no universal, one-size-fits-all theory. As with tools, student development theories have specific applications. Psychosocial theories, such as the theories of Chickering and Reisser (1993) and Arnett (2000), are focused on the content—the "what"—of development. Cognitive structural theories, such as those of Perry (1968) and

Kohlberg (1969), focus on "how" students are thinking, reasoning, and making decisions. Social identity theories, such as Cross and Fhagen-Smith's (2001) model of African American identity development, D'Augelli's (1994) model of LGB identity development, and Gibson's (2006) disability identity model, are focused on how one develops an understanding of their fit into social identity groups. It is as if each theory family is a different lens; as we change lenses, what was focused on becomes background and what was background now becomes the focus. It is necessary to pick the theoretical tool or tools best suited to the given application or population.

Theory is Generalization

The nature of theory is to generalize. However, individuals are complex. As Evans et al. (2010) observed, "While theories attempt to describe universal phenomena, students are unique individuals" (p. 37). Theories take the particulars of individuals' development and make general and generalizable statements about development. Therefore, a theory cannot be used to describe or account for the nuances of each student. Student affairs professionals need to keep individual differences of students in mind when using theory to inform practice (Patton et al., 2016).

The Student Body Changes

It is important to consider the empirical research that substantiated the development of a theory and the population that was studied at that time. For example, Chickering's (1969) theory was based on students at small colleges. Perry's (1968) theory was based on students at Harvard and Radcliffe but relied substantially on data from male Harvard students. Schlossberg's (1981) transition theory originated from her work in career development with adults outside of higher education. In each case, it is critical to understand the similarities or differences between the individuals whose experiences informed the development of the theory and students with whom we are working now. Think about how dramatically the college student population has changed since 1968. Then, ask what subsequent empirical research says about the applicability of the theory to those who were not represented in the original sample. What modifications to the use of the theory are suggested by this exploration? Patton et al. (2016) noted Perry's theory "is more than twice as old as today's youngest traditionally aged college students, yet it remains relevant when assessing contemporary students' ability to think" (p. 330).

Potential Challenges and Practical Solutions

It sometimes can be difficult to translate theory into practice. Translating student development theory into practice with online learners can be even more challenging, as most theories were developed based on populations of face-to-face learners. Following are some challenges one might encounter:

Potential Challenge: It is likely some individuals who support and serve online learners will be unfamiliar with student development theory. They may not understand the jargon associated with student development theory, which could potentially create resistance.

Practical Solution: When talking with stakeholders who are not familiar with theory, strive to substitute common language for jargon. This can help to facilitate understanding and buy-in.

Potential Challenge: The online learner population is diverse and is often different from one institution to another.

Practical Solution: Assess online learners at your institution to discover who they are and what they need. This can guide you as you think about applicable theories.

Using Theories in Combination

As Evans et al. (2010) observed, "Rarely . . . is an issue in student affairs so straightforward that one theory will adequately explain it or provide sufficient guidance to address it" (p. 349). This is why we need more than one tool in our toolbox. Supporting online learners is a complex challenge, particularly because online learners are a diverse population. Just as we might need a hammer, a screwdriver, and a level to build a bookcase, so too might we need to bring together two or more theories to design approaches to better support online learners at our institutions. In many cases, combining theories can help us address gaps in individual theories. This is very similar to how mental health counselors blend two or more counseling theories in their work with clients.

Conclusion

Student development theory serves as a tool student affairs professionals can use to understand students better and guide practice. This chapter presented theories that hold promise for guiding practice in supporting online learners; undoubtedly, there are also other helpful theories. Useful conceptual connections or overlaps exist between many theories. However, we also can employ disparate theories to the various parts of our approach as appropriate to diverse students and situations. Using theories thoughtfully, with their limitations in mind, and in combination when needed can lead to stronger programs and interventions for students. As the literature on college students expands, the number and diversity of models and theories will increase as well. As this happens, we may find new tools to add to our toolbox.

Questions for Reflection

- Which of the theories presented in this chapter do you think you will add to your professional toolbox? Why?

- According to Schlossberg (1989), rituals play an important role in helping to decrease feelings of marginalization for students in transition. What are some rituals you could create for online learners?

- What ways can your institution foster engagement for online learners? What might be effective "hooks" to encourage involvement?

- How does your institution currently support online learners at various stages of their transition? What new, additional approaches are suggested by this chapter?

References

Anderson, M. L., Goodman, J., & Schlossberg, N. K. (2012). *Counseling adults in transition: Linking Schlossberg's theory with practice in a diverse world* (4th ed.). New York, NY: Springer.

Arnett, J. J. (2000). Emerging adulthood: A theory of development from the late teens through the twenties. *American Psychologist, 55*, 569–480. doi:10.1037/0003-066X.55.5.469

Astin, A. A. (1984). Student involvement: A developmental theory for higher education. *Journal of College Student Development, 40*, 518–529.

Calhoun, D. W., Green, L. S., & Burke, P. (2017). Online learners and technology: A gap in higher education and student affairs professional preparation. *Quarterly Review of Distance Education, 18*, 45–61.

Chickering, A. W. (1969). *Education and identity.* San Francisco, CA: Jossey-Bass.

Chickering, A. W., & Reisser, L. K. (1993). *Education and identity* (2nd ed.). San Francisco, CA: Jossey-Bass.

Cole, D., Newman, C., Park, E., & Hypolite, L. (2018). *Learning communities, mattering, and sense of belonging: Structural equation modeling from Year 1 of a longitudinal study.* Paper presented at the annual meeting of the American Educational Research Association, New York, NY.

Cooperrider, D. L., Stavros, J. M., & Whitney, D. K. (2008). *The appreciative inquiry handbook: For leaders of change* (2nd ed.). Brunswick, OH: Berrett-Koehler.

Cross, W. E., Jr., & Fhagen-Smith, P. (2001). Patterns in African American identity development: A life span perspective. In C. L. Wijeyesinghe & B. W. Jackson, III (Eds.), *New perspectives on racial identity development: A theoretical and practical anthology* (pp. 243–270). New York, NY: New York University Press.

D'Augelli, A. R. (1994). Identity development and sexual orientation: Toward a model of lesbian, gay, and bisexual identity development. In E. J. Trickett, R. J. Watts, & D. Birman (Eds.), *Human diversity: Perspectives on people in context* (pp. 312–333). San Francisco, CA: Jossey-Bass.

Dungy, G., & Gordon, S. A. (2011). The development of student affairs. In J. H. Schuh, S. R. Jones, & S. R. Harper (Eds.), *Student services: A handbook for the profession* (5th ed., pp. 61–80). San Francisco, CA: Jossey-Bass.

Evans, N. J., Forney, D. S., Guido, F. M., Patton, L. D., & Renn, K. A. (2010). *Student development in college: Theory, research, and practice* (2nd ed.). San Francisco, CA: Jossey-Bass.

Gibson, J. (2006). Disability and clinical competency: An introduction. *The California Psychologist, 39*, 6–10. Retrieved from http://www.disabilitypsychology.com

Hart, T. L. (2018). *The relationship between online students' use of services and their feelings of mattering* (Doctoral dissertation). Retrieved from ProQuest Dissertation and Theses database. (Order No. 10264100)

Kahn, R. L. (1975). *Memorandum to SSRC Committee on Work and Personality in the Middle Years.* Ann Arbor, MI.

Knefelkamp, L. L., Golec, R. R., & Wells, E. A. (1985). *The practice-to-theory-to-practice model.* Unpublished manuscript, University of Maryland, College Park.

Kohlberg, L. (1969). Stage and sequence: The cognitive developmental approach to socialization. In D. A. Goslin (Ed.), *Handbook of socialization theory and research* (pp. 347–480). Skokie, IL: Rand McNally.

Kruger, K., & Jarrat, D. (2018, December 16). Student affairs goes digital: Translating student support to the world of online learning. *Diverse: Issues in Higher Education.* Retrieved from https://diverseeducation.com/article/134371

Kuh, G. D. (2009). What student affairs professionals need to know about student engagement. *Journal of College Student Development, 50*, 683–796.

Patton, L. D., Renn, K. A., Guido, F. M., & Quaye, S. J. (2016). *Student development in college: Theory, research, and practice* (3rd ed.). San Francisco, CA: Jossey-Bass.

Perry, W. G., Jr. (1968). *Forms of intellectual and ethical development in the college years: A scheme.* New York, NY: Holt, Rhinehart, & Winston.

Perry, W. G., Jr. (1981). Cognitive and ethical growth: The making of meaning. In A. W. Chickering (Ed.), *The modern American college* (pp. 76–116). San Francisco, CA: Jossey-Bass.

Rosenberg, M., & McCullough, B. (1981). Mattering: Inferred significance and mental health among adolescents. *Research in Community and Mental Health, 2,* 163–182.

Schlossberg, N. K. (1981). A model for analyzing human adaptation to transition. *The Counseling Psychologist, 9,* 2–18. doi:10.1177/001100008100900202

Schlossberg, N. K. (1989). Mattering and marginality: Key issues in building community. In D. C. Roberts (Ed.), *Designing campus activities to foster a sense of campus community* (pp. 5–15). San Francisco, CA: Jossey-Bass.

Seaman, J. E., Allen, I. E., & Seaman, J. (2018). *Grade increase: Tracking distance education in the United States.* Retrieved from Babson Survey Research Group website: http://onlinelearningsurvey.com/reports/gradeincrease.pdf

Strayhorn, T. L. (2019). *College students' sense of belonging: A key to educational success for all students* (2nd ed.). New York, NY: Routledge.

Wetzel, E. M., Haynes, W., & Holley, P. W. (2017). Evaluation of self-modification of hand tools in the construction industry. In *53rd ASC Annual Conference Proceedings* (pp. 537–544). Retrieved from http://ascpro0.ascweb.org/archives/cd/2017/paper/CPRT164002017.pdf

Wolf-Wendel, L., Ward, K., & Kinzie, J. (2009). A tangled web of terms: The overlap and unique contribution of involvement, engagement, and integration to understanding college student success. *Journal of College Student Development, 50,* 407–428. doi:10.1353/csd.0.0077

CHAPTER 2

Title IX Programming for Online Learners

Andrea N. Hunt and Madeleine D. Frankford

ONLINE EDUCATION at many colleges and universities is increasing and is often included as a part of the institutional strategic plan (Sun & Chen, 2016). With this growth, student affairs professionals have to shift how Title IX educational programming is developed and implemented to include the needs of online learners. This chapter uses Title IX efforts at the University of North Alabama (UNA) as a case study to address how higher education institutions can deliver Title IX educational programming for online learners. First, the relevant literature on online Title IX programming is reviewed, and the third iteration of UNA's Student Campus Climate Survey data on the experiences of students who take 100% of their coursework online is reported. Second, best practices for providing Title IX training to online learners are examined by reviewing how UNA's Office of Title IX has tried to address the gap in outreach to online learners through a training presentation in the online First Year Experience (FYE) class. This chapter concludes with a list of recommendations for Title IX offices and other student affairs professionals to consider as higher education offers more online learning opportunities.

Title IX

There has been an increasing focus on higher education institutions around the Title IX of the Education Amendments Act of 1972. To develop guidelines to assist colleges and universities in implementing effective sexual assault prevention and intervention programming, former President Barack Obama convened the White House Task Force to Protect Students From Sexual Assault (2014), co-chaired by the Office of the Vice President and the White House Council on Women and Girls. In its first report, *Not Alone: The First Report of The White House Task Force to Protect Students From Sexual Assault,* the task force recommended a four-step process for all colleges and universities:

1. Identify the problem by conducting campus climate surveys.
2. Prevent sexual assault—and pay special attention to engaging men in this process.
3. Effectively respond when a student is sexually assaulted.
4. Increase transparency and improve enforcement.

In 2017, newly appointed Secretary of Education Betsey DeVos rescinded the 2011 *Dear Colleague* letter and announced changes to the Obama-era federal policies on investigations of sexual assault claims. The proposed guidelines for Title IX were posted to the

Federal Register for an open commenting period. During the time between open commenting and before the guidelines were implemented, institutions nationwide faced the unique challenge of educating students about Title IX, knowing procedures and processes were subject to change. While expectations for college and university policies and procedures are outlined in Title IX, this federal law also mandates institutions be proactive in educating students on their rights and resources. This education is necessary for all survivors of sexual assault and other forms of sexual violence, such as stalking and intimate partner violence (IPV; Oswalt, Wyatt, & Ochoa, 2018). The Sexual Violence Resource Center also identified how many institutions failed to define acts of sexual violence consistently across different levels of reporting (National Center for Victims of Crime, 2018). Nonetheless, even with inevitable changes underway from the federal government, best practices include education, prevention, and support services for all students, regardless of whether they take courses on campus or online.

Title IX and Online Learners

The number of students taking online courses has increased over the last decade. Allen and Seaman (2017) reported 6 million students were registered in at least one online course in 2015, with 14% of those students taking exclusively online courses and 15% taking at least one class online while also taking other classes on campus. As a result of the increase in the percentage of online learners, student affairs professionals need to rethink how Title IX education is offered to provide ongoing support to survivors of sexual assault.

There are some specific challenges in providing services to students who take 100% of their coursework online, including how content is delivered. While using a third-party platform can be cost effective and the content or services can be more easily distributed to a larger audience, it can be difficult to develop engaging and relevant content for online learners (Jaffe et al., 2018; Salazar, Vivolo-Kantor, & McGroarty-Koon, 2017). As a result, many technology companies have created prevention-focused platforms with educational modules to meet this need. Companies such as EverFi, SafeColleges, Catharsis Productions, and 3rd Millennium Classrooms integrate campus-specific policies and procedures into programming and allow for content customization. EverFi's "Sexual Assault Prevention for Undergraduate Students" training (formerly referred to as HAVEN) was found to increase rates of students' self-reported ability and intention to intervene, empathize, and support victims compared to using an in-house online intervention module (Zapp, Buelow, Soutiea, Berkowitz, & DeJong, 2018). However, Zapp et al. (2018) found the HAVEN online training had less effect in changing the rates of rape myth acceptance (i.e., the misinformation or misperceptions about sexual assault) among first-year students across campuses in the sample.

Engaging students with scenarios, videos, and inclusive and diverse language is imperative. Specifically, understanding the demographic characteristics—an institution's fully online learner population— can assist student affairs professionals in identifying the best online platform to use to provide resources and programming to students (Salazar et al., 2017). Student affairs professionals can use web-based programming to portray nonheteronormative relationships, represent minority groups, and acknowledge and challenge Greek-letter and athlete subculture norms, standards, and behaviors. The focus of such modules can include topics ranging from consent, alcohol abuse, and incapacitation to oppression, bystander intervention, and reporting protocol (Jaffe et al., 2018; Worthen & Wallace, 2017). The type of feedback students receive while taking the online training modules affects their level of engagement (Jaffe et al., 2018). For example, platforms that provide personalized feedback have been found to be the most effective (Gilmore, Bountress, Selmanoff, & George, 2018), while receiving corrective feedback may reduce engagement (Jaffe et al., 2018).

Addressing Online Learners' Mental Health Needs

Educational modules on Title IX prevention have been successfully implemented online (Zapp et al., 2018), whereas less is known about the effectiveness of online mental health services, especially for survivors of sexual assault and IPV (Nguyen-Feng et al., 2016). While online services for prevention, information, screening, and self-reflection are useful, in a recent Association for University and College Counseling Center Directors' survey, LeViness, Bershad, and Gorman (2017) found 63% of student counseling centers did not provide any telehealth services to students. Of the centers providing services, online screening tools were the most prevalent. Online screenings for mental health conditions, risk factors, and previous victimization can help university counselors implement appropriate measures to reinforce protective factors (LeViness et al., 2017). Conley et al. (2017) suggested rates of prior victimization as a significant predictor of sexual assault in college for both men and women; thus, understanding and acknowledging students' experiences prior to college enrollment can play an important role in programming, regardless of whether they are taking courses online.

Räsänen, Lappalainen, Muotka, Tolvanen, and Lappalainen (2016) found telehealth programs increase mindfulness, wellbeing, and satisfaction among students. However, Räsänen et al. did not focus specifically on students seeking support for Title IX-related issues, and the students in their sample had opportunities to meet counselors in person. Nguyen-Feng, Greer, and Frazier (2017) focused on telehealth services for students with a history of IPV and found they needed a more structured approach than mindfulness to help increase their present control. Nguyen-Feng et al. also found adding online interventions to address control and stress management were effective for IPV survivors.

Counseling with survivors requires specialized knowledge and experience, and these clients often need more time with counselors than do other clients (Chakaryan, 2018). Survivors may also benefit from professional wraparound services to develop coping mechanisms for the recovery process. While online resources and services may be helpful initially to support survivors as they start the recovery process, it is difficult to retain students when you do not see them. Therefore, there should be a specific focus on leveraging technology to establish positive affective bonds and therapeutic alliances between students and therapists (Doss, Feinberg, Rothman, Roddy, & Comer, 2017; Fu & Cheng, 2017). Institutional size and institutional commitment to counseling services will affect how successful colleges and universities are in developing and implementing a range of supports and services for online learners (Cornish et al., 2017).

Technology and Innovative Tools

Title IX resources	
bMOREsafe	Question-driven resource app for students after experience of abuse or assault *https://www.bmoresafemercy.org/get-the-app*
myPlan	Tool for creating safety plan for individuals experiencing intimate partner violence *https://www.myplanapp.org/home*
Noonlight (formerly SafeTrek)	Emergency response app that signals alarm and dispatches first responders *https://noonlight.com*
ReachOut (Capptivation)	On- and off-campus resource app for students that includes reporting options, policy information, and educational content *https://www.capptivation.com*
ReDawn	Reporting resource for survivors of sexual assault with interactive question and response texting with "Dawn" *https://itunes.apple.com/us/app/redawn/id1438769921?mt=8*
UNA Bluelight	University of North Alabama's Campus Police emergency assistance app *https://iphone.apkpure.com/una-bluelight/com.unifyed.unabluelight*
You are a Survivor (UCASA)	Resource app for survivors of sexual assault *https://www.ucasa.org/app*
Telecounseling resources	
BetterHelp	Online counseling platform with access to licensed therapists *https://www.betterhelp.com*
MyTherapist	Online counseling platform with access to licensed and accredited psychologists (PhD/PsyD), therapists (LMFT), clinical social workers (LCSW/LMSW), and licensed professional counselors (LPC) *https://www.mytherapist.com*
Sibly	A text-based service that connects people with life coaches *https://www.sibly.co*
Talkspace	A text-based service with licensed therapists *https://www.talkspace.com*
Telehealth	Provides information on training, consulting, and credentialing for telebehavioral health, telemental health, and telemedicine *https://telehealth.org/psychology*
TherapySites	A secure and HIPPA-compliant software used for interacting with clients *https://www.therapysites.com/tele-counseling*

Collaborative Approaches to Title IX

As the need for prevention education has increased, many colleges and universities have centralized these efforts within divisions of student affairs (Landreman & Williamsen, 2018). Title IX programming that involves offices of student conduct, student counseling services, and case management (or behavioral intervention teams) becomes more collaborative, relevant, and effective. Because of this approach, in fall 2014 UNA implemented a Title IX Advisory Board composed of students, faculty, staff, and community members and launched its first Title IX student campus climate survey. Of the 978 surveys completed in 2014, 68 students (7%) reported at least one incident of unwanted sexual contact in the previous year. Some students reported more than one incident, resulting in an incidence rate of 12%. The prevalence rate was higher for IPV at 16% and stalking/bullying at 36%.

In fall 2016, UNA administered a second survey to assess the effectiveness of the institution's efforts to educate students and the campus community on Title IX. By this time, all incoming freshmen and first-year transfer students were required to take an FYE course that contained mandatory Title IX and bystander intervention training. This FYE course is offered to students in both in-person and online formats. During the fall semester, incoming freshman and first-year transfer students also complete EverFi's Sexual Assault Prevention training, an online educational module for students on issues associated with sexual assault and relationship violence. Incidence rates were defined as a count of how many unique incidents of a particular act occurred during a given period of time (i.e., within the previous year); prevalence rates were defined as a count of how many unique people experience a particular act during a given period of time. The results from the 2016 survey were based on 1,457 completed surveys and indicate a prevalence rate of 7.7% (112 students) and an incidence rate of 13.7% of unwanted sexual contact. The prevalence rate for IPV was nearly 13% and stalking/bullying was 30.8%. Questions to measure experiences of emotional abuse were added to the 2016 survey, with 616 students (42%) reporting at least one experience with control and/or abusive tactics in an intimate relationship. Additional questions were also added to this survey to assess perceptions on campus among LGBTQIA students.

All of the efforts since 2014 have resulted in a continued commitment to the national It's on Us Campaign and additional trainings with Greek life, housing and residence life, athletics, and numerous registered student organizations, all of which serve online learners who may live on or near campus. A series of Title IX informational briefs are released each year by the university, and a set of spotlight videos of campus leaders discussing different components of the findings are also featured on the university website and social media platforms; all of these materials are accessible to the public. While these efforts are extraordinary in scope, UNA has yet to assess the difference in the experiences of on-campus students and students who take all of their classes online.

 Tips for Getting Started

Taking on the challenge of incorporating Title IX education within the online environment may seem overwhelming, but even the smallest of changes can make a significant difference for students. Here are some tips that can be helpful throughout all stages of programming implementation.

- **Don't do it alone.** Create a committee, task force, or advisory board delegated with making educational programming decisions.
- **Define your scope and purpose.** Is the online format to provide prevention and support or intervention and response?
- **Identify your resources.** Consider creating a line item within your department's budget for online educational programming. Reach out to key stakeholders across campus for feedback and support.
- **Create a list of learning objectives.** Like any other educational course, online programming should be intentional and SMART (specific, measurable, achievable, realistic, and timebound).
- **Review and reassess periodically.** You may find the demographics of your online learner community change rapidly. Evaluate the effectiveness of the programming regularly and make changes as needed.

Efforts at the University of North Alabama to Implement Title IX Programming for Online Learners

In fall 2018, the third iteration of the UNA Student Campus Climate Survey was disseminated, this time with an added measure to learn more about the population of students taking all of their courses online versus in traditional, face-to-face classes. Of the 1,034 students who completed the survey, 35 reported taking 100% of their classes online, including 10 men and 25 women. Of the 35 students, 11.8% of students identified as either lesbian, gay, bisexual, or questioning. Ages ranged from 19 to 56, with 30 as the median age of online-only students. In terms of race/ethnicity, the majority of this subsample of 35 students identified as White (66%), 14% identified as Asian, and 20% identified as Black or African American. Around 40% of the online-only students reported previously or currently having anxiety, and 18.75% reported previously or currently having a mood disorder (e.g., depression, bipolar disorder). Almost all of the students (90%) who reported taking all of their courses online were aware of on-campus student counseling services.

Of the online-only students, 6% had a current class standing of freshman; 6% were sophomores, 18% were juniors, 32% were seniors, and 38% were graduate students. Nearly half of the online-only students (49%) had received training from UNA in Title IX policies and procedures related to incidents of sexual assault either online or on campus (e.g., what is sexual assault, how to report an incident, confidential resources, procedures for investigating). Of the students who received this training, 71% found it very useful, 23% found it moderately useful, and 6% found it slightly useful. About half of the online-only students (49%) also received bystander intervention training focused on sexual assault prevention; of those who received the bystander intervention training, 59% found it very useful, 35% found it moderately useful, and 6% found it slightly useful. Moreover, 17% of the online-only students reported belonging to a social fraternity or sorority. While this is a low percentage, it does provide some information on the nature of online learners who are often characterized or thought of as nontraditional students. This may indicate some scenarios within educational platforms that include fraternity/sorority party scenes may still be relevant for those who reported having/maintaining Greek-letter affiliation. Understanding students' level of involvement in Greek-letter organizations may provide clarification for this approach. Approximately 11% of the students who received the Title IX and Bystander Intervention training were international students, which indicates a need for student affairs professionals to address discernable social and cultural differences in risk reduction training related to alcohol use and sexual activity.

Although UNA has already implemented online Title IX and bystander intervention training, these responses highlight a need for ongoing (and revised) Title IX and bystander intervention training specifically for the online learner population. Interestingly, 97% of fully online learners reported not having observed a situation that was or could have led to sexual assault. This is likely due to taking all of their courses off campus and not having some of the same risk factors as students who take a majority of their classes on the physical campus. Online learners *do* participate in campus life at many colleges and universities and may experience bullying or sexual harassment in online classes or through social media; however, the survey's investigators did not examine these specific areas. Only one student reported experiencing unwanted sexual contact with someone since becoming a student at UNA, and one student reported experiencing unwanted sexual contact while they were unable to provide consent or stop what was happening because they were passed out, under the influence of drugs and/or alcohol, incapacitated, or asleep. One student reported experiencing stalking (i.e., a pattern of repeated and unwanted attention, harassment, or contact) within the previous calendar year; and four fully online learners reported experiencing violence or abuse from an intimate partner of any kind (e.g., sexual, physical, emotional, psychological).

Of the fully online learner population, roughly 2% completed the Student Campus Climate Survey compared to 6% of students taking a majority of their classes on the physical campus. With an increasing population of online learners, student affairs professionals need to design and implement educational programming with a new level of creativity. As Allen and Seaman (2017) noted in their study of trends and patterns of distance education enrollments among U.S. higher education institutions, on-campus students are also beginning to take some online courses, indicating the number of online learners will likely continue to increase.

In addition to the Sexual Assault Prevention online education training on issues related to sexual assault and relationship violence, the Title IX education and prevention coordinator at UNA recorded a voiceover of the Title IX and bystander intervention training PowerPoint presentation used in face-to-face classes and uploaded it to the online FYE course. Traditional students are encouraged to take pre and posttraining surveys before watching the presentation to evaluate Title IX content. UNA plans to incorporate this survey technique into the online FYE course in the upcoming semester. To address multiple learning styles, the FYE course instructor facilitated an open discussion in which students participated after watching the Title IX training presentation. The instructor encouraged self-reflection by posing realistic case scenarios, and students answered questions on how they would react and/or what they would do in various situations. This method of disseminating Title IX information was found to be engaging and reflective for students and the instructor. It is important to note not all students are required to take the FYE course, including students who transfer in or return to school with more than 24 credit hours.

UNA also created an online support group for survivors. The education and prevention coordinator partnered with the women's center and the community organization called Shoals Diversity Center to create a Sexual Assault Survivor Support Group Committee. The group first organized in-person group counseling sessions with a local counselor for survivors. After several months, the committee was forced to reevaluate the support group environment due to low attendance at counseling sessions. To better meet students' needs, the committee planned and created a private Facebook group for all local survivors of sexual assault. The goal of the group is to provide survivors an accepting, supportive, and empowering space to connect and share openly about their experiences. A UNA graduate student and advocate for survivors was selected to facilitate the Facebook group discussions and reflections. This support group operates outside the scope of the Title IX office; however, the Title IX coordinator provides information on how to connect with the support group for survivors of sexual assault with whom she comes in contact through her work. While the number of members in the Facebook group is still relatively small, the group facilitator received feedback simply providing this space sends a positive message to survivors. It is expected engagement in this Facebook group will grow over time.

The Student Campus Climate Survey results have been used to direct educational programming efforts. While UNA conducts this campuswide survey every two years, institutions can benefit from periodically surveying their student population within a timeframe that works best with their resources. With a campus climate survey, campuses can gather relevant student demographic information, such as age, race, student classification, perception of resources, and knowledge of services. Because of this process, UNA has seen enrollment trends grow as more online degrees and programs are offered. Including measures that capture whether a student takes 100% of their coursework online can help an institution pinpoint that population's understanding of policies, awareness of support services, and perceptions of campus climate. Working in tandem with others on campus (e.g., academic affairs, university communications, faculty) can increase student participation in educational programming. UNA has even cultivated relationships with community agencies and organizations to promote and cosponsor events for on-campus and fully online learners. Sharing this information and promoting such events through UNA's e-mail and social media platforms keeps fully online learners who live in the surrounding area in the know on how to get involved in campus life.

Potential Challenges and Practical Solutions

Encountering challenges to implementing an effective online education model is inevitable. Such obstacles will vary based on each institution; however, this list provides where to anticipate resistance when developing a strategy for your institution's online Title IX education. There are also several solutions to consider when facing these challenges. Much of what can be resolved or transformed relies on access to resources and a willingness to collaborate. Be creative!

Potential Challenges:

- Jurisdiction
- Changing guidelines (federal, state, and institutional levels)
- Administration buy-in
- Resources (e.g., staff, funding)
- Student participation

Practical Solutions:

- Increase communication among students, staff, administration, state representatives, and company representatives.
- Join professional organizations to learn best practices (e.g., Association of Title IX Administrators and Campus Advocacy and Prevention Professionals Association).
- Collaborate with departments across campus and community organizations/ agencies to divide tasks and expenses.

Implications of Online Title IX Programming

There are unique implications to consider when moving educational programming to an online environment. The age of online learners may affect programming details, including accessibility, relevance, and ease of navigation. It is imperative to consider whether and how the education and prevention will be tailored to different needs. It may no longer be appropriate to include scenarios of college partying if the majority of the online learners are over the age of 30. Instead, providing scenarios that occur in the workplace, restaurants, or home environments may resonate more with older adult learners—the context is important for the success of Title IX education. Campuses must check in periodically and systematically with their online learners to understand the challenges they face; when needs and challenges are identified, trainings should be modified accordingly.

Another element to consider with online Title IX education and programming is accessibility. To what extent can the college or university make content accessible for all students, regardless of ability? Is the platform for online programming functional with computer screen reader programs, such as JAWS? Providing content in an accessible format may also meet the needs of students with different learning styles. Proper accessibility ensures, no matter the viewing format, students can attain the information they need.

Telehealth services are increasingly important as the number of online learners grows. Institutions need to consider licensure issues, types of services to offer, and how services are meeting the needs of online learners. For example, not all counselors are licensed to practice through a medium (e.g., screen, computer) where service use occurs in a different place from their licensing state. This could be an issue if fully online learners who reside in another state or country seek your institution's counseling services. In these circumstances, understanding your counselors' scope of practice becomes imperative. It is also important to consider where Title IX falls within an institution's hierarchy and how this affects approaches to programming. If an institution's Title IX coordinator reports directly to the university president, they may have more leverage to ask for additional programming resources.

Conclusion

For all institutions, regardless of the organizational structure, there are vital questions to address. What is the intention of the programming? Is the goal to provide prevention and support, or intervention and response, to the aftermath of sexual violence? Answering this question will determine an institution's next steps. Campus climate surveys also provide vital information to guide programming and supports based on the needs of a student population. It is our responsibility as student affairs professionals to pair our understanding of sexual violence and student growth and development to proactively respond to negative campus culture and create a safe environment for all students (Landreman & Williamsen, 2018).

When it comes to Title IX implementation, consideration of online learners cannot be lost. As institutions continue to incorporate relevant, accessible programming for traditional students, they must also provide corresponding education for students who take 100% of their coursework online. As participation in online courses and degree programs increases, it is imperative institutions take advantage of the tools and technologies available to meet the needs of the online learner population.

Questions for Reflection

- What is the size and demographic of your institution's online learner population?
- How can you ensure online learners are aware of how institutional policy defines sexual assault?
- Does your institution already offer services to online learners?
- Can your institution's Title IX office offer an online reporting option for online learners to use?
- How are you incorporating the mission and goals of the institution and/or division into your programming for online learners?
- In what ways are you using culturally appropriate language and scenarios specific to your institution's online learner population?
- How will online learners evaluate your institution's ongoing prevention strategies?
- Who are the key stakeholders you need to engage at your institution to promote educational prevention programming for online learners (e.g., administration, counselors, administrative assistants)?

References

Allen, E. I., & Seaman, J. (2017). *Digital learning compass: Distance education enrollment report 2017.* Retrieved from https://onlinelearningsurvey.com/reports/digtiallearning compassenrollment2017.pdf

Chakaryan, H. (2018). Effective ways to approach sexual assault response. *Counseling Today.* Retrieved from https://ct.counseling.org/2018/07/effective-ways-to-approach-sexual-assault-response

Conley, A. H., Overstreet, C. M., Hawn, S. E., Kendler, K. S., Dick, D. M., & Amstadter, A. B. (2017). Prevalence and predictors of sexual assault among a college sample. *Journal of American College Health, 65,* 41–49. doi:10.1080/07448481.2016.1235578

Cornish, P. A., Berry, G., Benton, S., Barros-Gomes, P., Johnson, D., Ginsburg, R., . . . Romano, V. (2017). Meeting the mental health needs of today's college student: Reinventing services through Stepped Care 20. *Psychological Services, 14,* 428–442. doi:10.1037/ser0000158

Doss, B. D., Feinberg, L. K., Rothman, K., Roddy, M. K., & Comer, J. S. (2017). Using technology to enhance and expand interventions for couples and families: Conceptual and methodological considerations. *Journal of Family Psychology, 31,* 983–993. doi:10.1037/fam0000349

Fu, M., & Cheng, A. W. (2017). College counseling services: Meeting today's demands. *Psychological Services, 14,* 403–406. doi:10.1037/ser0000219

Gilmore, A. K., Bountress, K. E., Selmanoff, M., & George, W. H. (2018). Reducing heavy episodic drinking, incapacitation, and alcohol-induced blackouts: Secondary outcomes of a web-based combined alcohol use and sexual assault risk reduction intervention. *Violence Against Women, 24,* 1299–1313. doi:10.1177/1077801218787934

Jaffe, A. E., Bountress, K. E., Metzger, I. W., Maples-Keller, J. L., Pinsky, H. T., George, W. H., & Gilmore, A. K. (2018). Student engagement and comfort during a web-based personalized feedback intervention for alcohol and sexual assault. *Addictive Behaviors, 82,* 23–27. doi:10.1177/1077801218787934

Landreman, L. M., & Williamsen, K. M. (2018). Addressing sexual violence as student affairs work. In J. Jessup-Anger & K. E. Edwards (Eds.), *Addressing sexual violence in higher education and student affairs* (New Directions for Student Services, No. 161, pp. 35–45). San Francisco, CA: Jossey-Bass. doi:10.1002/ss.20251

LeViness, P., Bershad, C., & Gorman, K. (2017). *The Association for University and College Counseling Center Directors annual survey.* Retrieved from Association for University and College Counseling Center Directors website: https://www.aucccd.org/assets/documents/Governance/2017%20aucccd%20survey-public-apr26.pdf

National Center for Victims of Crime. (2018). *2018 National Crime Victims' Rights Week resource guide: Crime and victimization fact sheets—Sexual violence.* Retrieved from https://ovc.ncjrs.gov/ncvrw2018/info_flyers/fact_sheets/2018NCVRW_CrimeAndVic_508_QC.pdf

Nguyen-Feng, V. N., Frazier, P. A., Greer, C. S., Meredith, L., Howard, K., & Paulsen, J. (2016). Testing the efficacy of three brief web-based interventions for reducing distress among interpersonal violence survivors. *Translational Issues in Psychological Science, 2,* 439–448. doi:10.1037/tps0000099

Nguyen-Feng, V. N., Greer, C. S., & Frazier, P. (2017). Using online interventions to deliver college student mental health resources: Evidence from randomized clinical trials. *Psychological Services, 14,* 481–489. doi:10.1037/ser0000154

Oswalt, S. B., Wyatt, T. J., & Ochoa, Y. (2018). Sexual assault is just the tip of the iceberg: Relationship and sexual violence prevalence in college students. *Journal of College Student Psychotherapy, 32,* 93–109. doi:10.1080/87568225.2017.1350122

Räsänen, P., Lappalainen, P., Muotka, J., Tolvanen, A., & Lappalainen, R. (2016). An online guided ACT intervention for enhancing the psychological wellbeing of university students: A randomized controlled clinical trial. *Behaviour Research and Therapy, 78,* 30–42. doi:10.1016/j.brat.2016.01.001

Salazar, L. F., Vivolo-Kantor, A., & McGroarty-Koon, K. (2017). Formative research with college men to inform content and messages for a web-based sexual violence prevention program. *Health Communication, 32,* 1133–1141. doi:10.1080/10410236.2016.1214219

Sun, A., & Chen, X. (2016). Online education and its effective practice: A research review. *Journal of Information Technology Education: Research, 15*, 157–190. doi:10.28945/3502

Title IX of the Education Amendments Act of 1972, 20 U.S.C. §§1681–1688. Retrieved from http://www.dol.gov/oasam/regs/statutes/titleIX.htm

The White House Task Force to Protect Students from Sexual Assault. (2014). *Not alone: The first report of The White House Task Force to Protect Students From Sexual Assault.* Retrieved from https://www.justice.gov/archives/ovw/page/file/905942/download

Worthen, M. G. F., & Wallace, S. A. (2017). Intersectionality and perceptions about sexual assault education and reporting on college campuses. *Family Relations, 66*, 180–196. doi:10.1111/fare.12240

Zapp, D., Buelow, R., Soutiea, L., Berkowitz, A., & DeJong, W. (2018). Exploring the potential campus-level impact of online universal sexual assault prevention education. *Journal of Interpersonal Violence,* 1–22. doi:10.1177/0886260518762449

CHAPTER 3

Partnering With Business Vendors to Enhance Student Affairs Services for Online Learners

Sherry A. Benton and Melissa M. Vito

IN THE EARLY years of online education, attention was focused on producing and delivering courses and academic programs with little attention to student support needs beyond those that were purely academic, proving "student support infrastructure for these students is still a nascent field" (Kruger & Jarrat, 2018, para. 3). When online learning was first developing, chapter coauthor Sherry Benton was working at the University of Florida as the director of the counseling and wellness center and a professor in the psychology department when she decided she should participate in the committee formed to develop student services for the new online university. Up until that time, the university had formed a committee, made a couple of hires, and started asking the academic departments to create some online courses and programs. Little thought was given to student services for online learners initially.

One early assumption made by the the committee developing the online university was online learners would not need many of the services student affairs provided since the students would not be on campus. Online learners would pay less because they would not need to be charged health, activity, and other student-affairs-related fees. These assumptions proved to be wrong and lead to ineffective decisions. Students were often enrolled in a combination of online and on-campus courses. Online learners regularly called counseling services seeking consultations, and, as the director of the counseling and wellness center, this left Benton in a quandary. Counseling and wellness services were not funded to work with these students, services were overwhelmed with demand from on-campus students, and staff could not, in good conscience, turn away online learners who were in crisis. The overwhelming majority of the university's online learners lived in state, so there was little reason not to serve these students.

In addition, online learners were disappointed to be excluded from participation in clubs and organizations, particularly when these clubs could readily meet by video conferencing, and participation in organizations was helpful for résumé building and job searches. This lack of ability to participate fully in the university experience can leave students feeling disconnected from the university and more likely to transfer to other institutions (Salter, 2012).

The Need for Services for Online Learners

As online education evolved and grew, educational leaders across the country who were developing online programs increasingly recognized the importance of student services in supporting online learner success. Chapter coauthor Melissa Vito spent most of her career in various aspects of student affairs, including as senior vice president of student affairs and enrollment management and senior vice provost for academic initiatives and student success, overseeing student life, orientation, student retention, counseling, campus recreation, campus health, and auxiliaries (bookstore, student union, and residence life). She was leading these areas at the University of Arizona when university leadership asked her to develop and implement the university's strategy and plans for fully online degree programs, especially undergraduate programs. Online degree programs would be integrated into overall enrollment management plans, making it simple to take a comprehensive view of online learner support. Key online goals included improving access and supporting retention for all students—student support was critical. The following sections describe the approach, including assessing whether or not to use outside vendors in providing specific areas of student support.

Student Retention and Attrition

Student retention and matriculation to graduation are major concerns for colleges and universities. A decision to leave school or transfer is a major decision for a residential student. Changing schools typically involves moving to a new city with all of the accompanying complications, including finding housing, making deposits, arranging utilities, and finding new friends and supports. In contrast, changing online institutions is relatively easy. The change can often be accomplished with a few clicks on a computer. Attrition rates for online learners are as much as 20% higher than for face-to-face students (Herbert, 2006). Some scholars have found attrition rates of 40% to 80% among online learners (Smith, 2010). A recent study commissioned by the National Postsecondary Education Cooperative reported mixed and limited results in terms of student outcomes for online learners (Miller, Topper, & Richardson, 2017). Researchers have long validated the value of belonging and community for student success, and, for fully online learners who frequently lack physical presence, this need is more acute (Hrastinski, 2009).

Online orientation programs, cohort learning, interaction with fellow online learners, and connections to a suite of student support options all help build a sense of connection and belonging to the institution (Thomas, Herbert, & Teras, 2014). Most important, retention is the top concern for those who oversee online learning (Magda, 2018). Therefore, using support services to promote student success is critical. Several factors are most likely to lead to attrition among online learners, including discomfort or frustration with technology, feeling disconnected from instructors and the university community, and the institution not responding to the needs of distance learners (Bawa, 2016).

Establishing Universal Supports

At the University of Arizona, a key first step was to establish an institutionwide committee to assess what types of student support would be important to the success of fully online learners. The next step was to make sure whatever financial model was developed for online programs included a way to support these services for fully online learners.

In assessing areas of support for online learners, the committee also examined student services' internal capacity and ability to build support for online learners, including potentially engaging outside vendors to provide support. Regardless of whether the service was built internally or contracted through a vendor, it was critical students experienced it as a University of Arizona service. Moreover, it is important to note about 78% of fully online learners live within 100 miles of the institution at which they are enrolled (Magda, 2018), with almost half living less than 25 miles away. These students need a way to opt in to campus services to provide them the ability to access physical services on campus, especially campus recreation, campus health, and counseling and academic support. Given this, the University of Arizona committee also focused on internal capacities, including physical plant.

As noted, the committee evaluated both the capacity and expertise of support units and the specific needs of online learners to help determine whether to seek vendor support or work to adapt or expand services within units on campus. While using a vendor may seem expensive, frequently it is a more cost-effective way to provide a specific support than building it internally. In addition, because the modalities of online and hybrid learning are prevalent among face-to-face students, a guiding principle was to build or use support that had a beneficial impact on all students. An example of where there was a clear benefit for all students was in the expansion of virtual tutoring sessions. The goal was to make sure math and writing tutoring was available to online learners. Offering online tutoring was found to benefit all students. This modality of tutoring offered more flexibility for face-to-face students, and the result was an increase in access for both student populations.

Some of the health and wellness tools initially built for online learners also proved beneficial for face-to-face students. All support was initially designed for a fully online learner and was generally in an online modality. However, there was also an intent to have the services available for all students, if possible. In thinking about providing student services for online learners, a case could often be built that these services would actually be more universal and serve all students.

Considerations for Using Outside Vendors and Technology in Online Education

There is a plethora of products and vendors with software that sell to colleges and universities. Administrators may find themselves bewildered by the number and variety of options. At times, the volume of sales pitches for products can be taxing and overwhelming. In considering any software purchase, the most important question should be whether the software solves a significant problem that is worth the expense. The following examples offer a sampling of the types of tools available for different student service needs with a description of their usefulness.

Using Online Program Management Systems

One common approach to building online programs involves using online program management (OPM) tools, such as those offered by Pearson and Academic Partnerships. These are different than learning management systems (LMS) that primarily focus on delivering academic courses online. OPM tools also provide student services and have the advantage of requiring fewer internal resources. The disadvantages include a lack of flexibility and institutional control and, potentially, some loss of university branding. The use of OPM tools to deliver online education seems to be declining (Lurie, 2018). OPM tools frequently deliver the full spectrum of online program support including marketing, enrollment coaching, course development, and academic support, which can limit an institution's ability to use vendors for a specific function. This may be one reason the use of OPM tools is declining.

Financial Planning for Student Services

When planning to provide services to online learners, using vendors often makes sense and enables the college or university to provide better services and support than it would without these vendor tools (Kretovics, 2015). In this case, there will be a need to build an encompassing financial model to include student support. In researching pricing when developing online program financial models at the University of Arizona, the committee sought information from a number of institutions that were already offering online programs and learned technology and library fees are frequently embedded in online learner costs, but other support services may not be. Student affairs leaders must have the ability to include optional fees for online learners who either want to come to campus for services or who will be accessing services remotely. If student committees are involved in the funding process, it is important to work with them early in planning to gain their support for this fee extension. As financial models for online programs are built for the approval of governing boards and institutional leadership, it is critical to include online student services to help demonstrate the impact these services will have on online student success and the need for them.

Choosing Where and When to Use Vendor Products

Vendor use may limit upfront costs and provide equivalent or more targeted support, while there may be institutional offices or areas that can easily develop specific support for online learners and will want this opportunity. As noted earlier, an assessment of internal capacity by involving leadership from these areas is fundamental to planning.

Buying Versus Building

For colleges and universities with considerable technological resources, it may be an option to build digital tools for working with online learners. This can be an expensive enterprise and often involves long-term commitments to revisions and further development as new operating systems develop. With app development, ensuring apps work on every version of smart phones is a considerable process. However, if there simply are no tools available to solve the problem, this may be an option. Nevertheless, if there are good and affordable tools available to solve a problem or meet a need, then a commercial product may save headaches and expenses. Many of these useful tools are described later in this chapter.

Maintaining Ownership of the Student Relationship

There is an abundance of online tools from dozens of companies to help engage online learners. Some outside vendors provide a complete online suite of courses, programs, and services for colleges and universities. While these may seem like an easy solution, students are likely to feel more connected to the company than to the higher education institution, which can increase attrition and transfers if students feel a weakened affiliation with the campus. It is vitally important the college or university "own" the relationship with the student. This both improves retention and increases students' sense of connection and well-being. Two ways to reinforce students' connection to the institution include using white label products and single sign-on. White labeling minimizes references to the vendor while placing college or university names and logos prominently on digital products. This assures students their interactions are with the institution and not an outside company. Similarly, if your institution uses single sign-on for services, it is helpful to include vendor products in single sign-on so students have the clear sense they are signing into the institution even when they are using vendor products.

In addition to maintaining ownership of the student relationship, it is also important to maintain ownership of student data. An especially inexpensive opportunity may be misleading, as the vendor will now own the data for students who use the product. Institutions typically must pay extra to access or own this data. To ameliorate this concern, contracts should be reviewed with someone well versed in this area.

Technology and Innovative Tools

General resources

EDUCAUSE	A nonprofit organization focused on the use of IT in higher education *http://www.nsf.gov/eng/iip/sbir/documents/Phase_I_Proposal_Preparation_Booklet.pdf*
Education Advisory Board	Provides research on a wide array of topics in higher education *https://eab.com*
Eduventures	Proprietary research, analysis, and advising services to support decision making throughout the student lifecycle *https://encoura.org/products-services/eduventures-research-and-advisory-services*
The Evolllution	Enrollment strategies *https://evolllution.com*
Inside Higher Ed	Online news with topics in higher education *https://www.insidehighered.com*
Online Learning Consortium	Online learning community *https://onlinelearningconsortium.org*
University Professional and Continuing Education Association	Professional organization for continuing education providers *https://upcea.edu*

Vendors

Adobe Captivate Prime	Learning management system, online course creation software *https://www.adobe.com/products/captivateprime.html*
Campus Labs	Provides data collection and visualization software that enables colleges and universities to make impactful, data-driven decisions *https://www.campuslabs.com*
Canvas	Learning management system *https://community.canvaslms.com*
Civitas	Uses institutional learning data to improve student outcomes *https://www.civitaslearning.com*
Elucian	Software aimed to boost student success & retention with modern technological strategies and resources *https://www.ellucian.com*
GradLeaders	Software for student recruitment and career services *https://www.gradleaders.com*
GuidebookEDU	App builder designed to create custom guidebook apps for colleges and universities *https://guidebook.com*
Handshake	An online community for job searching and career networking *https://www.joinhandshake.com*

I.M. Well	Integrated mental wellness app, wellness resources, mood tracking, counselors, and live chat *http://imwell.ca*
Moodle	Open source learning management system *https://moodle.org*
Protocall Services	Mental health emergency and after hours services by telephone *https://protocallservices.com*
Purple Briefcase	Career services and employer contact management *http://www.purplebriefcase.com*
Qualtrics	Online survey system *https://www.qualtrics.com*
Signal Vine	Artificial-intelligence-based mass or individual texting for colleges and universities *https://www.signalvine.com*
Starfish	Artificial-intelligence-based student retention tools *https://www.starfishsolutions.com*
Survey Gizmo	Online survey tools *https://www.surveygizmo.com*
SurveyMonkey	Online survey tools *https://www.surveymonkey.com*
Symplicity	Career services software *https://www.symplicity.com*
TalkSpace	Online asynchronous chat with a counselor *https://lp.talkspace.com*
TAO Connect	Customizable online mental health and wellness tools for self-help, courses, student affairs offices, and counseling *https://www.taoconnect.org*
Tenlegs	An integrated platform for schools to engage their communities, deliver administrative services, and make data-driven decisions *http://www.tenlegs.com*
uConnect	Career education portal *https://www.gouconnect.com*
WayUp	Platform to find paid internships, part-time jobs, and entry-level opportunities at thousands of startups and Fortune 500 companies *https://www.wayup.com*
YOU at College	Brings together campus resources, assessments, and wellness content *https://youatcollege.com*

Helpful Vendor Tools for
Online Student Affairs Services

Any vendors with whom you partner should support and help your internal student affairs staff and enhance the relationship between on-campus and online learners. New companies and new products are being developed constantly. In addition, companies are continually merging, being acquired, and developing, so any review of products and companies is purely a one-point-in-time snapshot of a very fluid digital space. Regardless, the following are descriptions of some examples of the kinds of products available, and some that may be coming in the future, across different functional areas within student affairs. The products and companies described are intended only as examples and neither the authors nor NASPA–Student Affairs Administrators in Higher Education endorse any particular products.

Student Orientation and Integration

All online colleges and universities use an LMS to deliver courses. The LMS could be a native app for operating systems like Apple iOS and Android, home-grown (developed in-house) software in HTML, freeware such as Moodle, or a commercial product like Canvas or Adobe Captivate Prime. Creating a first-year experience class for new online learners can help quickly acclimate them to the institution and facilitate interactions with other students.

Student Retention and Early Intervention

Several companies and tools provide analytics to identify students at risk for withdrawing by detecting these students as early as possible. Signal Vine, Civitas Learning, and Starfish all provide variations of analytics to detect when a student starts to engage less with courses and institutional departments. These tools use advanced analytics and machine learning to detect problems and send timely messages to students. Artificial intelligence and machine learning require massive databases to make accurate predictions. Companies that work with many higher education institutions often have hundreds of thousands of cases, so they can create tools that are more accurate than anything one could build internally at one institution. Machine learning-based programs can detect changes in engagement very early and relay this information to an academic advisor or student affairs professional, thus allowing them to reach out to the student. The result is a product that uses artificial intelligence to enhance opportunities for personal relationships and responsiveness to online learners. Other products to consider include Ellucian Banner Finance, Ellucian Colleague Student Planning, and Ellucian PowerCampus.

Student Affairs Assessment and Evaluation

Assessing the impact and outcome of student affairs services and programs is a core activity in student affairs. In addition, surveying students and determining needs is important for every institution. These efforts can be resource intensive, requiring skills in methodology, measurement, data analysis, writing, and interpretation. Common survey tools such as Qualtrics, SurveyMonkey, Survey Gizmo, and others can help student affairs professionals format and deliver surveys, but administering the tools still requires considerable internal resources. Campus Labs provides consultation and tools in multiple areas beyond surveys, including analytics and insight, improvement and accountability, teaching and learning, retention and success, and student engagement. Campus Labs' very large databases allow the company to predict with some accuracy which students are likely to persist, and which students are at risk for withdrawing. They also integrate with many learning management systems.

Career Services

There are many vendor tools available for career services. Some focus on placement, while others provide more comprehensive career planning and career exploration services. Some tools for career services management include Symplicity, Tenlegs, and Purple Briefcase. Other career services tools are helpful for job and internship searches, including WayUp, Handshake, GradLeaders, and uConnect.

Generally, fully online undergraduate students are older (average age of 32) and frequently employed (84%; Friedman, 2017) while working on their education. Keeping in mind services relevant to an already employed population is important in evaluating career services tools.

Counseling and Wellness Services

Students tend to reach out to institutions they trust and to which they already feel connected. Consequently, online learners often contact college or university counseling services when they are in distress. Professional counselors are governed by U.S. laws that also govern the practice of psychologists and mental health counselors, limiting them to practice only within the jurisdiction for which they are licensed. If a counselor is licensed in Ohio, they cannot provide ongoing services to a student in Florida. By law, the location of practice is defined as the state in which the student is located. Ideally a therapist would be licensed in both the state in which the counselor is located and the state in which the student is located. This can be particularly problematic with students who often do internships, experiential learning, or study abroad programs that take them away from their home state for a period of time. In most jurisdictions, crisis and emergency services are allowed but not ongoing counseling. Jurisdictional laws seem antiquated and counterproductive, since there is considerable evidence online counseling via videoconference and telephone can be just as effective as face-to-face counseling. However, regulation of mental health services and professional licensure is the province of states, not the federal government. Consequently, any change would require every individual state to change its licensure law. In spite of these limitations, there are some services that can be provided to distance learners. All distance learners residing in the same state as the counseling center can receive online therapy services. For students outside of the state, a number of helpful resources can be provided.

Most students make some attempt at self-help before seeking services from a professional counselor. Counseling service websites can include recommended apps and additional websites. Some companies, such as YOU at College, TAO Connect, and I.M. Well, provide prevention and useful early intervention tools for online learners. YOU at College is primarily focused on immediate "just in time" tools. Just in time tools provide an immediate resource when students search a topic. Students' primary way of initially engaging with any wellness and mental health topic tends to be "grab and go": A student searches for a topic on a mental health app, gets the information they are seeking, and then may not engage with the app again for a few weeks. YOU at College has very broad coverage of many areas. In contrast, TAO Connect provides some quick resources but focuses on more in-depth, evidence-based programs for common mental health problems. TAO Connect's online tools have been demonstrated in research to be as effective as face-to-face counseling (Benton, Heesacker, Snowden, & Lee, 2016; Cornish et al., 2017). TAO Connect can be used for self-help, as resilience training for first-year experience courses, as customized content for a course, or as a tool for counseling and health centers.

Several companies provide online counseling services that can help both on-campus students and distance learners. Many of these companies have counselors across most states. A few of these are Betterhelp (now a division of Teladoc), Talkspace (which focuses on services delivered via text messaging), and I.M. Well, a more comprehensive company that is based in Canada. I. M. Well has recently begun providing services in the United States. I.M. Well provides mood tracking, live chat with a counselor, telephone counseling, and online mental health educational resources through TAO Connect. These companies can increase a counseling center's capacity during times of high demand. The disadvantage is services are not directly connected to the college or university brand, although some institution branding is available. Therapist selection, training, and vetting can vary across companies, so consideration of these factors and any resultant liability for the college or university is important. In addition, IT staff, general counsel, and student affairs professionals should carefully review services and agreements before contracting with an external provider.

Many colleges and universities contract with local resources, including crisis help lines for after-hours and emergency services. ProtoCall Services is a national company that provides after-hours and weekend on-call services. A national company has advantages for online learners since it can respond to crises anywhere and likely have some referral information in most states.

Chapter coauthor Sherry Benton founded TAO Connect. The company provides a suite of tools to help colleges and universities increase access, capacity, and efficacy for students using institutional resources. TAO Connect's evidence-based behavioral health tools can be used as self-enrolled self-help or in-group interventions. They can be used in combination with short sessions with a counselor, allowing a counselor to see two to three students per hour instead of one. In addition, TAO Connect's tools can be used to create courses on a variety of topics, including resilience, substance abuse, and relationship skills. All can be delivered remotely.

Student Involvement and Leadership

Developing and maintaining connections with a campus community can promote students' sense of affiliation with their institution. Presence is a software program that focuses on student engagement and also offers assessment tools. GuidebookEDU is used to help residential students connect with clubs and organizations and could also be used to help online learners find opportunities for campus involvement.

Resources for Student Affairs Professionals to Understand the Institutional Processes for Vetting, Selecting, and Contracting with Vendors

In addition to using individual request-for-proposal (RFP) processes, vice presidents for student affairs (VPSAs) should reach out to colleagues at other campuses with comprehensive online programs to seek feedback on vendors and specific support areas. Discussions and questions submitted on professional listservs can provide helpful information. Involving students can help to provide potential user feedback. Professional organizations, including University Professional and Continuing Education Association and Online Learning Consortium, are increasingly addressing student support for both online and on-campus students, and provide good resources.

Eduventures, Education Advisory Board, *Inside Higher Ed*, EDUCAUSE, and The EvoLLLution are all great resources for information about online program management specifically (Riter, 2017) and online education more generally. EDUCAUSE conducts an annual survey of students on a variety of technology issues that have significant value for VPSAs working to build more knowledge about online education and understand the student experience around technology. The WICHE Cooperative for Educational Technologies (2013) has a checklist for choosing and working with third-party vendors. In addition to reaching out to colleagues and engaging in careful RFP processes, this checklist is indispensable in helping frame questions and priorities.

Tips for Getting Started

- Begin by defining the problem(s) you want to solve.
- Understand the population being served to help guide and prioritize services.
- Identify what local and financial resources are available to address the problem.
- Explore both internal and vendor options for addressing the problem.
- Reach out to colleagues on campuses with significant numbers of online learners (2,000+) to learn how they approach student support, if there are vendors they would recommend, and how they are funding the support.
- Do not let a great sales pitch from a vendor redefine priorities.

While VPSAs will likely have only modest impact on an institution's decision about whether or not to use an OPM, they should use every opportunity to participate in these decisions. Some OPMs provide services one would expect from student affairs, and it is invaluable to understand the reputation of the OPM, the limits it may impose, and the opportunities that may be created. If possible, VPSAs should participate on RFP committees or make sure student affairs staff are engaged in as many of the institutional planning processes as possible. While less than half of VPSAs also oversee enrollment management, where enrollment is part of the portfolio, it is significantly important for VPSAs to understand the difference in marketing to, recruiting, admitting, and processing online learners versus face-to-face students. Systems must move within minutes rather than days or weeks. There are vendors that specifically work in this area, and an OPM relationship will embed this.

VPSAs should consider the following when partnering with third-party vendors to support the needs of online learners:

- **Experience.** Think about online learner experiences as similar in some ways to face-to-face experiences and completely different in others.

- **Support.** What support makes a difference? Assessment is as important for online learners as it is for face-to-face students. As noted, there are vendors that can support assessment efforts.

- **Retention.** Retention is a critical measure of success for students. For online learners, it is measured term to term, which is challenging and tends to lag retention numbers for face-to-face students.

- **Sense of belonging.** Helping students develop a sense of pride and affiliation with the institution is important—building online cohorts, creating opportunities for virtual peer support, making sure students get student IDs, sending a T-shirt upon admission, cross training advisors, and encouraging students to participate in student life.

- **Finances.** Research system or governing board policies about online pricing to make sure there is a way to create revenue to provide some support services, whether developed internally or through vendor support. Will fees be embedded in the pricing or charged separately?

- **Broader opportunities.** Areas like expanding online tutoring, online counseling, and online advising become ways of obtaining services face-to-face students can use. Strategic implementation of online support can result in an improved experience for face-to-face students. Broader use may impact the vendor relationship, so make sure to think through this when working with vendors in specific support areas.

Vetting Online and Digital Product Vendors

Vetting online and digital product vendors is critical to the long-term success and sustainability of any service for students. Some questions to ask a potential vendor include:

- **How secure is the vendor's software?** Privacy and security are crucial in higher education. Any service must be FERPA (Family Educational Rights and Privacy Act) compliant. If the software is connected to the healthcare area, it must also be HIPAA (Health Insurance Portability and Accountability Act) and HITECH (Health Information Technology for Economic and Clinical Health Act) compliant. Ask how the company ensures compliance with privacy and security laws. Vendors should do security audits annually and should contract with outside companies to conduct penetration testing. In penetration testing, the contracted company attempts to hack and otherwise tests for any weaknesses in the software's privacy and security systems. Does the vendor have an SOC (system and organizational control report) from an independent auditor? If so, ask if there were any deficiencies and what their remediation plans are. Are the data in the system encrypted? Is encryption for data both in motion and at rest? Many of the large breaches in data have occurred when companies encrypt data when the data are in use, but not when data are sitting in a data bank. Encryption should be end to end. Logical access control refers to systems that limit access to data, much like locks on doors and security systems limit access to materials in your office. How often does the company perform a logical access review?

- **Where are the data hosted?** Some systems allow hosting on college or university computer servers, while others are hosted in the cloud. There are tradeoffs for each. Hosting on the higher education institution's servers allows greater control but also means more institutional resources are needed for tech support. Cloud-based systems typically require fewer institutional resources to maintain but provide less direct control. Security can be very solid in either case. If the data are stored in the cloud, it is important to know where data are stored.

Ideally, data should be co-located on two servers at two different locations. This allows service to continue uninterrupted if a server goes down for some reason.

- **Is the information and documentation for the vendor's software clear and easy to read?** Difficult-to-read documentation is often related to difficult-to-use software. Documentation should include frequently asked questions, ideas for trouble shooting, and technical support. It is valuable to provide live humans with whom students, staff, and faculty can interact when questions arise. Trouble with the technology is a frequent reason students give for leaving an online higher education program.

- **Are the vendor's products accessible?** Accessibility is mandated in many states but is vitally important for students, faculty, and student affairs professionals. Does the software work with screen readers? Does it use captioning? Can it be navigated with tabs rather than with only a mouse? How does the vendor verify and test for accessibility?

- **How long has the vendor been in business and what is its retention rate?** Contracting with a vendor who promptly goes out of business can be expensive and frustrating. Be sure your vendor is financially stable and likely to be around in the future. What proportion of colleges and universities who contract with a company renew each year? If institutions are not renewing year to year, it indicates they are not satisfied with their experience.

- **How often is the software upgraded?** Most software systems are upgraded regularly. How often does the vendor upgrade its software, and how long do upgrades take? Is the system down or offline during an upgrade? If so, for how long? Are upgrades included in the price, or are their additional charges for upgrades?

- **Does the vendor have native apps for both Android and Apple iOS?** Many students prefer apps to web-based resources. Does the vendor have apps, and are these available in various app stores such as Apple and Android?

- **What support and training are required for college or university staff?** What institutional resources will be required to maintain the vendor tools? How much training is required for student affairs professionals and IT support staff? Who provides training? An SLA is a service-level agreement between a vendor and a university contracting for services. What is the level of SLA you can expect? Does the vendor offer different levels of support? The SLA should spell out what support the customer will receive.

- **What kind of reporting does the vendor provide?** Evaluate any software products in use. How does the vendor provide information on utilization, satisfaction, and efficacy? How are reports generated? Can data be downloaded to create reports?

- **How often does the vendor back up data?** When it comes to backing up data, the more frequently this is done, the better. If data are backed up once a day, then only one day of data could be lost if the system crashes for any reason. If it backs up hourly, then only one hour of data is lost. Is the backup offsite and encrypted? Imagine a system crashes for several days because of a local weather event such as a hurricane. If the backup data are in the same location as the primary server, the backup may be of limited use. However, if the server is in New Jersey and the backup is in Ohio, it is far less likely to lose all of the data.

- **Does the vendor have a disaster recovery plan?** Any software vendor should have a plan for how it will get back up and running in the case of a disaster. How long will it take to resume operations? Does the vendor perform tests of its disaster recovery plan?

Potential Challenges and Practical Solutions

Potential Challenge: Going through the vetting process holistically.

Practical Solution: Expect the process of vetting and purchasing software products to be lengthy. Make sure you have included everyone who will be affected in the decision process. Your general counsel's office will want to review any contract, and your IT department will want to review the company's software, privacy practices, and other policies and procedures.

Potential Challenge: All of these steps may take two weeks or up to a year, depending on the college or university.

Practical Solution: If you work at a public institution that is part of a state system, you may be able to move more quickly to vet and purchase software if other campuses within the system are using it.

Potential Challenge: Limited resources.

Practical Solution: Student affairs staff work hard and rarely have significant resources, and not all will see the opportunity to serve online learners as a positive. Recognize these challenges and work to educate staff so they understand the role of online education in increasing access and the growing acceptance of online education.

Conclusion

Fully online programs increasingly account for the growing number of students in higher education, while face-to-face student enrollment is declining (National Student Clearinghouse Research Center, 2018; Ortagus & Tanner, 2019). This change in enrollment emphasizes the importance of student affairs leaders becoming knowledgeable and involved in institutional online planning processes as early as possible. While more institutions now recognize the need to integrate broad student support into online program development, this area tends to take a back seat to course development and other aspects of online planning. As the student affairs profession has evolved, it has been important for leaders to develop knowledge about outsourcing, public-private partnerships, and other business aspects related to providing support to students. The growth of fully online programs has added a new dimension to knowledge and skill development required of student affairs leaders.

The goal of this chapter was to provide baseline information about internal options and outside vendors that can assist in meeting the escalating demand for student support for online learners. It included resources for continued learning as this is a dynamic area. The chapter also provided some thoughts on how to ensure online program financial models incorporate ways to pay for student support. Finally, the chapter emphasized the value of professional networks for informal guidance and information about experiences with and knowledge of vendors.

 Questions for Reflection

- What is your current knowledge about online learners? How prevalent is the conversation about student services for online learners at your institution? How do you make sure to engage in campus planning for online programs?

- How do you ensure members of your team are also engaged in campus planning for online learner support?

- What is a pain point or problem you face in your role right now that may be addressed with software?

- How might tools enhance student engagement and subsequently improve retention and student satisfaction?

- How comfortable are you and your staff members with technology and digital tools?

- How will you think about these opportunities as impacting all students, not just fully online learners?

References

Bawa, P. (2016). Retention in online courses: Exploring issues and solutions—A literature review. *SAGE Open, 6*(1). doi:10.1177/2158244015621777

Benton, S. A., Heesacker, M., Snowden, S. J., & Lee, G. (2016). Therapist-assisted, online (TAO) intervention for anxiety in college students: TAO outperformed treatment as usual. *Professional Psychology: Research and Practice, 47*, 363–371. doi:10.1037/pro0000097

Cornish, P., Berry, G., Benton, S., Barros-Gomes, P., Johnson, D., Ginsburg, R., . . . Romano, V. (2017). Meeting the mental health needs of today's college student: Reinventing services through stepped care 2.0. *Psychological Services, 14*, 428–442. doi:10.1037/ser0000158

Friedman, J. (2017, April 4). U.S. News data: The average online bachelor's student. *U.S. News & World Report.* Retrieved from https://www.usnews.com/higher-education/online-education/articles/2017-04-04/us-news-data-the-average-online-bachelors-student

Herbert, M. (2006). Staying the course: A study in online student satisfaction and retention. *Online Journal of Distance Learning Administration, 9*(4). Retrieved from http://www.westga.edu/~distance/ojdla/winter94/herbert94.htm

Hrastinski, S. (2009). A theory of online learning as online participation. *Computers & Education, 52*, 78–82. doi:10.1016/j.compedu.2008.06.009

Kretovics, M. (2015). Commuter students, online services, and online communities. In J. P. Biddix (Ed.), *Understanding and addressing commuter student needs* (New Directions for Student Services, No. 150, pp. 69–78). San Francisco, CA: Jossey-Bass. doi:10.1002/ss.20128

Kruger, K., & Jarrat, D. (2018, December 16). Student affairs goes digital: Translating student support to the world of online learning. *Diverse Issues in Higher Education.* Retrieved from https://diverseeducation.com/article/134371

Lurie, H. (2018, March 6). The OPM is dead. Long live the OPM. *encoura.* Retrieved from https://encoura.org/opm-dead-long-live-opm

Magda, A. J. (2018). *Online learning in continuing higher education: Current practices and planned initiatives.* Louisville, KY: The Learning House.

Miller, A., Topper, A., & Richardson, S. (2017). *Suggestions for improving IPEDS distance education data collection* (NPEC 2017). Washington, DC: U.S. Department of Education, National Postsecondary Education Cooperative.

National Student Clearinghouse Research Center. (2018). *Current term enrollment estimates—Spring 2018.* Retrieved from https://nscresearchcenter.org/currenttermenrollmentestimate-spring2018

Ortagus, J. C., & Tanner, M. J. (2018). Going to college without going to campus: A case study of online student recruitment. *Innovative Higher Education, 44*, 53–67. doi:10.1007/s10755-018-9448-9

Riter, P. (2017, March 13). Five myths about online program management. *EDUCAUSE Review.* Retrieved from https://er.educause.edu/articles/2017/3/five-myths-about-online-program-management

Salter, D. W. (2012). Online student retention. In A. Seidman (Ed.), *College student retention: Formula for student success* (2nd ed., pp. 211–228). Lanham, MD: Rowman & Littlefield.

Smith, B. G. (2010). *E-learning technologies: A comparative study of adult learners enrolled on blended and online campuses engaging in a virtual classroom* (Doctoral dissertation). Retrieved from ProQuest Dissertations and Theses database. (UMI No. 3413143)

Thomas, L., Herbert, J., & Teras, M. (2014). A sense of belonging to enhance participation, success and retention in online programs. *International Journal of the First Year in Higher Education, 5*, 69–80. doi:10.5204/intjfyhe.v5i2.233

WICHE Cooperative for Educational Technologies. (2013). *Best practice checklist for choosing and working with 3rd party vendors.* Retrieved from https://wcet.wiche.edu/sites/default/files/WCET-TalkingPoints-Vendor-Best-Practice-Checklist.docx

CHAPTER 4

Addressing Equity Through Online Learner Support Services

Jeannette Smith and Matt Smith

EFFORTS TO ADDRESS inequities in access (Agu, 2019), lack of affordability (Delaney, Kearney, & Hemenway, 2016), and sense of belonging (Griffin, 2017; Kretovics, 2015) in higher education are many. Online learning has the potential to mitigate disproportionate student outcomes. This chapter explores what connections may exist between the delivery of student services online and the advancement of institutional equity goals by student affairs practitioners.

A resource guide from the University of Southern California's Center for Urban Education (CUE; 2017) included this note: "An equity focus in policy recognizes the need to eliminate disparities in educational outcomes of students from underserved and underrepresented populations" (p. 2). This chapter identifies scholarly literature and research whose authors spoke to the intersections of equity and online learning to help inform student affairs practitioners on ways to address equity in student support services for online learners. Given the persistent equity gaps perpetuated by higher education institutions (Broido, Brown, Stygles, & Bronkema, 2015; Museus, Ledesma, & Parker, 2015), and the steady increase in college and university offerings of online courses and resources, this chapter's focus on the intersection of equity and online access to higher education is both timely and relevant.

Online Learning as an Avenue to Address Equity in Student Support Services

Much of the literature on online learner supports does not explicitly include an equity focus, and an equity lens must be applied by the practitioner who intends to adapt these practices on their campus. A recent report included case studies of six institutions that "have a strong track record of using digital learning to serve large, socioeconomically diverse student populations" (Bailey, Vaduganathan, Henry, Laverdiere, & Pugliese, 2018, p. 5) while expanding access and improving outcomes at an affordable cost. Of the participating institutions, three were four-year institutions, two were community colleges, and one was a statewide community and technical college system. The institutions' leaders tailored strategies and resources toward specific goals for online programs, and Bailey et al. (2018) emphasized the need for thoughtful, detailed approaches driven by student needs. For instance, a primary goal of increased revenue and overall enrollment requires a different set of strategies than increasing student retention and success. In sharing seven promising practices,

Bailey et al. (2018) noted the necessity to "provide the differential supports that students need in order to succeed fully in online learning" (p. 40). Although a variety of positive student outcomes related to digital learning broadly were mentioned in the report, no direct links between specific online learner support services and student outcomes were referenced.

In addition to a variety of instructional supports, including adaptive learning software, Bailey et al. (2018) highlighted the combinations of online student services provided to supplement instructional supports for five of the institutions studied (the sixth institution used an emporium model with few fully online courses). Three institutions leveraged software platforms for outreach and/or early alert systems, three institutions provided some form of online success coaching or mentoring, two institutions provided online tutoring resources, and two institutions provided fully online academic advising. The community and technical college system gave "guidance to students in 'degree mapping' to provide a standard interface across institutions" (Bailey et al., 2018, p. 45) via a third-party vendor. One of the community colleges profiled implemented an assessment for students to determine their technical readiness for online learning and also enrolled all online learners who had earned fewer than 12 credit hours in an online student success course.

Karp, Kalamkarian, Klempin, and Fletcher (2016) from the Community College Research Center examined six colleges' attempts to reform their advising and student support systems via technology-mediated advising systems, often referred to as integrated planning and advising for student success (iPASS). Karp et al. (2016) "sought to understand whether colleges could use iPASS to transform student services such that they were delivered in more sustained, strategic, intrusive and integrated, and personalized ways—and if so, how?" (p. 43). Karp et al. (2016) also noted implementation of a new system is distinct from adoption of new structures and processes aligned with a shared vision, and although all six colleges implemented reforms, transformative change was achieved at only three. The common threads between the three successful colleges were "functional technology and a positive vendor relationship; an orientation toward student success as a shared enterprise across the institution; a clear vision for iPASS reform; and cross-hierarchical, visionary leadership" (Karp et al., 2016, p. 44).

Wheelan (2016) advocated for flipping student services. Rather than a continual cycle of repeating basic information to student after student, flipped student support—particularly for advisors, coaches, and counselors—refers to asynchronous content that may enhance the quality and efficiency of one-on-one interactions between practitioners and students (either in person or remotely). Wheelan (2016) indicated "students can access critical support information from anywhere at any time, support professionals can spend their time engaged in personalized student interaction, and institutions can provide more tailored support to students in a cost-effective manner" (p. 36) when this approach is employed.

The five fundamental components of flipped student supports are technology, data analytics, methodology, content, and personnel (Wheelan, 2016), each of which require thoughtful consideration to be effective: A service traditionally delivered in person will not naturally maintain or increase its efficacy by shifting online. Flipped student supports should be implemented using an equity lens. Just as institutions focus support services on student populations experiencing equity and opportunity gaps, so should online learner supports be prioritized to help students who are not yet thriving in online or hybrid learning environments. For example, multiple vendors and platforms exist to provide predictive analytics, and "colleges are increasingly using models to predict student behavior and intervene to change that behavior" (Palmer, 2018, p. 1). These systems employ sophisticated algorithms to deliver data that can be used to help student affairs practitioners prioritize where to place their energies to support student enrollment, persistence, and completion, particularly for the most vulnerable students, many of whom take all of their courses online. Learning management systems can frequently be linked to predictive analytics, and many of these systems include online outreach tools that can be used to deliver tailored communications to particular groups of students efficiently, often in their preferred communication mode (Palmer, 2018) or the mode proven to reach the highest proportion of those students on campus (Wheelan, 2016).

Online Access to Student Services

Online education provides great benefit to nontraditional students (Bailey et al., 2018). Students with family and work obligations "are more likely to take courses online than traditional students" (Cohen, Brawer, & Kisker, 2014, p. 195). Furthermore, "62 percent of online community college students are women and over half are over age 26" (Cohen et al., 2014, p. 195). This phenomenon is not limited to urban community colleges. Rural community colleges often serve students who lack access to transportation and have limited education (Walker-Gibbs, Paatsch, Moles, Yim, & Redpath, 2016).

Although ample research literature exists related to online and hybrid instruction in higher education, researchers often indicate a dearth in examining student support services infrastructure (Shea & Bidjerano, 2018). Sundt, Berry, and Ortiz (2017) stated, "The online environment is a diverse environment" (p. 83), meaning there are various modes of delivering and sharing information, systems intentionally created for enhanced accessibility, and the ability to engage with people across a spectrum of identities, including ethnicity, gender, socioeconomic status, nationality, ability, and generation. Student affairs practitioners are tapping into this diverse learning environment to deliver services to their communities:

- Online orientation programs can be effective "especially among at-risk students" (Cohen et al., 2014, p. 217), particularly low-income students who are unable to attend a summer orientation session due to work obligations.

- Accessing mental health services online can provide "access, speed, and comfort" (Cohen et al., 2014, p. 221) to students who may not be in close proximity to mental health providers or who are concerned about stigmatization.

- Student unions provide access to guest speakers through live stream feeds.

- Academic advisors engage in individual and group video chat sessions with prospective students and connected cohorts.

- Career advisors offer online tutorials for interview tips, résumé writing, and job inventory assessments.

- Financial aid offices deliver financial literacy through video tutorials.

- Student governance and organizations offer online group registration, risk management, and student election options.

- Conduct offices use case management software (see the Technology and Innovative Tools sidebar for examples) to communicate processes and student rights.

Across the student affairs discipline, online technologies are an increasingly accessible tool for support, advocacy, community building, content creation, and transparency. Within this digital landscape is the opportunity to overlay an equity lens to better serve all students.

Technology and Innovative Tools	
AwardSpring	A platform for financial aid and scholarship administrators. The software allows for going beyond basic application processes to offering tools for relationship building and connectivity between donors, students, and staff. *http://awardspring.com*
CampusGroups	An online platform that allows student activities, student organizations, and student governance advisors to create and maintain online communities with students. UCLA, UW Stout, the Rochester Institute of Technology, the Northwest Kellogg School of Management, and the Wharton School have all been featured as case studies on this site. *https://www.campusgroups.com/product/success-stories*
CareerWISE (Women in Science and Engineering)	A free, asynchronous online coaching and mentoring platform designed to support women in graduate-level science, technology, engineering, and mathematics programs. Three empirical studies of the website and its content suggest the program provides psychosocial support and resilience training, which can lessen the risks and barriers women often face in STEM environments. *https://careerwise.asu.edu*
Engage UP	A platform through Campus Labs student unions are beginning to launch for club connectedness and funding applications. Administrators at the University of Portland are looking at how to use it for cocurricular transcript creation as well. *https://up.campuslabs.com/engage*

Equity in Supporting Underserved and Marginalized Student Populations Online

Student populations from communities or backgrounds that have traditionally been underserved, underrepresented, and marginalized are taking online courses. In some instances, they are more likely to stop or drop out than their counterparts from dominant populations (Museus et al., 2015). Shea and Bidjerano (2018) looked at a 2010 study by Jaggers and Xu where "male students, younger students, Black students, and students with lower GPAs" (p. 283) had lower academic performance in online courses than others in the same courses. While specific to instruction, there is an opportunity here for student affairs practitioners to provide targeted support for at-risk student populations. In a keynote speech to a group of faculty and student affairs practitioners at a statewide guided pathways institute, Estela Bensimon from the Center for Urban Education emphasized the historical context of equity work in higher education:

> Equity work is an expertise with history, theory, literature. Many using this word are not aware of its foundational principles. It is not about disaggregating data. It's about being able to interpret disaggregated data as dysfunction of institutional practices, not students. (personal communication, April 11, 2019)

This is a critical distinction. For instance, if disaggregated institutional data suggest a particular student group lacks readiness for online education, it is incumbent upon student affairs practitioners, along with faculty, to determine how best to meet those student needs from a growth mindset. Too often students are blamed when institutions and educational systems fail to meet their needs.

Students With Disabilities and Neurodiverse Students

Students with disabilities are recognized as a marginalized population that faces multiple challenges in higher education (Flink, 2019). The passage of the Technology-Related Assistance for Individuals With Disabilities Act of 1988 and its subsequent reauthorizations have led to great advances in assistive technology to support individuals with disabilities (Flink, 2019). Assistive technology is a general term that includes devices, software, and services spanning a range of low-tech innovations to the advanced and highly technical (Ahmed, 2018). Of the examples of advances provided by the National Institute of Child Health and Human Development (2018), the following are relevant to supporting online learning:

- Hearing aids to help people hear or hear more clearly.

- Cognitive aids, including computer or electrical assistive devices, to help people with memory, attention, or other challenges in their thinking skills.

- Computer software and hardware, such as voice recognition programs, screen readers, and screen enlargement applications, to help people with mobility and sensory impairments use computers and mobile devices.

- Closed captioning to allow people with hearing problems to watch movies, television programs, and other digital media.

Higher education has benefited from these advances by incorporating technology to support students on campus and online. For example, captioning increases access for students viewing videos and assistive listening devices as they "amplify and transmit voices to any place in a room" (Evans, Broido, Brown, & Wilke, 2017, p. 35). For a student with a disability taking an online class, these devices make for increased "autonomy and fuller access" (Evans et al., 2017, p. 35). How online student services are presented is just as important as the content itself. Colleges and universities are taking notice of how online programs can serve students with disabilities in ways on-campus support cannot. One example is St. Petersburg College's simplification of the presentation format of online courses by "decreasing the number of windows, using straightforward language, limiting excessive movement on web pages, and syncing videos in real time text" (Cohen et al., 2014, p. 223). Student affairs practitioners can also use this technology when delivering online first-year student experience courses, online orientation sessions, and online student leadership content for student government and clubs.

Applications such as Second Life (SL) are being used around the globe to serve neurodiverse students online (Hartley, Ludlow, & Duff, 2015). Neurodiverse students can interact with their neurotypical peers, free from the labels and stereotypes associated with learning disabilities (Daley & Rappolt-Schlichtmann, 2018). Flink (2019) made a compelling case for SL, as it is not a video game where students are competing but rather a tool that "can mirror in person class work" (p. 35). Students can use this open virtual world to create content, participate in discussions, or build community through self-created avatars (Flink, 2019). For a person who experiences anxiety because of speech or language, Flink (2019) posited SL can be used as a tool to remove this barrier as well, allowing for students to engage on their own timeline, with the opportunity to practice that engagement until they have mastered it to their desired level.

Student affairs practitioners can use tools such as SL, where community building between diverse students can take place in a virtual world. This technology may aid student clubs and other student groups within campus activities with online recruitment and member engagement, thereby promoting a more inclusive environment by offering a virtual campus with gathering spaces that do not require students to visit the physical campus and allow for meeting times unconstrained by building operating hours. Any online activity that aims to pull students together could make use of this technology as a tool to advance equity for students with disabilities.

Practitioners should consider providing captions for students who are deaf or hearing impaired so they can be included in digital streaming of guest speakers, participation in online common reading chat rooms, and online student employment training materials. Digital written materials should be formatted to ensure optimization for screen readers used by students with visual impairments (Moriña & Morgado, 2018), including all web content and official communications to students from the institution (Zahra, 2017). Screen readers may prove helpful for better access to online handbooks created for

Tips for Getting Started

Determining whether your institution's equity gaps vary by modality (e.g., online only, hybrid, face-to-face only) and understanding the capacity of what your campus technology can support and maintain is a great foundational step to help determine capacity and cost. To aid that inquiry, the following tips may be of use:

- **Learn from other institutions.** Look to schools currently providing student services online, such as Berkeley College, Columbia Southern University, or Oregon State University, for lessons learned. Not only will you gain valuable insight, you may build a relationship or partnership for continued support and sharing of experiences.

- **Assess program impacts.** Assess how your institution could infuse equity into both an online presence and address equity gaps within the student population. Sundt, Cole, and Wheaton's (2017) guidance is a solid foundation for addressing program design and assessing program impacts explicitly for marginalized and minoritized students. Although the framework is not explicitly designed for students' online experiences, the thought process can be easily adapted to the focused scope of online and hybrid students.

- **Identify gaps in student representation.** Review your institution's existing student organizations for student representation based on data from your institutional research office. This will allow you to see where gaps are and how online learners are being included or excluded.

- **Deliver services at the right time.** Use existing data analytics in collaboration with your technology department to assess when students are accessing online resources. Once you have that data, you can review your offerings for online chat sessions, tutoring, and other support services and align the timing and dates offered with when students are accessing your websites.

activities, conduct, rights and responsibilities, and orientation. Sign language interpreters may also be recorded and viewable, particularly for events happening in real time, such as budget presentations and requests for student fee-funded groups or legislation being debated by student governance groups. Educating colleagues and decision makers on these technologies and related supports may be made easier by citing relevant statutes and regulations. There are examples of nondiscriminatory legislation in the following paragraph that can help guide campus leaders in expanding access for students with disabilities.

The United States has the Americans With Disabilities Act and the Rehabilitation Act, Canada has provincial legislation like the Integrated Accessibility Standards for Ontarians With Disabilities and the Web Content Accessibility Guidelines, and the United Kingdom has the Special Education Needs and Disability Act (Kumar & Owston, 2016). Although this legislation exists, Kumar and Owston (2016) said, in practice "there is evidence to suggest [legislation] has not effectively increased e-learning accessibility to acceptable levels for all students" (p. 266). They suggest limitations within the legislation contribute to institutions' lack of compliance in expanding e-learning accessibility. Kumar and Owston (2016) said those limitations include "lengthy and ambiguous" language, "minimal representation of learning disability experts" (p. 26) creating and interpreting the legislation, and limited understanding of the intersection of various learning disabilities and web access. These limitations provide an opportunity for student affairs practitioners to serve as advocates for students with disabilities. Using existing data on usage, researching and publishing more on the lived experiences of students with disabilities who use online services, and sharing best practices as technology is implemented are tools at their disposal.

Student Parents

The research on the intersection of online learners who are parents framed as an equity issue is a definite gap in the literature (Lawson, 2018). Lawson (2018) noted this group is "an underrepresented population" (p. 1) whose experiences are lacking in the literature in terms of equity. Students with children younger than 6 years old completed online courses at significantly lower rates than their peers with no children, and "these results suggest that without adequate support for student parents (e.g., childcare, financial aid to reduce work hours)" (Wladis, Conway, & Hachey, 2016, p. 103), the online delivery of curriculum may not be enough to offset the workload of parenting.

In this spirit, financial aid staff should consider allocating funds from institutional grant aid specifically for student parents. Those who work in registration and orientation can look to offer asynchronous content and online support outside of traditional business hours, recognizing student parents have varied time constraints with caretaking responsibilities (Lawson, 2018). Finally, student activities professionals could program family-friendly online workshops aimed at identifying the specific challenges student parents face, such as balancing bedtime routines with homework or budgeting daycare expenses. If we "treat the unique challenges of pregnant and parenting students in college as a social justice and equity issue" (Lawson, 2018, p. 2), student affairs practitioners can contribute to the gap in this research, allowing for a stronger rationale to further support these students.

Potential Challenges and Practical Solutions

Potential Challenge: Efficacy of those presenting the information, and how comfortable with the technology the staff are who deliver online support, can be a challenge when assessing efficacy and capability, providing access to training and development, and offering continued support to staff (Walker-Gibbs et al., 2016).

Practical Solution: Connect with tech-savvy community members on and off campus for guidance, advice, and support. For instance, instructional designers and marketing professionals on campus may have specialized skills and training in content development that can be shared with faculty and student affairs staff. Alumni and friends of the college may have backgrounds in coding, information technology, or mobile app development and have yet to be asked to support the institution with their time and talent. All of these talents and expertise can be tapped to serve online learners.

Potential Challenge: There are limited tools for auditing digital experiences delivered and digital resources offered (Ross, Volz, Lancaster, & Divan, 2018). Contrary to limited tools, it is possible to have too much data and not know what to do with it to create systemic changes through an equity lens (Sundt, Berry, et al., 2017).

Practical Solution: One way to address this challenge is to start with basic analytics available from your institution's instructional technology department and work with your institutional research office to understand your data. A second option is to enlist campus partners, such as faculty and grad students, who have interest in this area and are knowledgeable of survey and research methods. Staff may also choose to outsource to a consultant or undergo an external evaluation where there are intentional steps taken to assess equity and online services.

Potential Challenge: Financial resources to support the increasing demand, need, and evolution of the technology and tools necessary may pose a challenge.

Practical Solution: Results from external evaluations, accreditation reports, and even employee professional evaluations can all aid in making a compelling story for budget support. Mining existing data for inferences is a stop gap that will help build your case while you plan to collect strategic data moving forward. It may also help to look at what funding already exists and where equity can be applied. For example, a student technology fee may be flexible enough to provide funding to perform a digital equity audit. Also consider adjusting student technology fees on a sliding scale based on expected family contribution.

Student Veterans and Active Service Members

Due to the transient nature of their careers, online learners who are also active military personnel may benefit from services such as online registration and orientation programs, access to online coaching and mentorship support, online group and individual counseling, online student club offerings, and online financial aid courses. There are few studies on the online delivery of student services for student veterans and active service members that focus strongly on instruction and access, although "the need to provide retention and graduation impacting support services [for veterans] is critical" (Kirchner, 2015, p. 117). Similarly, when Mentzer, Black, and Spohn (2015) researched military students at an online university, they found students exhibited "stronger persistence when built on a foundation of institutional and academic support" (p. 12). Mentzer et al. (2015) looked at financial, social, and academic supports with a slight nod to advising in their survey.

Adams, Lee, and Holden (2017) studied "student veteran perceptions regarding the development of a web-based support group" (p. 24). The small sample of 21 student veterans was diverse by gender, age, race, ethnicity, and type of service. Adams et al. (2017) found students used social media to stay connected, recruit for student clubs and organizations, and participate in support groups facilitated by college staff. More specifically, "the student veterans were generally nontraditional students who had family and work responsibilities" (Adams et al., 2017, p. 26), and the online communities contributed to the veterans developing their sense of identity as students.

To support the military-connected student population, student affairs practitioners should examine where professionals are positioned within their institution to provide the best online support to a community of learners who may be deployed at any moment. Researchers have suggested military-connected students thrive when they can be in community with peers and educators who have personal experience and knowledge of their lived experiences (Karp & Klempin, 2016). One strategy would be to ensure an institution's veterans resource center has strong partnerships with other community builders on campus and then provide a digital space for those partners to connect with veteran students. For campuses without a veterans resource center, an option may be to empower certifying officials to build capacity on campus through strategic relationships with key campus and community partners who may work toward using online tools to help students transition to college life.

Van Sack (2016) reported "Athletes of Valor is an online platform that connects college coaches with athletes who have served their country in the armed forces" (p. 1) who may be seeking a college to attend as a student-athlete. This communication can be sustained online and can serve as a recruitment tool to assist with sense of belonging and community building before the student arrives to campus or maintain communication while the student is deployed. In this way, student affairs practitioners can provide critical online support for a group of students who function uniquely as both online learners and on-campus learners because of deployment.

First-Generation, Low-Income Students

Researchers have found students who are first generation and/or low income can experience difficulties in navigating college, accessing resources, understanding material and content, and having a sense of belonging (Means & Pyne, 2017; Pichon, 2016; Plaskett, Bali, Nakkula, & Harris, 2018). Although Wladis et al. (2016) did not find significant differences between low-income students' course and college outcomes by modality, "lower-income students likely still need significant support in online courses, just as they do in face-to-face courses" (p. 107). When student affairs practitioners take advantage of delivering online services, they can "monitor student performance, flag issues, and intervene in real and with potentially greater effectiveness than in the past" (Sundt, Berry, et al., 2017, p. 83). While crucial to supporting this population of students, this success can be replicated for any student experiencing crisis or in need of support, particularly online learners.

Bensimon (2016) created a series of 12 questions designed for college and university leaders to develop a practice of equity-minded indicators. The first question is: "Do you routinely examine and report racial/ethnic participation in [transfer from community college to four-year college]?" (Bensimon, 2016, para. 1). The question includes 10 suggested examples of reporting indicators. None of the examples reference online learning. Student affairs practitioners can advocate to expand these reporting indicators from 10 to 13 to include access to online learning and support services:

- Do online learners at your institution succeed at different rates when disaggregated by race/ethnicity, ability, parent, income, veteran status, etc.?

- Do online learners at your institution access online support services (if available) at disproportionate rates when disaggregated by race/ethnicity, ability, parent, income, veteran status, etc.?

- If so, what potential causes could explain such disproportionality within your institution's specific campus and community contexts?

In particular, advisors, coaches, counselors, and tutors should be thoughtful in determining which student groups should be prioritized when providing online support. Historically marginalized groups likely need more additional supports than their higher income, dominant culture peers. This axiom of student affairs practice should be tempered with a reliance on both individual and institutional level data rather than conventional wisdom, as well as a focus on contributing factors in success and avoidance of deficit-oriented theories (Sundt, Cole, et al., 2017).

Conclusion

Student affairs practitioners have been adapting digital resources and tools from the outset of online learning (Westra, 2018). The very nature of the work of student support is bolstered by access to a diversity of online platforms. While universities and colleges include equity and access in strategic plans, more and more are beginning to focus on how to promote "inclusivity in a digital world" (Walker-Gibbs et al., 2016, p. 1) by prioritizing flexible learning through online deliverables that can be used to build digital literacy.

To offer a student a holistic academic experience, college personnel have begun to offer student services traditionally accessed on campus to their online community of learners, thus closing the equity gap between students on campus and distance learners who pay the same student fees but have different levels of access to services. Equity is addressed twofold in that students who could not access services in person were given options to do so remotely, and of the students being served remotely, those who identified as women or as from underserved communities were served more efficiently than before.

This chapter has identified the need for an equity lens in regard to online learner support services to address the critical needs of the most vulnerable students. Student affairs practitioners must adapt existing best practices to include both equity frameworks and institution-specific data on equity gaps to create digital spaces that help students to thrive and minimize disproportionate student outcomes.

```
┌─────────────────────────────────────────────┐
│ (?) Questions for Reflection                  │
```

- How are online learners included in your institution's definitions of equity, diversity, and inclusion?
- Are the services provided on campus offered in an equitable fashion for online learners?
- Where are the biggest gaps in your institutional support for online learners?
- What systemic policies, processes, and/or guidelines pertaining to technology, social media, and online access currently impede your ability to advance equity goals?
- Where will you place your initial focus to shift practice to improve student support services for online learners?

References

Adams, P., Lee, H. S., & Holden, B. (2017). A needs assessment for developing a web-based social support program for student veterans. *Journal of Military and Veterans' Health, 25*, 23–29. Retrieved from https://jmvh.org/article/a-needs-assessment-for-developing-a-web-based-social-support-program-for-student-veterans

Agu, C. (2019). Higher education access: Filling in the cracks versus rebuilding the foundation. *Harvard Kennedy School Review, 19*, 70–78. Retrieved from https://ksr.hkspublications.org/ksr-2018-2019-edition

Ahmed, A. (2018). Perceptions of using assistive technology for students with disabilities in the classroom. *International Journal of Special Education, 33*, 129–139. Retrieved from https://files.eric.ed.gov/fulltext/EJ1184079.pdf

Bailey, A., Vaduganathan, N., Henry, T., Laverdiere, R., & Pugliese, L. (2018). *Making digital learning work: Success strategies from six leading universities and community colleges.* Boston, MA: Boston Consulting Group.

Bensimon, E. M. (2016). *Developing a practice of equity minded indicators.* Retrieved from Center for Urban Education website: https://cue.usc.edu/files/2016/02/Developing-a-Practice-of-Equity-Mindedness.pdf

Broido, E. M., Brown, K. R., Stygles, K. N., & Bronkema, R. H. (2015). Responding to gendered dynamics: Experiences of women working over 25 years at one university. *Journal of Higher Education, 86*, 595–627. doi:10.1080/00221546.2015.11777376

Center for Urban Education. (2017). *Improving postsecondary attainment: Overcoming common challenges to an equity agenda in state policy.* Los Angeles, CA: Author.

Cohen, A. M., Brawer, F. B., & Kisker, C. B. (2014). *The American community college.* San Francisco, CA: Jossey-Bass.

Daley, S. G., & Rappolt-Schlichtmann, G. (2018). Stigma consciousness among adolescents with learning disabilities: Considering individual experiences of being stereotyped. *Learning Disability Quarterly, 41*, 200–212. doi:10.1177/0731948718785565

Delaney, J. A., Kearney, T. D., & Hemenway, B. (2016). Balancing tuition predictability and affordability: The pitfalls of guaranteed tuition plans. *Change: The Magazine of Higher Learning, 48*, 59–66. doi:10.1080/00091383.2016.1167568

Evans, N. J., Broido, E. M., Brown, K. R., & Wilke, A. K. (2017). *Disability in higher education.* San Francisco, CA: Jossey-Bass.

Flink, P. (2019). Second Life and virtual learning: An educational alternative for neurodiverse students in college. *College Student Journal, 53,* 33–41. Retrieved from https://www.projectinnovation.com/college-student-journal.html

Griffin, K. A. (2017). Campus climate and diversity. In J. Schuh, S. R. Jones, & V. Torres (Eds.), *Student services: A handbook for the profession* (6th ed., pp. 73–88). San Francisco, CA: Jossey-Bass

Hartley, M. D., Ludlow, B. L., & Duff, M. C. (2015). Second Life: A 3D virtual immersive environment for teacher preparation courses in a distance education program. *Rural Special Education Quarterly, 34,* 21–25. doi:10.1177/875687051503400305

Karp, M. M., Kalamkarian, H. S., Klempin, S., & Fletcher, J. (2016). *How colleges use integrated planning and advising for student success (iPASS) to transform student support* (CCRC Working Paper No. 89). New York, NY: Columbia University, Teachers College, Community College Research Center.

Karp, M. M., & Klempin, S. (2016). *Supporting military veteran students: Early lessons from Kohlberg prize recipients.* Retrieved from https://ccrc.tc.columbia.edu/media/k2/attachments/supporting-military-veteran-students-early-lessons-kohlberg.pdf

Kirchner, M. J. (2015). Supporting student veteran transition to college and academic success. *Adult Learning, 26,* 116–123. doi:10.1177/1045159515583813

Kretovics, M. (2015). Commuter students, online services, and online communities. In J. P. Biddix (Ed.), *Understanding and addressing commuter student needs* (New Directions for Student Services, No. 150, pp. 69–78). San Francisco, CA: Jossey-Bass. doi:10.1002/ss.20128

Kumar, K. L., & Owston, R. (2016). Evaluating e-learning accessibility by automated and student-centered methods. *Educational Technology Research and Development, 64,* 263–283. doi:10.1007/s11423-015-9413-6

Lawson, J. (2018). The student equity problem of parent-students. *Medium.* Retrieved from https://medium.com/highered-insider/the-student-equity-problem-of-parent-students-df5b138154a0

Means, D. R., & Pyne, K. B. (2017). Finding my way: Perceptions of institutional support and belonging in low-income, first-generation, first-year college students. *Journal of College Student Development, 58,* 907–924. doi:10.1353/csd.2017.0071

Mentzer, B., Black, E. L., & Spohn, R. T. (2015). An analysis of supports for persistence for the military student population. *Online Learning, 19,* 31–47. doi:10.24059/olj.v19i1.500

Moriña, A., & Morgado, B. (2018). University surroundings and infrastructures that are accessible and inclusive for all: Listening to students with disabilities. *Journal of Further and Higher Education, 42,* 13–23. doi:10.1080/0309877X.2016.1188900

Museus, S. D., Ledesma, M. C., & Parker, T. L. (2015). Systemic racism in higher education. *ASHE Higher Education Report, 42,* 49–71. doi:10.1002/aehe.20067

National Institute for Child Health and Human Development. (2018). *What are some types of assistive devices and how are they used?* Retrieved from https://www.nichd.nih.gov/health/topics/rehabtech/conditioninfo/device

Palmer, I. (2018). *Choosing a predictive analytics vendor: A guide for colleges.* Retrieved from New America website: https://www.newamerica.org/education-policy/reports/choosing-predictive-analytics-vendor-guide/introduction

Pichon, H. W. (2016). Developing a sense of belonging in the classroom: Community college students taking courses on a four-year college campus. *Community College Journal of Research and Practice, 40,* 47–59. doi:10.1080/10668926.2014.964429

Plaskett, S., Bali, D., Nakkula, M. J., & Harris, J. (2018). Peer mentoring to support first-generation low-income college students. *Phi Delta Kappan, 99,* 47–51. doi:10.1177/0031721718767861

Ross, S. R. P-J., Volz, V., Lancaster, M. K., & Divan, A. (2018). A generalizable framework for multi-scale auditing of digital learning provision in higher education. *Online Learning, 22,* 249–270. doi:10.24059/olj.v22i21229

Shea, P., & Bidjerano, T. (2018). Online course enrollment in community college and degree completion: The tipping point. *International Review of Research in Open and Distributed Learning, 19*, 281–293. doi:10.19173/irrodl.v19i2.3460

Sundt, M. A., Berry, S., & Ortiz, A. (2017). Using data to support online student communities. In K. M. Goodman & D. Cole (Eds.), *Using data-informed decision making to improve student affairs practice* (New Directions for Student Services, No. 159, pp. 83–91). San Francisco, CA: Jossey-Bass. doi:10.1002/ss.20229

Sundt, M. A., Cole, D., & Wheaton, M. (2017). Using data to guide diversity work and enhance student learning. In K. M. Goodman & D. Cole (Eds.), *Using data-informed decision making to improve student affairs practice* (New Directions for Student Services, No. 159, pp. 93–103). San Francisco, CA: Jossey-Bass. doi:10.1002/ss.20230

Walker-Gibbs, B. A., Paatsch, L., Moles, J., Yim, B., & Redpath, T. (2016). A view through the long lens: Pre-service teachers' perceptions of multi-campus course delivery. *Journal of University Teaching & Learning Practice, 13*, 1–8. Retrieved from http://ro.uow.edu.au/jutlp/vol13/iss5/23

Westra, K. (2018, October 29). Online student services: What, where, who, when, how, and most importantly, why. *EDUCAUSE Review*. Retrieved from https://er.educause.edu/articles/2018/10/online-student-services what-where-who-when-how-and-most-importantly-why

Wheelan, P. (2016). Flipping student support services to improve outcomes. *Change: The Magazine of Higher Learning, 48*, 36–41. doi:10.1080/00091383.2016.1247581

Wladis, C., Conway, K. M., & Hachey, A. C. (2016). Assessing readiness for online education: Research models for identifying students at risk. *Online Learning, 20*, 97–109. doi:10.24059/olj.v20i3.980

Van Sack, J. (2016, May 31). Cambridge firm connects college coaches with military athletes. *Boston Herald*. Retrieved from https://www.bostonherald.com/2016/05/31/cambridge-firm-connects-college-coaches-with-military-athletes

Zahra, S. A. (2017). *How people with disabilities use the web*. Retrieved from Web Accessibility Initiative website: https://www.w3.org/WAI/people-use-web

CHAPTER 5

Assessing Student Affairs Programs and Services for Online Learners

Nicole Long and Stephanie Smith Budhai

A CENTRAL TENET of student affairs is the education of the whole person, as articulated in the profession's early years through *The Student Personnel Point of View* (American Council on Education, 1949). Student affairs personnel are charged to create educational experiences where students engage in active, purposeful learning along an array of dimensions (ACPA–College Student Educators International & NASPA–Student Affairs Administrators in Higher Education, 1998). Moreover, student affairs staff are not only facilitating these experiences, they are essential experts within the fabric of higher education institutions (Schuh & Gansemer-Topf, 2010).

In its progression over the years, student affairs assessment has been approached from the standpoint of traditional learning environments, with applications and exemplar implementation of assessment in brick-and-mortar institutions. Traditional approaches to student affairs assessment assume students interact with personnel and other students in face-to-face contexts, along with physically experiencing the campus environment. Movement toward online and hybrid courses embedded within primarily face-to-face academic programs and completely online course delivery has changed what it means to learn and interact with other students, faculty, and staff (Boling, Hough, Krinsky, Saleem, & Stevens, 2012; Bryan et al., 2018). Additionally, in the past two decades, traditional higher education learning environments have leveraged technology (e.g., automated scheduling, social media, web conferencing) to not only increase efficiencies but also to meet contemporary college student expectations (Cabellon & Junco, 2015; Hornak, Akweks, & Jeffs, 2010; Lowery, 2004; Pullan, 2009).

Much has been written on facilitating and assessing pedagogical practices in distance education (Baleni, 2015; Swan, Schen, & Hiltz, 2006). Similarly, assessment has been a critical aspect of student affairs administration since the mid-1990s when Upcraft and Schuh (1996) pioneered the student affairs assessment movement with *Assessment in Student Affairs: A Guide for Practitioners*. These parallel emphases of assessment in online learning environments *and* in student affairs have yet to fully converge in the literature. This chapter provides an overview of assessment while exploring how these practices can be used to evaluate the effectiveness of student services for online learners and environments.

Common Types of Assessment in the Context of Online Student Services

Broadly, *assessment* is the systematic and purposeful collection of information or data for the purpose of improvement (Henning & Roberts, 2016). Although primarily for the purpose of improvement, assessment is often associated with helping an organization or unit demonstrate its effectiveness, thus being an important component of engaging stakeholders and establishing a commitment of accountability toward them (Banta, Jones, & Black, 2009; Schuh, 2013). Indeed, Schuh (2015) noted, "Student affairs educators owe it to their constituents, from students and their parents to benefactors and graduates, that they are adding to the value of the education offered to students enrolled in their institutions" (p. 8). While attending to the diversity of stakeholders, assessment is conducted for a variety of purposes and includes an array of activities. Specific types of assessment commonly used in student affairs include needs, learning outcomes, satisfaction, and operational assessment.

Needs Assessment

By conducting a needs assessment, organizations collect information to assist in determining the necessary services, experiences, and goods to meet stakeholder needs (Bresciani, Gardner, & Hickmott, 2009). A needs assessment of current online student services being offered and areas online learners feel are missing can be conducted to ensure a comprehensive suite of student services are provided by all functional areas with offices that serve on-campus students. Although needs assessments are routinely conducted, there are common challenges associated with them, including distinguishing needs versus wants, assuming stakeholder needs, and collecting information from stakeholders that is not actionable. One such way to not succumb to these challenges is to stay abreast of current trends and research to inform decisions about student needs and related assessments

(Henning & Roberts, 2016). This may be even more so true when carrying out a needs assessment of online student services, as student affairs functions in exclusive online learning environments continue to evolve.

Learning Outcomes Assessment

Student learning occurs in both the curricular and cocurricular landscapes of the higher education context (Borrego, 2006). Simply put, learning outcomes assessment "takes our natural curiosity about our work's effectiveness and puts it in a systematic framework, where we explicitly articulate what we hope a student participating in a program will take away from the experience—the learning outcomes" (Bresciani, 2011, p. 1). In many functional areas of student affairs, student learning is assessed by measuring the knowledge, awareness, and skills of students before, after, and sometimes during a program or activity. For example, an academic integrity unit may leverage a learning management system (LMS) to deploy modules on an institution's academic honor code to support online learners rather than conducting face-to-face workshops that would likely occur in a traditional learning environment.

Satisfaction Assessment

Through satisfaction assessment, an organization collects information from stakeholders to determine if they are satisfied with the services, experiences, programs, and goods they provide. At times, online learners may have different expectations and needs than on-campus students. For example, in a qualitative study of online learners, Taylor and Holley (2009) noted academic support programs for online learners were of greater importance than peer connections, which were also part of the online learning experience. However, Boling et al. (2012) found engaging with peers in online learning environments helped students to develop a greater sense of belonging to the campus. As such, student affairs professionals should exercise caution when making assumptions about the campus experiences necessary to assess with satisfaction assessment. Having a complete understanding of student satisfaction with multiple areas of the online learning experience can yield robust, actionable data to meet student expectations.

Operational Assessment

This type of assessment focuses on the operations of a department and may include considerations of cost effectiveness, efficiencies, usage tracking, and communication metrics. When working with online learners, operational assessment may focus on how often students access and stay on particular webpages or within a resource. Student affairs practitioners may also consider the types of devices (e.g., laptop, smart phone, tablet) students use to access relevant content. This information may be beneficial to student affairs practitioners in the design of programmatic experiences or assessment data collection instruments.

Approaches to the Online Student Affairs Assessment Process

The assessment arena in student affairs has expanded, and scholars have called for a deepening of professional expertise in engaging in sound assessment practice. ACPA and NASPA (2015) named assessment, evaluation, and research as a competency area for student affairs administrators. This competency area includes essential skills, increasing in complexity, at the design, implementation, and dissemination phases. Developing assessment competence allows student affairs practitioners to attend to their organizational and professional responsibility and to "ask hard questions about student learning, program effectiveness, and contribution[s] to higher education" (Henning & Roberts, 2016, p. 17), and, more importantly, to answer such questions. This call has to transcend into the online environment to accurately assess the effectiveness of student services offered to online learners.

To ensure online student services are needed, effective, and produce desired outcomes, student affairs professionals must engage in the assessment process. Numerous authors have written about the assessment process, and this process is used to guide assessment for multiple purposes: (a) individual, (b) organizational, (c) curricular, and (d) cocurricular (Henning & Roberts, 2016; Suskie, 2009; Upcraft & Schuh, 1996). Common across all of these purposes is the primary goal of using assessment to demonstrate the effectiveness of programs, services, and experiences, as well as to provide evidence for their improvement. This section outlines the components of the assessment cycle and identifies key considerations within each of them, specific to student services delivered for online learners.

Components of the Assessment Process

At the core of an assessment cycle is the mission of a department or program. Mission statements serve as a public statement to stakeholders of department goals and the work the department does to achieve those goals. Even if a department or functional area already has a mission statement and plan to determine the effectiveness of services, the mission may need to be modified or adapted to ensure the needs of online learners are truly being addressed.

Outcomes. Student services departments are likely to focus on student learning and program outcomes as they articulate what a student should achieve upon participating in a learning experience (Suskie, 2009). While there are many commonly used resources on the domains of cocurricular learning, including *Learning Reconsidered* (Keeling, 2004) and the Council for the Advancement of Standards in Higher Education's (2019) Learning and Development Outcomes, student affairs professionals working with online learners may need to modify the articulated outcomes within these resources to fit the online environment. Komives and Schoper (2006) also offered a detailed checklist of considerations to take into account when developing learning outcomes.

Educators who lead online student services also need to attend to program outcomes. These outcomes entail what the program or service should achieve upon its completion. Program outcomes are different in that they do not focus on what an individual student is able to learn or achieve. These outcomes may include important metrics, such as utilization targets, or other aggregate student success metrics, such as academic achievement or retention. For example, a math tutoring service for online learners may develop a program outcome such that the failure rates for a gatekeeper math course are reduced by a certain percentage within a year.

Program and assessment design. Once outcomes have been identified, strategies for program implementation and assessment should be developed. Often times, well-intentioned practitioners design programs (or services and experiences) without first thinking about (a) how the program relates to and will fulfill the departmental or organizational mission, and (b) the specific outcomes (student learning or program) the program is designed to address. Clarity around program purpose as it relates to mission and outcome(s) is especially important when implementing new programs or when considering holding programs and offering services online. *Backward design* (Wiggins & McTighe, 2005) is a commonly used approach for program design to achieve learning goals. By using this approach, emphasis is first placed on what a student should learn and then placed on designing a learning experience to achieve stated learning outcomes. While this approach is grounded in curricular design, the underlying philosophy can be applied to program outcomes to assess effectiveness. For example, many institutions are concerned about the retention of online learners. A first step would be to gain more specificity on retention goals. This may include determining courses and other related curricular experiences where online learner attrition is most pronounced. Once goals are identified, the practitioner can then think about creating a virtual retention program intervention. If a problem point for students is writing within their first year of college, the retention program may include support services related to academic writing offered virtually through an online writing center. The assessment design takes into account important considerations that address the who, what, how, when, and where of assessment.

Technology and Innovative Tools	
Gather	
Blackboard	https://www.blackboard.com
Canvas	https://www.instructure.com/canvas
Kahoot!	https://kahoot.com
Poll Everywhere	https://www.polleverywhere.com
Qualtrics	https://www.qualtrics.com
Survey Monkey	http://www.surveymonkey.com
Zoho Survey	https://www.zoho.com/survey
Analyze	
IBM SPSS	https://www.ibm.com/analytics/academic-statistics-software
Microsoft Excel	https://www.microsoft.com/excel
Nvivo	https://www.qsrinternational.com/nvivo/home
Qualtrics	https://www.qualtrics.com
R	https://www.r-project.org
SAS	https://www.sas.com/en_us/home.html
Stata	https://www.stata.com
Report, visualize, and disseminate	
Google Data Studio	https://datastudio.google.com
Picktochart	https://piktochart.com
Power BI	https://powerbi.microsoft.com/en-us
Tableau	https://www.tableau.com

Program implementation. The next component of the assessment process is to implement the program or learning experience. During this aspect of the process, it is important to ensure the experience has been implemented as planned. This is known as *fidelity*. Practitioners can ensure the fidelity of a program by communicating planned activities with partnering colleagues and making sure all individuals involved in program implementation understand how to carry out the experience *prior* to implementation. If individuals are working remotely or not on the same campus, shared communication tools such as Google Drive or SharePoint can be used to cocreate and review implementation protocols. Failure to implement the program or learning experience as intended could adversely affect achievement toward the stated outcomes. Additionally, if program fidelity is compromised, it may be difficult to use the data for program improvement.

Gather evidence. Collecting the appropriate evidence is an essential step in assessing outcomes. *Evidence* is any information that can support or demonstrate intended goals. Most commonly, practitioners refer to evidence as data. The necessary data obtained as part of the assessment process can be qualitative, quantitative, or both. Quantitative data are numbers used as a means of interpreting information (Maki, 2010). A quantitative approach assumes there is a reality that can be understood through numbers. Quantitative data commonly used in the assessment process include self-reported ratings, scores, usage statistics, and expenditures. On the other hand, qualitative data are words and descriptions used to examine and understand a phenomenon. Quotes from focus groups or interviews, journal entries, and open-ended survey questions are commonly used qualitative evidence in the assessment process. The use of qualitative and quantitative data together, known as the mixed methods approach (Creswell & Plano Clark, 2017), can provide the most complete information necessary to assess outcomes.

Essentially, the assessment of online student affairs services should occur in various ways (Yin, 1994), including online documents, archival records of online learner event attendance, interviews with students about their experiences, and observations of the overall online learner culture. Collecting data from multiple sources to triangulate information can bolster the validity of assessment data (Maxwell, 2005). Depending on the nature of the assessment, data may be obtained directly from program participants or from other sources, such as institutional records and databases.

Analyze and interpret evidence. Once all of the appropriate evidence (qualitative and/or quantitative) has been obtained as part of the assessment process, the next step is to analyze it. The type of data collected determines the process practitioners will use for data analysis and interpretation. The primary goal of qualitative data analysis is to understand the data that have been collected and organize the data in a meaningful way using codes to generate themes for interpretation. Various software tools can be used to support qualitative data analysis, such as Microsoft Excel and NVivo. Quantitative data may be acquired through existing static reports. Most often, however, practitioners need to work with raw data that have been collected through surveys or other reporting measures.

Analyzing raw quantitative data requires varying levels of expertise depending on the complexity of the data and the needs of the assessment project. Complexity of analysis may range from conducting descriptive analyses (e.g., frequencies, percentages, means) to inferential statistical analyses (e.g., correlations, t tests, regression). Again, Microsoft Excel is a data analysis tool that can be used to achieve desired quantitative data analyses, along with other statistical software packages, such as IBM SPSS, R, SAS, and Stata. Ultimately, it is important to know what technology resources and practitioner expertise are available, regardless of the type of evidence, to complete the required analyses.

In addition to preparing and analyzing data, the meaning-making process is an important aspect of this work and is often undervalued. Including time in the assessment process to involve other colleagues in interpreting assessment findings can provide a richer understanding to the data. Additionally, asking others, such as members of the practitioner's work team, trusted colleagues, experts, and even students, to review findings is very beneficial to drawing sound conclusions about the data and making corresponding recommendations for action.

Report findings and recommendations. Sharing assessment findings is a step in the process that often is overlooked because reporting was not built into the initial assessment strategy. Reporting of assessment findings in public, accessible formats is a central part of transparency (National Institute for Learning Outcomes Assessment, 2011). Reports can take on a variety of forms, such as full-length and one-page hard copy documents to infographics displayed through social media. Authors of assessment reports need to take into consideration the intended audience and reflect the needs and expertise of stakeholders who will view the report.

Recently, some student affairs practitioners have turned to more contemporary approaches to reporting. A couple of these approaches include using data storytelling and data visualization technologies. Data visualization tools move beyond standard graphical reports that have been commonly produced through programs such as Microsoft Excel. By design, data visualizations are intended to be dynamic and interactive, leading to insights into data that may not otherwise have been obtained through static charts and tables. Commonly used data visualization programs include Google Data Studio, Piktochart, Power BI, and Tableau. Access to a variety of open-source and proprietary software programs to produce data visualizations allows practitioners to meet the increasing demands for finding ways to visually present engaging information in an accessible way to multiple audiences. These data visualization tools may be particularly useful in online student services as they are designed to readily interface with communication portals, such as SharePoint, and be published on websites.

However, data visualization tools on their own do not always provide audiences with all of the information they need to make decisions or act. Data storytelling continues to be a concept increasingly referenced in higher education assessment communities. According to Dykes (2016), "Data storytelling is a structured approach for communicating data insights and involves a combination of three key elements: *data*, *visuals*, and *narrative*" (para. 4). Data storytelling requires a level of intentionality that has not previously been prioritized in traditional approaches in that the focus is on crafting compelling, intriguing, and visually appealing stories through data. These approaches to sharing may be especially beneficial when sharing assessment findings for online learning stakeholders as they are often designed to engage individuals through the use of dynamic, web-based technologies.

Implement change. The final and commonly avoided aspect of the assessment process involves using assessment findings. This is commonly referred to as "closing the loop" in the higher education assessment community. How departments and institutions use their assessment to guide decision making and influence change varies. Online learning is still new compared to traditional brick-and-mortar learning environments, and assessing student support services will involve change. Specific ways assessment findings may be used include activities such as priority setting, reflecting on current practices and processes, improving support services, and improving learning experiences (Baker, Jankowski, Provezis, & Kinzie, 2012) in the online learning environment.

Tips for Getting Started	
Examples of Assessment Design Considerations	
Who	• Practitioner(s) responsible for oversight of the entire assessment strategy • Students who are being assessed (student learning outcomes) or tracked (effectiveness outcomes) • Practitioner(s) responsible for data collection and/or analysis
What	• Clearly articulated outcome(s) for student learning or effectiveness • Specific aspect of the program that relates to an intended outcome
How	• Data collection strategies (use of existing data sources or newly collected data) • Measures employed to assess the outcome(s) • Data analysis techniques
When	• Timeline for overall assessment strategy • Time points at which data will be collected, analyzed, and reported
Where	• In person at the program site • Virtually via online survey software

Applications: Assessment for Effectiveness in Online Student Services

Student affairs is called to provide assessment related to effectiveness, learning, and rising issues in the profession (Henning & Roberts, 2016). Online student services are no different from traditional student affairs environments in that they, too, must attend to the need to demonstrate the effectiveness of the operations and services they provide to students. Following are three applications of how some forms of assessment and their related processes may be carried out in online student services.

Operational Assessment in an Orientation Services Program

To assess the effectiveness of programs, usage tracking is often a starting place for most practitioners. Often times, department tracking starts and stops with a simple count of the number of students who participate in an activity, use a service, or access a facility. However, these counts can serve as a springboard for more interesting and actionable information that can help a practitioner or department better understand not only how many students access their services and programs but also *with whom* the department engages. This can be a critical starting point for information gathering.

An essential role in student affairs units includes assisting students in their transition to college. Within online learning environments, students may participate in transition programs (e.g., new student orientation) prior to the start of the academic term and other extended orientation activities. These initiatives promote student success by attending to the academic and social (e.g., interpersonal, intrapersonal) transition experiences for students (Upcraft, Gardner, & Barefoot, 2005). While participation in orientation programs is often required for students, some institutions either do not require participation or allow students to self-select specific program offerings within the overall orientation experience. Given there may be some variability, participant tracking can provide important information to better understand the effectiveness of the reach of orientation offerings.

Tracking who participates in orientation programming can provide powerful insights for ensuring student success and successful program delivery. In the simplest fashion, tracking participation in individual offerings can yield important information on student interests and perceived needs. For example, if there are optional online sessions, tracking participation and length of time students stayed logged in can provide useful insights into the numbers of student participants and potentially the populations of students who participated, along with the extent to which they engaged with the content.

Widely attended online sessions may indicate areas of greatest importance for students or areas students deem essential to their success. Offerings such as academic advising appointments would likely fall into this category since advisors play a critical role in communicating academic policies and assisting students with course selection. On the other hand, sessions with lower attendance or less time spent on session content may indicate students do not perceive the content as essential for their transition to college, even though staff might deem the information important to their success. Taking note of low attendance may result in actions to provide students with the same information in an alternative format outside of the online orientation or with content woven into a session with higher attendance.

Tracking participation can also yield rich, important information to help student affairs professionals determine the effectiveness of an orientation program. By knowing who attended orientation sessions, staff can compare data about the experiences of those who attended orientation against those who did not to determine marked differences in success indicators at mid and end-of-term points. For example, staff may be interested in examining fall-to-spring retention rates, midterm grades, and first semester grade point averages (GPAs) among those who participated and those who did not. Furthermore, with the appropriate tracking data, staff can engage in follow-up data collection related to overall program effectiveness by obtaining valuable information from students about their experiences with the orientation program, such as knowledge gained about resources and important deadlines, expectations, and satisfaction.

Satisfaction Assessment in Academic Support Services

Academic support services can be a primary means by which online learners interact with staff and other students outside of the course environment. These support services may include areas of focus such as tutoring, mentoring, and skill building. The effectiveness of these services often has a direct impact on student success (e.g., degree attainment, GPA) and fulfillment of departmental and institutional missions. As such, assessment of these services is critical.

Most academic services departments likely track the numbers of students accessing services already. For example, academic tutoring services can track and report the number of students accessing services throughout an academic term. The unit may also account for the specific content areas for which students receive tutoring. Furthermore, participant tracking data can be used to help the unit determine if it is actually reaching the students with the most need. Within academic services, sometimes it is the most academically motivated students who reach out for support, not those who need the services the most. As such, an academic support services department may be interested in conducting a satisfaction assessment to address perceptions of its services, operations, and personnel.

To conduct this assessment, the academic services department may first want to identify students who have experienced academic challenges (e.g., academic probation status, D-F-W in specific courses). Second, staff will need to identify the focus of the satisfaction assessment. If the department is concerned students with the greatest academic need are not using the services, staff may want to focus their inquiry on knowledge of services, marketing strategies, and perceptions of help seeking in the academic environment.

To collect data in these areas, the department may want to consider two approaches for this population. First, the department could use the campus LMS to deploy a brief questionnaire to this population of students upon logging in to the system at a certain point in time during the academic term. Using the LMS to collect data would require minimal effort from the department and students since campus members and online learners regularly use the platform for courses. The department may also consider conducting online interviews or virtual focus groups using a semistructured interview questionnaire so online learners have a voice in the process. This can be achieved by using video conferencing software, such as Google Hangouts or Zoom, which contain recording capabilities to document student responses. Analysis of student interviews would likely be time intensive, compared to LMS data collection, though highly beneficial to fully understanding online learner perceptions of academic support services.

Student Learning Assessment in Diversity and Inclusion

Services and activities to promote diversity and inclusion efforts in online learning environments may involve a number of activities, such as mentoring, training, and other types of educational opportunities. Skills-based diversity and inclusion training is a common activity promoted in educational environments given the increased diversity of college students. Within online learning environments, a game-based approach may be ideal for implementing training on inclusive practices. As an example, this approach may be used to help online learners learn about microaggressions in the educational environment. Student affairs professionals could provide content knowledge to online learners about microaggressions and their impact using video-based vignettes of interactions between students. Students could be asked to identify the microaggression along with possible responses or interventions.

Given the focus of this training is on student learning, the designer of the learning experience would first want to identify appropriate learning outcomes for the scope of the training. For example, baseline learning outcomes for this training may include: (a) define the term *microaggression*, (b) identify two negative impacts associated with microaggressions, and (c) determine appropriate interventions when witnessing a microaggression.

To assess the effectiveness of this learning experience, a practitioner would want to employ pre and posttraining questionnaires to determine if participants already have the desired knowledge about microaggressions covered in the training. The questionnaire may include an open-ended question where students write out the definition of a microaggression to address the first learning outcome. The practitioner may include a series of closed-ended quiz questions where students need to select the correct choice(s) to assess the other learning outcomes. As an alternative to a posttraining questionnaire, quiz items could be embedded throughout the training so if students select incorrect choices, they could receive immediate follow-up information to reinforce learning. Aggregate reporting on students' knowledge of microaggressions before and after the training will yield important information on students' baseline knowledge and learning as a result of the training.

These examples provide snapshots on how to get started with carrying out different forms of assessment in online student services. To fully implement each form of assessment, practitioners need to attend to all aspects of the assessment process from mission to change implementation.

Potential Challenges and Practical Solutions

As new approaches to the delivery of student services in online learning environments emerge, assessment will continue to play an important role in ensuring the effectiveness of strategies geared toward supporting the success of online learners. Moreover, student services staff are tasked with demonstrating expertise in a specific functional area, while developing the requisite skills to obtain and use information to improve their services. Following are two potential challenges and corresponding solutions student services staff may experience in online educational contexts:

Potential Challenge: Some student services are not yet offered online and cannot be fully assessed.

Practical Solution: As an example, mental health and well-being is a leading student issue in higher education and an area of primary concern for student affairs divisions (Wesaw & Sponsler, 2014). Although these services are bound by strict privacy laws (i.e., the Health Insurance Portability and Accountability Act of 1996), assessment of these services remains feasible. Given the increased demand for and attention toward mental health and well-being services, assessment of these resources is of the utmost importance at this time. If your institution has not started offering online mental health and wellness services, you can start by assessing the most widely used of these services on campus. Then, create a task force to look at how to translate those services in an online forum. The Higher Education Mental Health Alliance recently published the guide *College Counseling From a Distance: Deciding Whether and When to Engage in Telemental Health Services* (http://hemha.org/wp-content/uploads/2018/04/HEMHA-Distance-Counseling_FINAL.pdf) to assist in this area.

Potential Challenge: Staff in student services departments do not have the expertise to conduct assessment.

Practical Solution: All staff in a unit do not need to be experts in all aspects of assessment. It is common for even the most experienced assessment professionals to have expert-level knowledge in certain areas while maintaining intermediate and sometimes introductory-level knowledge in others. There are many ways a working professional can enhance assessment competence without going back to graduate school. A primary way to learn more about student affairs assessment is through the numerous assessment texts (e.g., Henning & Roberts, 2016; Schuh, Biddix, Dean, & Kinzie, 2016). Listservs hosted by the Association for the Assessment of Learning in Higher Education (https://www.aalhe.org) and Student Affairs Assessment Leaders (SAAL; http://studentaffairsassessment.org) also offer opportunities to pose assessment questions and search previous listserv conversations. Finally, SAAL offers a number of opportunities to learn more about assessment at no cost through its blog, online open course, and *Structured Conversations* YouTube series.

Conclusion

This chapter highlighted key aspects of how student affairs assessment can move beyond the traditional higher education learning environment to online learning environments. By learning about types of assessment and components of the assessment process, online student services staff can begin to think through how to use assessment to better inform decisions and, most importantly, exercise their commitment to the online learner.

Student affairs divisions have been tasked with engaging in assessment practices related to students in all learning environments to meet internal and external accountability demands. Such practices include articulating and documenting student learning, engaging in rigorous data collection, and making evidence-based decisions for improvement. Increasingly, more attention has been devoted to culture building as a means of developing and sustaining systematic assessment processes and practices across student affairs divisions.

Although initially written for infusing assessment practice across student affairs divisions, many of these divisional conceptual frameworks (Culp & Dungy, 2012; Henning, 2015; Schuh, 2013) can be easily used to guide assessment culture development in online student services. Selecting and employing a framework for assessment within an online student services department is essential to developing common language, knowledge, and expectations that can contribute to employing successful assessment strategies. Online student services professionals must rely on assessment results to make decisions about the use of online technologies they will use to implement virtual student services (e.g., telehealth, virtual wellness counselors, online orientation, diversity and inclusion training). A commitment to developing a culture of assessment in online student services can ensure multiple department staff members are equipped to engage in the assessment process with the knowhow to embed assessment practices in all online programs and services and the appropriate resources to complete this work.

? Questions for Reflection

- How would you describe the current approaches to assessing online student services at your institution?
- How do you currently track online student services usage?
- To what assessment collection tools do you already have access? To what tools would like to gain access?
- Who are the stakeholders you would include in online student services assessment? How would you share assessment findings with those stakeholders?

References

ACPA–College Student Educators International & NASPA–Student Affairs Administrators in Higher Education. (1998). *Principles of good practice for student affairs.* Retrieved from https://www.naspa.org/images/uploads/main/Principles_of_Good_Practice_in_Student_Affairs.pdf

ACPA–College Student Educators International & NASPA–Student Affairs Administrators in Higher Education. (2015). Professional competency areas for student affairs educators. Retrieved from https://www.naspa.org/images/uploads/main/ACPA_NASPA_Professional_Competencies_FINAL.pdf

American Council on Education. (1949). *The student personnel point of view.* Washington, DC: Author.

Baker, G. R., Jankowski, N. A., Provezis, S., & Kinzie, J. (2012). *Using assessment results: Promising practices of institutions that do it well.* Urbana, IL: University of Illinois and Indiana University, National Institute for Learning Outcomes Assessment.

Baleni, Z. G. (2015). Online formative assessment in higher education: Its pros and cons. *Electronic Journal of e-Learning, 13,* 228–236. Retrieved from https://www.learntechlib.org/p/160781

Banta, T. W., Jones, E. A., & Black, K. E. (2009). *Designing effective assessment: Principles and profiles of good practice.* San Francisco, CA: Jossey-Bass.

Boling, E. C., Hough, M., Krinsky, H., Saleem, H., & Stevens, M. (2012). Cutting the distance in distance education: Perspectives on what promotes positive, online learning experiences. *The Internet and Higher Education, 15,* 118–126. doi:10.1016/j.iheduc.2011.11.006

Borrego, S. E. (2006). Mapping the learning environment. In R. Keeling (Ed.), *Learning reconsidered 2: Implementing a campus-wide focus on the student experience* (pp. 11–16). Washington, DC: ACPA–College Student Educators International, Association of College and University Housing Officers–International, Association of College Unions International, National Academic Advising Association, National Association for Campus Activities, NASPA–Student Affairs Administrators in Higher Education, & National Intramural-Recreational Sports Association.

Bresciani, M. J. (2011, August). *Making assessment meaningful: What new Student affairs professionals and those new to assessment need to know* (NILOA Assessment Brief: Student Affairs). Urbana, IL: University of Illinois and Indiana University, National Institute for Learning Outcomes Assessment.

Bresciani, M. J., Gardner, M. M., & Hickmott, J. (2009). *Demonstrating student success: A practical guide to outcomes-based assessment of learning and development in student affairs.* Sterling, VA: Stylus.

Bryan, T. K., Lutte, R., Lee, J., O'Neil, P., Maher, C. S., & Hoflund, A. B. (2018). When do online education technologies enhance student engagement? A case of distance education at University of Nebraska at Omaha. *Journal of Public Affairs Education, 24,* 255–273. doi:10.1080/15236803.2018.1429817

Cabellon, E. T., & Junco, R. (2015). The digital age of student affairs. In E. J. Whitt & J. H. Schuh (Eds.), *New directions for student services, 1997–2014: Glancing back, looking forward* (New Directions for Student Services, No. 151, pp. 49–61). San Francisco, CA: Jossey-Bass. doi:10.1002/ss.20137

Council for the Advancement of Standards in Higher Education. (2019). CAS learning and development outcomes. In J. B. Wells & N. Henry-Darwish (Eds.), *CAS professional standards for higher education* (10th ed., pp. 16–19). Washington, DC: Author.

Creswell, J. W., & Plano Clark, V. L. (2017). *Designing and conducting mixed methods research* (3rd ed.). Thousand Oaks, CA: Sage.

Culp, M. M., & Dungy, G. J. (2012). *Building a culture of evidence in student affairs: A guide for leaders and practitioners.* Washington, DC: NASPA–Student Affairs Administrators in Higher Education.

Dykes, B. (2016, March 31). Data storytelling: The essential data science skill everyone needs. *Forbes.* Retrieved from https://www.forbes.com/sites/brentdykes/2016/03/31/data-storytelling-the-essential-data-science-skill-everyone-needs

Henning, G. W. (2015). Tenet 2: Cultivating a culture of assessment. In E. Bentrim, G. W. Henning, & K. Yousey-Elsener (Eds.), *Coordinating student affairs divisional assessment: A practical guide* (pp. 11–34). Sterling, VA: Stylus.

Henning, G. W., & Roberts, D. (2016). *Student affairs assessment: Theory to practice.* Sterling, VA: Stylus.

Hornak, A. M., Akweks, K., & Jeffs, M. (2010). Online student services at the community college. In R. L. Garza Mitchell (Ed.), *Online education* (New Directions for Community Colleges, No. 150, pp. 79–87). San Francisco, CA: Jossey-Bass. doi:10.1002/cc

Keeling, R. P. (Ed.). (2004). *Learning reconsidered: A campus-wide focus on the student experience.* Washington, DC: ACPA–College Student Educators International & NASPA–Student Affairs Administrators in Higher Education.

Komives, S. R., & Schoper, S. (2006). Developing learning outcomes. In R. Keeling (Ed.), *Learning reconsidered 2: Implementing a campus-wide focus on the student experience* (pp. 17–41). Washington, DC: ACPA–College Student Educators International, Association of College and University Housing Officers–International, Association of College Unions International, National Academic Advising Association, National Association for Campus Activities, NASPA–Student Affairs Administrators in Higher Education, & National Intramural-Recreational Sports Association.

Lowery, J. W. (2004). Student affairs for a new generation. In M. D. Coomes & R. DeBard (Eds.), *Serving the millennial generation* (New Directions for Student Services, No. 106, pp. 87–99). San Francisco, CA: Jossey-Bass. doi:10.1002/ss.127

Maki, P. L. (2010). *Assessing for learning: Building a sustainable commitment across the institution.* Sterling, VA: Stylus.

Maxwell, J. A. (2005). *Qualitative research design: An interactive approach* (2nd ed.). Thousand Oaks, CA: Sage.

National Institute for Learning Outcomes Assessment. (2011). *Transparency framework.* Urbana, IL: University of Illinois and Indiana University, National Institute for Learning Outcomes Assessment.

Pullan, M. C. (2009). Student support services for Millennial undergraduates. *Journal of Educational Technology Systems, 38,* 235–251. doi:10.2190/ET.38.2.k

Schuh, J. H. (2013). Developing a culture of assessment in student affairs. J. H. Schuh (Ed.), *Selected contemporary assessment issues* (New Directions for Student Services, No. 142, pp. 89–98). San Francisco, CA: Jossey-Bass. doi:10.1002/ss.20052

Schuh, J. H. (2015). Assessment in student affairs: How did we get here? *Journal of Student Affairs Inquiry, 1*(1). Retrieved from https://jsai.scholasticahq.com/article/366-assessment-in-student-affairs-how-did-we-get-here

Schuh, J. H., Biddix, J. P., Dean, L. A., & Kinzie, J. (2016). *Assessment in student affairs.* San Francisco, CA: Jossey-Bass.

Schuh, J. H., & Gansemer-Topf, A. M. (2010, December). *The role of student affairs in student learning assessment* (Occasional Paper No. 7). Retrieved from National Institute for Learning Outcomes Assessment website: https://www.learningoutcomeassessment.org/documents/StudentAffairsRole.pdf

Suskie, L. (2009). *Assessing student learning: A common sense guide.* San Francisco, CA: Wiley.

Swan, K., Shen, J., & Hiltz, S. R. (2006). Assessment and collaboration in online learning. *Journal of Asynchronous Learning Networks, 10,* 45–62. doi:10.24059/olj.v10i1.1770

Taylor, B., & Holley, K. (2009). Providing academic and support services to students enrolled in online degree programs. *College Student Affairs Journal, 28,* 81–102. Retrieved from https://www.sacsa.org/page/CSAJ

Upcraft, M. L., Gardner, J., & Barefoot, D. (2005). *Challenge and support: Creating climates for first-year student success.* San Francisco, CA: Jossey-Bass.

Upcraft, M. L., & Schuh, J. H. (1996). *Assessment in student affairs: A guide for practitioners.* San Francisco, CA: Jossey-Bass.

Wesaw, A. J., & Sponsler, B. A. (2014). *The chief student affairs officer: Responsibilities, opinions, and professional pathways of leaders in student affairs*. Washington, DC: NASPA–Student Affairs Administrators in Higher Education.

Wiggins, G. P., & McTighe, J. (2005). *Understanding by design*. Alexandria, VA: ASCD.

Yin, R. K. (1994). *Case study research: Design and methods* (2nd ed.). Thousand Oaks, CA: Sage.

CHAPTER 6

The Role of Students Affairs in Cultivating Integrity in Online Education

Christian K. Wuthrich and Madison L. Hansen

WHEN PROMPTED TO DEFINE the word *integrity*, students consistently bring up a few points we have found in our experience: Integrity is about being hardworking, trustworthy, having a strong moral compass, and doing the right thing when no one is looking. Upholding integrity at the student and institutional levels is easier said than done. Often, student and institutional goals do not reflect each other when taken at face value. A major function of student affairs is to intermediate between the goals of an institution and the students it serves, which are generally course progression, retention, and graduation. The realities of postsecondary education are they reflect the societal zeitgeist of the current time. Today, students want convenient online access to education and other institutional resources. The aforementioned can be exacerbated in the online learning environment due to miscommunication and differing expectations about the goals of educational programs.

Informed by the basic foundation online instruction provides educational access for students, this chapter (a) explores the role of student affairs in supporting engagement with integrity in online education; (b) suggests ways in which student affairs practitioners cultivate not just a basic understanding of integrity but an academic culture that promotes fairness, full engagement with learning, and students being accountable to a community, even when that learning community is online; and (c) provides examples, resources, and suggestions, guided by case studies, on how student affairs practitioners can ensure all students, and specifically students who take their courses online, are behaving ethically within their institutions *and* that those institutions are treating them fairly.

The Role of Student Affairs

Traditional student affairs concepts can contribute significantly to the online learning environment, facilitating ethical behaviors, feelings of mattering and belonging, and better understanding between students and their institutions (Strayhorn, 2019). In short, student affairs practitioners can help provide an experience in which the integrity of higher education's broader purposes are not compromised, ensuring online learners are receiving an experience that is whole, complete, and on par with their on-campus peers through the implementation of new approaches.

The urgency to find new ways to support online learners is illustrated in the decline of for-profit and community college enrollment and a corresponding increase in the online environment. Since 2012, overall traditional brick-and-mortar enrollment at public and nonprofit post-secondary institutions has grown by 5% on average, and the for-profit and community college sector has seen decreases of 32.3% and 14%, respectively (Seaman, Allen, & Seaman, 2018). Online enrollment has increased every year since 2012 and, as of 2016, comprises 31.6% of all postsecondary enrollment, or 6.3 million students (Seaman et al., 2018).

Practitioners are challenged by contemporary tensions in higher education, including a shift toward revenue-driven models, an expectation for transactional interactions between students and their institutions, and the particular expectations and circumstances of online learners (Fielding, 2016; Shumar, 2018). All of these tensions call for new methods to support the online learner-institution relationship and to ensure online learners experience a sense of mattering and belonging. This chapter is organized around a conceptual framework used to consider the intersections of student concerns and motivations related to obtaining an education side by side with common institutional pressures. In considering where students and institutions share common ground, student affairs practitioners can play a role to improve outcomes for all participants.

The Online Academic Environment

Assuming the advent or growth of an institution's online programs were intentional, the following questions were likely asked: Who are student affairs professionals trying to serve? What will the curriculum be? How will students enroll and for what cost? What do industry or stakeholders demand? What are the institutional costs for such an effort? In a rudimentary way, the development of online education mirrors the founding of U.S. higher education from hilltop colleges in New England, land-grant universities following the passage of the Morrill Act, and even the 20th-century growth the University of California and California State University systems. Then and now, there are a mix of economic and humanistic educational goals (Nodine, 2016; Thelin, 2011).

The unique environment that fostered the development of online programs deserves further examination. Higher education in the 21st century is juxtaposed between neoliberal policies and postmodern educational pedagogy requiring "consumption before knowledge" (Farrow & Moe, 2019, p. 277). Neoliberalism is a broad political and economic construct that serves to promote capitalistic goals of which higher education is a part (Gray, O'Regan, & Wallace, 2018). In the online environment, some postmodern educational theory explores the concept of humanity through recognizing the diversity of student identities, goals, and learning styles (van Rooij & Zirkle, 2016). One of several intersections in postmodern theory is the metanarrative, which, simply defined, is a societal-level belief or interpretation of circumstances that provides a foundation for the way people understand and make meaning of experiences (Bennett, Grossberg, & Morris, 2005). Online education in the postmodern frame is viewed with incredulity (Lyotard, 1984) by participants and providers. For example, in a context where academic integrity and academic quality are difficult to achieve, neoliberalism would assume there is no need to provide student affairs support to students. In other words, because education is now considered a commodity, neoliberalism suggests student success hinges simply on the basis of ability. Embedded here is the crisis of knowledge, which is twofold and contradictory. In the era of fake news, educators face challenges about the legitimation of knowledge and students who demand to cocreate the curriculum. Students are also influenced by economic markets and social media (Hauke, 2019; Hughes, 2019), seeking coursework not for the pursuit of knowledge but for a credential that will hopefully lead to higher income.

Neoliberal educational policies support free market economic values, which have encouraged many educational entities to consider students as consumers or revenue producers (Shumar, 2018).

Academic managers have accepted the model due to declines in state funding, competition in the marketplace, which includes private and for-profit institutions, and instructional technology innovation. Detractors of this model protest the commodification of education. Critics of the model believe "neoliberal ideology to be dynamic and contradictory, and aimed at discursive representations of individuals and social, cultural, and political institutions" (Saunders & Ramirez, 2016, p. 189). In the neoliberal model, professional education, such as business, engineering, and nursing, thrives over liberal arts.

Online degree and certificate programs are by and large competency based (Nodine, 2016). Competency-based education sits at the intersection of neoliberal ideals and postmodern educational theory and must be recognized as a binding factor, whether a practitioner serves as an academician or administrator. Programs are specialized and cocreated by students, industry, and institutions. Obtaining knowledge for theoretical purposes is not the goal; rather, mastering a narrow set of competencies associated with learning outcomes is key.

Economic and social changes of the late 21st century have created new opportunities for innovation, and higher education leaders embraced the challenge. Higher education faces pressure to remain relevant, competitive, and financially sound. The response is to balance the needs of students with the demands of governing boards requiring measurable outcomes, industry demands, cost control, and scaling. Student affairs practitioners are uniquely positioned to address the needs of online learners. Possibilities exist in everything from maintaining virtual libraries that increase access to course materials to educating instructional designers and faculty to ensure cultural competency and inclusion.

Online Learner Demographics and Expectations

The college online learner population looks quite different than the on-campus student population. Over 125,000 online learners from 175 institutions were surveyed in preparation of Ruffalo Noel Levitz's (2018) *National Student Satisfaction and Priorities Report*. As presented in the report, online learners are far more likely to be female, working, and older than their on-campus peers, and 70% of online learners are female, 88% are 25 and older, and 69% are employed full time. While students who identified as White made up the largest racial/ethnic group among online learners in this study, there was a slightly higher percentage of African American online learners than other student populations surveyed at four-year institutions and technical/community colleges.

In a *U.S. News & World Report* article, Friedman (2017) found between July 2015 and 2016, only 5% of online learners were attending college for the first time, and 61% were enrolled in programs in the business and health sciences disciplines. This indicates online learners are bringing to their academic program significant responsibility, diversity, prior education and career experience, and the desire to move up in professional fields. This is consistent with the common perception of online education as a tool for access and mobility for students for whom a more "traditional" campus-based experience is not feasible.

As such, online learners may be extremely likely to experience many life pressures and circumstances before they even make the decision to start school, which can impact their expectation that an online education should fit into their lives with some degree of ease and convenience (Ruffalo Noel Levitz, 2016). According to Ruffalo Noel Levitz's *2015–16 National Online Learners Satisfaction and Priorities Report*, the factors of most importance to potential online learners as they make the decision to enroll are convenience, flexible pacing, their work schedule, and cost (Ruffalo Noel Levitz, 2016). Once enrolled, online learners place significant importance on clarity of expectations, convenience of processes and receiving assistance, and purposeful use of their time. Online learners also place high importance on the perception "tuition paid is a worthwhile invest-ment" (Ruffalo Noel Levitz, 2016, p. 5), but a gap exists between the rate of importance and satisfaction, demonstrating online learners approach their education at least in part from the perspective of a consumer purchasing a service. Online learners also rated student services, including quick response time, knowing where to go for information, bookstore services, ease of filing complaints, and online career services, as having high importance.

Optimal online learning environments mirror those in the traditional educational setting of engagement, timely feedback, relevance, and application (Valai, Schmidt-Crawford, & Moore, 2019). In addition to the skills required of instructors teaching face to face, online instructors must also keep up with technologi-cal advancements, design effective instructional tools in the context of new technologies, and closely facilitate conversation (Courtney & Wilhoite-Mathews, 2015; Easton, 2003; Markova, Glazkova, & Zaborova, 2017). Further, effective student affairs practice in the area of well-being, cross cultural communication, and administration calls for collaborative academic partnerships that close the gap between these two functions (King, 2017). In the context of academic integ-rity described here, student affairs practitioners will be more effective in strengthening partnerships by developing a comprehensive under-standing of online education, faculty pedagogical concerns, and pres-sures individual students and institutions face.

Student Well-Being and Behavior

Student affairs practitioners are keenly aware of contemporary issues impacting students, such as social or political concerns, food scarcity, and school-life balance (Broton & Goldrick-Rabb, 2016; Eagan et al., 2016). According to the American College Health Association (2018), there are also significant issues around mental health and safety materializing in ever-increasing and complex ways higher education as a whole is only beginning to understand. These concerns of the student affairs field are due for consideration in the online learning space.

However, making sure online learners can be connected to mental health support should be of high importance for institutions and practitioners. The American College Health Association (2018) found in the past 12 months, significant numbers of college students had been diagnosed or treated for mental health concerns, including 22% for anxiety, 11% for panic attacks, 6.7% for attention deficit hyperactivity disorder, and 17.3% for depression. Nearly one in five students "felt so depressed they couldn't function" (American College Health Association, 2018, p. 14) or felt overwhelming anxiety over the past 12 months, and 6.9% had seriously considered suicide. These data do not account for whether students took their classes primarily online or face to face, and the population studied was generally younger and included more males than the online learner population. Still, it is clear mental health is of major concern in higher education. Student affairs can improve student well-being by coordinating or contracting services, such as teleheath (using telecommunication) for delivery of counseling and some healthcare services where allowed by law.

While student demographics, such as racial/ethnic identity or socioeconomic status, can contribute to students' experiences with mental illness, few mental health services are delivered online, and students may depend on just one faculty member to help them feel connected to the university (Barr, 2014). The people who serve as connection points for online learners need to be prepared to respond appropriately and make referrals when students disclose mental health concerns, but the infrastructure and resources to make this happen are not always in place (Barr, 2014). Student affairs practitioners can create interventions and training on relevant topics to help staff and faculty navigate those connection points, including identifying and responding to mental health concerns, strategies for engaging in difficult or uncomfortable dialogue with students, and generally understanding how an institution's suite of resources is accessible to distance students.

In addition to concerns around well-being, institutions and practitioners should pay close attention to student behavior online, including academic misconduct. The challenge that exists in the online environment is practitioners depend on studies of academic misconduct that rely on student self-reporting, are not particularly recent, and have different research objectives, sample sizes, and institution types. The research on academic integrity in online classes mostly explores moral reasoning and points to some key themes. While student misconduct does not necessarily occur with greater frequency online, students often report expectations for ethical academic behavior are different online than in face-to-face classes, and they may believe it is easier to cheat and plagiarize in online classes (Raines et al., 2011; Selwyn, 2008; Stephens, Young, & Calabrese, 2007). Further still, leaders in the academic integrity field continue to grow increasingly concerned about the most egregious forms of academic misconduct, such as contract cheating, a practice that is generally unregulated (Bertram Gallant, 2019).

Technology and Innovative Tools	
Noncommercial technology for student and practitioner use	
Purdue Online Writing Lab (OWL)	A hub for understanding various citation styles *https://owl.purdue.edu/owl/purdue_owl.html*
Stanford University, Measure of Software Similarity (MOSS)	Plagiarism checker designed specifically for analyzing code *https://theory.stanford.edu/~aiken/moss*
Unicheck	A free online plagiarism checker *https://unicheck.com/free-plagiarism-checker-online*
Commercial technology for plagiarism checking, digital identity verification, and online proctoring	
ProctorU	One of several services offering digital and remote proctoring *https://www.proctoru.com*
SafeAssign	Plagiarism detection software offered through Blackboard *https://www.blackboard.com/safeassign/index.html*
TurnItIn	Plagiarism detection software that can be integrated into other learning management systems *https://www.turnitin.com*

A number of tools, such as those identified in the Technology and Innovative Tools sidebox above, both freely available resources and commercial products, can monitor potential plagiarism and serve as digital identity verification. Student affairs practitioners can leverage these tools in a few ways, including encouraging the use of ubiquitous resources by students as part of their writing and learning processes, advocating their institutions license with particular vendors that best fit the needs of distance students, and discussing openly with online learners why the institution makes use of certain tools. In our experience, students share fairly frequently they believe they are being held to higher standards of integrity than their university, often because they feel their behavior and writing are being closely watched via tools like ProctorU or SafeAssign while they perceive little oversight of staff and faculty behavior.

How Practitioners Can Facilitate Integrity Online

To consider these factors, a model is offered to demonstrate the unique pressures faced by online learners and institutions, the interests that intersect for students and institutions, and the ways student affairs practitioners can have the most meaningful influence As Figure 6.1 illustrates, student affairs practitioners have the ability to interpret the educational environment and influence outcomes. Student affairs work sits at the intersection of students' personal lives and their academic and cocurricular pursuits.

While keeping in mind academic outcomes are paramount, student affairs' role is to pressure institutional functioning by synthesizing intersecting activities for the benefit of students. For example, online learners are impacted by work and personal matters outside of class (Bourdeaux & Schoenack, 2016). They also bring specific goals to online programs and expectations that their investment of time and money will be valuable and matched by convenient service by the institution (Ruffalo Noel Levitz, 2016). Furthermore, universities face significant institutional pressures, such as attending to budget and personnel, maintaining academic quality, developing curriculum, and meeting the needs of stakeholders, including students and their families, staff, faculty, donors, community and business partners, and governing bodies (Shumar, 2018).

In addition, students are increasingly linking their postsecondary education with their employment as is the case with companies such as McDonalds, Starbucks, UPS, and Bank of America. In these examples, employer paid tuition is based on meeting certain metrics, such as hours worked per week. These various pressures may seem to be in competition with each other at first glance, but when life and learning intersect, there are substantial interests at the heart of higher education, such as facilitating learning, creating knowledge, upholding integrity, earning and awarding degrees, and doing all of this with trust and respect so all involved have a valuable experience.

Figure 6.1. A Model for Interpreting Educational Environments and Influencing Outcomes

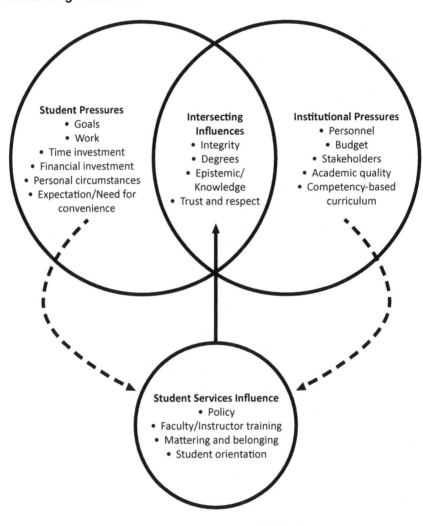

Tips for Getting Started

As you prepare to use the conceptual framework presented in this chapter, consider the following:

* **Define how your department's values, purpose, and services are articulated for online learners.** Consider where there is room for improvement in terms of your department's inclusion of online learners and their particular needs.

* **Know your institution's policies and rules that are relevant to integrity and online learner success.** Consider where there might be gaps in these policies and rules that do not account for the logistics of the online learning environment.

* **Develop a framework for response and support to online learner concerns.** Consider if units with which you usually partner (e.g., writing center, ombudsperson, student services offices, network of department chairs, academic deans, academic program advisors) are prepared to support online learners in addition to face-to-face students.

* **Locate allies among faculty who teach online and staff in your institution's e-campus unit, if your institution has one.** Consider how they can help you better understand online learner needs at your institution, what opportunities exist to work together on projects that support online learners, and how you might call on these people in tricky situations.

* **Ask how new programs and policies will impact online learners.** This is particularly important when others involved do not seem to be asking that question. Encourage explicit and transparent attention to online learners and integrity in every initiative.

These shared interests connect students and institutions to each other in meaningful ways that can improve online learners' engagement and sense of community. Student affairs practitioners offer influence in this area through individualized service and support; training for faculty, staff, and students; and policy development by understanding the needs of students and developing tools to assist. To this end, the importance of creating online environments for students to connect cannot be understated. For example, a virtual student union and online veteran's success hub, or tutoring and success coaching, can provide support and increase community, a virtual student union can store academic lectures for download, electronic bulletin boards can be provided for student messages, or authenticated and moderated hangouts can allow students to converse about their experiences and seek help on pertinent matters.

Commercial products such as Cognito, which provides online suicide prevention training, are available for developing faculty and staff skills to confront student mental health concerns. Student government and student organizations can help students meet their peers and stay connected through civic engagement. Finally, new student orientation, a traditional avenue to bring awareness to student affairs services and expectations, can be provided by a learning management system portal. A learning management system can support videos and tutorials, encourage journaling, and serve as an initial resource hub as students begin their academic journey. However, such projects to support online learners should not be initiated without first understanding the unique needs and experiences of online learners.

Practicing Solutions to Common Challenges

A major goal of online learning is access, followed closely by student course persistence, completion, retention, and graduation. A student's holistic academic experience hinges on social, cognitive, and institutional factors (Mayhew et al., 2016). The intersectionality of student affairs practitioners, spanning both the enrollment management and cocurricular functions of institutions, places these professionals in a position to influence policy, enhance communication across the enterprise, coach and train instructors, and problem solve in new and unique cases.

Analyzing case studies is generally formulaic in that the reader determines the decisions being presented and the relevant facts. Case study analysis also fills the theory-to-practice gap, helps break static thinking, and offers new ways to solve challenges (Stage & Hubbard, 2017). Working a case begins with an initial assessment and is followed by, if possible, collecting more information; determining the role of decision makers; and using relevant theory when possible. The final step of analysis includes exploring options for resolution, along with benefits and potential pitfalls of each, before making a decision or taking action. There are no right or wrong answers; rather, these cases

Potential Challenges and Practical Solutions

Potential Challenge: As student affairs professionals engage in their work and advocate for the needs of online learners, they may experience push back or lack of participation from some institutional partners. These issues can be exacerbated when discussing projects and policies that impact online learners because there may be a lack of understanding, experience, or buy-in with the online learning environment among colleagues.

Practical Solution: Show up prepared with a firm knowledge base and personal framework. When it comes to online learning, think about the areas where you need to learn more. Determine the code of ethics and sense of purpose you have as you engage in your work.

Practical Solution: Work on meaningful relationship building with those who may be less willing to collaborate or make adjustments to their practice. Engaging in open communication; showing genuine interest in understanding others' roles, interests, and the pressures they experience; and taking the initiative to find common ground are a few ways to navigate through challenges.

Practical Solution: Try to shift the focus away from who is in control of a situation and instead toward finding the best outcome for a situation. This approach makes it easier to gain collaborators, have difficult conversations, and provide information people do not always want to hear.

are intended to help the reader explore issues they might encounter at their institution. The authors encourage readers to apply the model (see Figure 6.1) shared in this chapter to the following cases.

Case Study 1: Collaboration Online

Imagine you work in the student conduct area of student affairs and have responsibility for adjudicating potential violations of your institution's student code of conduct. Dr. Khan teaches an online Contemporary Narratives 250 and requires students to submit their assignments for his course through plagiarism detection software. A report generated by the software indicates students Manuel and Karina wrote papers that are 67% similar. Dr. Khan's syllabus is clear students may not collaborate on assignments because individual, original personal reflection and analysis of the assigned texts are what he needs to assess.

Upon contacting Dr. Khan, you learn he is an adjunct instructor teaching this course and is using the detection software for the first time. Dr. Khan views himself as an educator and is concerned the university will ask him to address the situation punitively, which will break trust with the students. Upon contacting the students, Karina freely shares she and Manuel text frequently about the course and share documents with each other. She is willing to share text messages and e-mails to support her story. Manuel denies any involvement with Karina and passionately defends his integrity as a student. Manuel feels he is being treated unfairly and says the only way to avoid getting in trouble is to not speak to any of his peers ever again.

Questions to consider:

- The practitioner responding to this situation knows what learning analytics data say, and also needs to know more about what the students have to say. How would you go about creating an environment where online learners can share the information they have openly and honestly?

- As a student affairs professional, what kind of guidance would you give the faculty member that will ultimately help online students learn from their actions and develop?

- How do you respond to Manuel's plan to not talk to his peers anymore?

- How do you bring integrity to this scenario as a student affairs practitioner?

Case Study 2: Well-Being Online

Imagine you work in the student outreach and assistance area of student affairs, and you are responsible for responding to reports of concern regarding distressing or disturbing student behavior from institutional community members. Dr. Gomez teaches Accounting 355.

She submitted a report of concern regarding an online learner named Oscar who recently stopped attending synchronous team meetings, is falling behind on assignments, and wrote an e-mail that sounded defeated. Later, she writes you a brief e-mail with a copy of a homework assignment Oscar submitted and a link to a file and answer sharing website nearly identical to Oscar's homework, indicating he copied the solution from the Internet. Dr. Gomez shares she tried to connect with Oscar and offer him support, but this type of cheating behavior will not be tolerated in her class, and she wants him administratively removed from the course roster.

During a video conference with Oscar, he opens up about what he has been experiencing in his life. His mother is ill, and he has become her primary caretaker, which takes up a significant amount of time he previously used to complete homework. He has recently changed his medication to treat his depression and anxiety and has not had time to keep up with counseling sessions or make sure he is taking his correct dosages at the right time each day. His employer is paying for the majority of his tuition as part of a continuing education program. Facing pressure and limited time, Oscar says he copied the homework solutions from a file and answer sharing website in a last-ditch effort to pass the class. He is deeply ashamed of this choice but says Dr. Gomez made him feel unwelcome in class because she only paid attention to his plagiarism and did not respond directly when he shared he was struggling. Oscar feels no one at the university will trust him anymore or listen to him. He had already been feeling very alone and started to consider online classes might not be a good fit for him, so he is considering withdrawing.

Questions to consider:

- As you evaluate how to offer support to Oscar, would you partner with Dr. Gomez to make the appropriate referrals to address Oscar's needs and concerns? In what ways does your institution allow for this collaborative approach for online learners?

- As you assess this case, you determine taking time away from his studies may be the best choice for Oscar. How would you advise him and carry out this difficult conversation?

- What other factors pertaining to the online learning environment do you need to consider in the resolution of this case?

- How do you bring integrity to this scenario as a student affairs practitioner?

Case Study 3: Inclusivity Online

Imagine your institution has developed and revised policies on academic integrity without considering their impact on online courses and students, and, as such, the practical application of these policies is difficult to implement. For example, students found to be engaging in academic misconduct may be expelled on the second offense without differentiating whether the offense was intentional or unintentional or what kind of academic misconduct occurred. This is problematic because you believe online learners are more likely to engage in academic misconduct unintentionally, and because you know cheating is the most common violation among online learners, while plagiarism and unauthorized collaboration are widespread in courses delivered face to face. Further, policy requires students to meet with faculty in person to discuss alleged offenses and mandates reporting the incident to the student conduct office. You see a pattern in reporting nontraditional age students and multilingual students whose first language is not English. You have been meeting with an increasing number of online learners, so you are aware these concerns will disproportionately impact them.

Questions to consider:

- Without having been invited to the initial conversations about policy development and revision, what would be your first steps in becoming involved?

- To improve outcomes for online learners, which stakeholders at your institution would you need to bring to the table?
- How would respond to the alleged discrimination at your institution in terms of who is reported most frequently?
- How do you bring integrity to this scenario as a student affairs practitioner?

Common elements in these cases were the use of policy, resources, and pedagogy to prevent or address issues. In the case of unique issues, there is room for empathy, encouragement, and referral to professionals who can assist students. Regardless of the type of case, a solid understanding of faculty work life, issues of the professoriate, and management concerns should also be at the forefront for consideration. In all matters of academic integrity, faculty are our partners and care should be taken to cultivate relationships both to socialize faculty to student affairs work and to understand discipline-specific approaches that influence instructional decisions.

Conclusion

In full transparency, navigating these issues in the neoliberal context of higher education can prove not just challenging but disheartening as some practitioners may question if it is possible to make a meaningful impact among the tensions created by substantial cultural shifts regarding the purpose of higher education, the nature of knowledge, and substantial difficulties faced by students. The case studies you just read prompted you to reflect on just a few of the challenges student affairs practitioners encounter when supporting students who take their courses within the online learning environment. However, it is a worthwhile pursuit to approach student affairs work for online learners with a focus on creating ethically sound circumstances and doing what is needed to support individual students.

To do this work to the fullest and help facilitate further engagement from online learners, practitioners must be prepared to assert themselves and push back in ethical ways based on their understanding of the environment and what will best serve students. Online learners are working to navigate an educational landscape that can often feel new, blurry, and liminal. Student affairs practitioners must be prepared to meet them where they are and engage within murky spaces as well. Stepping into the challenges presented by the online learning environment with a focus on integrity, honesty, soundness, and doing what is right for the student in each new situation can facilitate meaningful experiences for online learners.

? Questions for Reflection

These questions are intended to help you map out your institution and role onto the conceptual framework presented in this chapter.

- How does your role fit into your institution's overall goals to uphold integrity and provide quality online education? With this in mind, how might you develop your interactions with students and stakeholders to create more meaningful engagement?

- How do topics like online education, integrity, and trust/respect fit into your student affairs department's mission and strategic plan?

- What demographic factors or other characteristics present in your student body might create particular challenges for online learners or reveal opportunities for leadership and involvement for online learners?

- What are the needs of your online faculty body, and where might there be opportunities for collaboration or support to address those needs from your position in student affairs?

References

American College Health Association. (2018). *Fall 2018 reference group executive summary.* Retrieved from https://www.acha.org/documents/ncha/NCHA-II_Fall_2018_Reference_Group_Executive_Summary.pdf

Barr, B. (2014). Identifying and addressing the mental health needs of online students in higher education. *Online Journal of Distance Learning Administration, 17*(2). Retrieved from https://www.learntechlib.org/p/152958

Bennett, T., Grossberg, L., & Morris, M. (2005). *New keywords: A revised vocabulary of culture and society.* Malden, MA: Blackwell.

Bertram Gallant, T. (2019). Contract cheating in the news [Blog post]. *ICAI: International Center for Academic Integrity Blog.* Retrieved from https://academicintegrity.org/blog/contract-cheating-in-the-news

Bourdeaux, R., & Schoenack, L. (2016). Adult student expectations and experiences in an online learning environment. *Journal of Continuing Higher Education, 64,* 152–161. doi:10.1080/07377363.2016.1229072

Broton, K., & Goldrick-Rab, S. (2016) The dark side of college (un)affordability: Food and housing insecurity in higher education. *Change: The Magazine of Higher Learning, 48,* 16–25. doi:10.1080/00091383.2016.1121081

Courtney, M., & Wilhoite-Mathews, S. (2015). From distance education to online learning: Practical approaches to information literacy instruction and collaborative learning in online environments. *Journal of Library Administration, 55,* 261–277. doi:10.1080/01930826.2015.1038924

Eagan, M. K., Stolzenberg, E. B., Ramirez, J. J., Aragon, M. C., Suchard, M. R., & Rios-Aguilar, C. (2016). *The American freshman: Fifty-year trends, 1966–2015.* Los Angeles, CA: University of California, Higher Education Research Institute.

Easton, S. S. (2003). Clarifying the instructor's role in online distance learning. *Communication Education, 52,* 87–105. doi:10.1080/03634520302470

Farrow, R., & Moe, R. (2019). Rethinking the role of the academy: Cognitive authority in the age of post-truth. *Teaching in Higher Education, 24,* 272–287. doi:10.1080/13562517.2018.1558198

Fielding, H. (2016). "Anytime, anyplace": The myth of universal access and the semiprivate space of online eduation. *Computers and Composition, 40,* 103–114. doi:10.1016/j.compcom.2016.03.002

Friedman, J. (2017, April 4). U.S. news data: The average online bachelor's student. *U.S. News & World Report.* Retrieved from https://www.usnews.com/higher-education/online-education/articles/2017-04-04/us-news-data-the-average-online-bachelors-student

Gray, J., O'Regan, J. P., & Wallace, C. (2018). Education and the discourse of global neoliberalism. *Language and Intercultural Communication, 18,* 471–477. doi:10.1080/14708477.2018.1501842

Hauke, E. (2019). Understanding the world today: The roles of knowledge and knowing in higher education. *Teaching in Higher Education, 24,* 378–393. doi:10.1080/13562517.2018.1544122

Hughes, G. (2019). Developing student research capability for a post-truth world: Three challenges integrating research across taught programmes. *Teaching in Higher Education, 24,* 394–411. doi:10.1080/13562517.2018.1541173

King, K. (2017). *Technology and innovation in adult learning.* San Francisco, CA: Jossey-Bass.

Lyotard, J. F. (1984). *The postmodern condition: A report on knowledge.* Manchester, England: Manchester University Press.

Markova, T., Glazkova, I., & Zaborova, E. (2017). Quality issues of online distance learning. *Procedia – Social and Behavioral Sciences, 237,* 685–691. doi:10.1016/j.sbspro.2017.02.043

Mayhew, M. J., Rockenbach, A. N., Bowman, N. A., Seifert, T. A., Wolniak, G. C., Pascarella, E. T, & Terenzini, P. T. (2016). *How college affects students: 21ˢᵗ century evidence that higher education works.* San Francisco, CA: Jossey-Bass.

Nodine, T. R. (2016). How did we get here? A brief history of competency-based higher education in the United States. *Journal of Competency-Based Education, 1,* 5–11. doi:10.1002/cbe2.1004

Raines, D. A., Ricci, P., Brown, S. L., Eggenberger, T., Hindle, T., & Schiff, M. (2011). Cheating in online courses: The student definition. *Journal of Effective Teaching, 11,* 80–89. Retrieved from https://uncw.edu/jet/articles/vol11_1/raines.pdf

Ruffalo Noel Levitz. (2016). *2015–16 national online learners satisfaction and priorities report.* Cedar Rapids, IA: Author.

Ruffalo Noel Levitz. (2018). *Appendix: 2018 national student satisfaction and priorities report.* Cedar Rapids, IA: Author.

Saunders, D. B., & Ramirez, G. B. (2016). Resisting the neoliberalization of higher education: A challenge to commonsensical understandings of commodities and consumption. *Cultural Studies—Critical Methodologies, 17,* 189–196. doi:10.1177/1532708616669529

Seaman, J. E., Allen, I. E. & Seaman, J. (2018). *Grade increase: Tracking distance education in the United States.* Retrieved from Babson Survey Research Group website: https://onlinelearningsurvey.com/reports/gradeincrease.pdf

Selwyn, N. (2008). "Not necessarily a bad thing . . .": A study of online plagiarism amongst undergraduate students. *Assessment & Evaluation in Higher Education, 33,* 465–479. doi:10.1080/02602930701563104

Shumar, W. (2018). Caught between commodification and audit: Concluding thoughts on the contradictions in U.S. higher education. In B. Urciuoli (Ed.), *The experience of neoliberal education* (pp. 215–234). New York, NY: Berghahn.

Stage, F. K., & Hubbard, S. M. (2017). Case analysis in action. In F. K. Stage & S. M. Hubbard (Eds.), *Linking theory to practice: Case studies for working with college students* (pp. 36–51). New York, NY: Routledge.

Stephens, J. M., Young, M. F., & Calabrese, T. (2007). Does moral judgment go offline when students are online? A comparative analysis of undergraduates' beliefs and behaviors related to conventional and digital cheating. *Ethics & Behavior, 17,* 233–254. doi:10.1080/10508420701519197

Strayhorn, T. L. (2019). *College students' sense of belonging: A key to educational success for all students* (2nd ed.). New York, NY: Routledge.

Thelin, J. R. (2011). *A history of American higher education* (2nd ed.). Baltimore, MD: Johns Hopkins University Press.

Valai, A., Schmidt-Crawford, D. A., & Moore, K. J. (2019). Quality indicators for distance learning: A literature review in learners' perceptions of quality. *International Journal of e-Learning, 18,* 103–124. Retrieved from https://www.learntechlib.org/primary/p/171392

van Rooij, S. W., & Zirkle, K. (2016). Balancing pedagogy, student readiness and accessibility: A case study in collaborative online course development. *The Internet and Higher Education, 28,* 1–7. doi:10.1016/j.iheduc.2015.08.001

Toward a Paradigm Shift:
Bringing Traditional Student Affairs Online

CHAPTER 7

Student Engagement Opportunities for Online Learners

Andrew M. Goretsky

AS STUDENT AFFAIRS professionals, we may think about an online learner and visualize them in their home, working independently on their coursework and mostly spending time where student engagement is limited to connections with faculty and students via an online learning management system (e.g., Canvas, Blackboard). In addition, we might envision online learners engaging directly with college or university systems through an online portal and not wanting or needing to be involved with a physical campus. Much of the literature on engaging with online learners centers around engaging with them through their online coursework (Baker & Taylor, 2010; Das, 2010; Dixson, 2015; Glazier, 2016; Harrington & Floyd, 2009; Hew, 2016; Kelly, 2010; Mandernach, 2010; Scheuermann, 2010). However, there are opportunities to engage with online learners in person, either on campus and/or within the region where students live, but it is up to student affairs practitioners to intentionally design and help cultivate those experiences. This chapter examines the literature on in-person engagement for online learners and explores ideas and opportunities for engaging with online learners in person.

The Case for Engaging With Online Learners

Increasing numbers of students are enrolling in online coursework instead of at brick-and-mortar campuses. Researchers have demonstrated a continuous trend of decreasing enrollments at institutions of higher education, while the number of students enrolling in online coursework has increased (Allen & Seaman, 2017; Lederman, 2018). From 2012 to 2015, overall enrollments at higher education institutions decreased by 662,076 students; during that same period, students taking at least one online course increased by 596,699 students (Allen & Seaman, 2017). More recently, according to a 2018 report from the U.S. Department of Education's National Center for Education Statistics, enrollment decreased nationally at colleges and universities by nearly 90,000 students; however, the number of students who took some online coursework increased by 350,000 (Lederman, 2018). In addition, the number of college students who took courses solely through online methods grew by 15.4% (Lederman, 2018).

Importance of Student Engagement for Online Learners

Student engagement theory suggests students develop and learn better when they engage in both academic and nonacademic activities in college (Astin, 1984; Campbell & Cabrera, 2011; Kuh, 2003, 2009). Simply put, the time and energy students invest in cocurricular activities and programs within the larger structures of higher education institutions is considered student engagement (Kuh, 2003). In addition, it has been demonstrated several desired outcomes have been connected to student engagement, including persistence, leadership development, identity development, moral development, academic performance, and critical thinking skills (Campbell & Cabrera, 2011). For student growth and development, student engagement theory emphasizes the importance of both peer-to-peer interactions and faculty-to-student interactions (Kuh, 1993). It is important to ensure engagement also occurs with online learners.

Online learners interact with fellow students and faculty through learning management systems such as Blackboard or Canvas, where online courses are housed and facilitated (Sood, 2018; Wei, Peng, & Chou, 2015). While there are many ways to provide online learners with active and experiential learning experiences (Budhai & Skipwith, 2017), I have observed online learners generally only interact with students in their courses and have limited opportunity to engage with peers outside of their coursework. As more students are enrolling in online academic programs, it is imperative higher education institutions do their part to foster engagement among online learners; therefore, student affairs professionals need to dedicate time and resources to engage with this population.

Desire to Be Part of the Larger Campus Community

Online learners want to be part of a community (Clinefelter & Aslanian, 2017). The Aslanian Market Research company publishes an annual report on online college students. The participants consist of 1,500 students from all across the United States, where the participants were recently enrolled, are currently enrolled, or are planning to enroll in a fully online undergraduate, graduate, or certificate academic program. In the 2017 study, more than 50% of respondents shared peer and faculty interactions were important, and 59% of respondents reported they traveled to the physical campus anywhere from one to five times per year (Clinefelter & Aslanian, 2017). In the 2018 study, 76% of online learners reported visiting the campus at least once a year, with 45% reporting doing so three or more times per year (Magda & Aslanian, 2018). The findings from the study revealed a couple of factors that likely contribute to students' decisions to attend online programs at institutions close to home, including familiarity with the institution and how often students perceive they need to travel to the campus (Clinefelter & Aslanian, 2017). Online learners are not just sitting in their homes working on their coursework from their computer. They want to connect with faculty and peers, and they do so by visiting the physical campus.

In a study of online learners in business and information technology programs, Burton, Chicone, and Ferebee (2018) suggested online learners want to engage in cocurricular activities. Eighty percent of respondents did not participate in cocurricular activities for two primary reasons: (a) lack of knowledge of available cocurricular opportunities, and (b) perceived lack of time needed to participate in cocurricular activities (Burton et al., 2018). In addition, less than 5% of respondents stated they had no interest in participating in cocurricular activities, which Burton et al. (2018) suggested was an indication students find value in cocurricular participation. The fact online learners are interested in connecting with the larger campus community and are willing and able to travel to campus presents tremendous opportunities for student affairs professionals to carry out their overarching mission. Student affairs professionals who effectively market activities and demonstrate a manageable time commitment for online learners will have success engaging this population because there is already a built-in interest and buy-in from online learners looking to connect with the larger campus community.

The Need to Stay Competitive

Students exploring online academic programs are researching more options, as "more students contacted or requested information from three or more schools (52%), an increase from 2016 (29%)" (Clinefelter & Aslanian, 2017, p. 6), while "the number of students considering only one institution fell from 30% to 18%" (p. 6). Price and quality of academic programs have been longstanding factors when students choose a specific online program (Clinefelter & Aslanian, 2017). However, as students investigate more options, having a vibrant engagement model that goes beyond coursework will help colleges and universities recruit students to their programs. With the number of online learners increasing (Allen & Seaman, 2017; Lederman, 2018), facilitating cocurricular engagement for these students will foster student growth and development and engage them as part of the larger institutional community.

In-Person Engagement Opportunities With Online Learners

Student affairs professionals do not need to limit their engagement with online learners to virtual means (Burton et al., 2018; Clinefelter & Aslanian, 2017; Magda & Aslanian, 2018). There are opportunities to connect with online learners that will engage them in cocurricular opportunities and help them to feel they are part of the larger institutional community. The following sections will focus on: (a) strategies to enable regional engagement of online learners with peers, and (b) online learner engagement with the institution when students travel to the physical campus.

Regional Engagement of Online Learners

Since online learners desire to be part of a community (Clinefelter & Aslanian, 2017), student affairs professionals can leverage opportunities to help them engage with other students and staff and faculty from the institution nearest to where they live. There are five key opportunities for regional engagement: (a) social media, (b) academic working groups, (c) student organizations, (d) alumni association events, and (e) athletic events.

Social media. Creating a regional social media group for online learners can facilitate meaningful peer-to-peer engagement opportunities. Social media platforms provide an opportunity to help connect students who might be in the same or different online programs at their institution but live in the same region. For example, a student who is in a distance nursing program might never take an online course with someone who is in an online information technology program; however, they could live minutes from each other. Creating a regional social media group where students from different academic disciplines have an opportunity to connect potentially creates opportunities for networking and support that might help to retain students.

Technology and Innovative Tools

Regional social media groups

* Develop regional social media groups for your institution's online learners, whether you use Facebook or another platform. LinkedIn recently added features to meet the increased user demand for social media group engagement (Hutchinson, 2019).

* When choosing a social media platform, stay consistent with the social media platforms your institution is using.

* Determine which geographical areas have a high concentration of online learners. If you have a significant number of online learners from the Western New York region, you could create a Western New York social media group for online learners to join. This will provide a platform for students in that region who are taking online learners at your institution to connect with one another, and then in-person meetings can then be planned.

* For ideas, look up Regional Alumni Chapter Facebook Group pages (e.g., Howard University Alumni Club of Atlanta Facebook page, Penn State Alumni Associate, New York City Chapter Facebook page). These types of social media groups can be used to facilitate connections for online learners.

Kowalik (2011) discussed strategies for and the benefits of engaging with both alumni and prospective students through social media platforms. Social media provides opportunities for individuals to socialize with other people and build community and trust (Kowalik, 2011). The benefit of engaging through social media could also extend to online learners. As Driver (2018) noted:

> It is important for online students to establish social connections because isolation and loneliness can have a negative effect on their physical and mental health. There are some educators and social scientists who believe that online education can exacerbate feelings of loneliness because studying remotely eliminates face-to-face communication. (para. 1)

Peer-to-peer connections are paramount for student engagement and related positive outcomes (Campbell & Cabrera, 2011; Kuh, 2003). Furthermore, mobile devices enable continuous peer engagement where students can connect with each other 24 hours a day (Goretsky, 2016). Students now have the ability to meet virtually, continue the conversation in person, and then part ways and continue the conversation through social media platforms on a mobile device. Furthermore, regional social media groups can be a stepping-stone for students connecting with each other and then engaging in the subsequent regional opportunities discussed in this chapter.

Academic working groups. Online coursework can be a lonely experience for students (Driver, 2018). There is another academic experience that is lonely too, which is the dissertation writing experience (Sternberg, 1981). There is much advice that can be found on the benefits of developing a writing group for individuals who are in the process of writing their dissertation (Cassuto, 2018; Hunter, 2017; Lee & Golde, 2019). I have taken several online courses through University of Maryland Global Campus (formerly University of Maryland University College) and successfully defended my dissertation in 2016 from The George Washington University, and I can speak to the loneliness associated with online coursework and the dissertation process. I found participation in a writing group to be invaluable to the dissertation process, and an academic working group could have been beneficial to the experience of taking online courses. Lee and Golde (2019) discussed several benefits of developing a dissertation writing group, including providing online learners with a source of emotional support, an accountability team, and a community of individuals with shared goals.

Similar to writing groups for doctoral students who are working on their dissertation, online learners could come together to form academic working groups with benefits similar to dissertation writing groups. Social media platforms can serve as an initial connection opportunity for online learners who are from the same region but attend different programs or campuses, and students could come together at a local library or coffee shop to engage in academic coursework together. This has the potential to combat the isolation of online work and provide additional accountability as students work to meet school project deadlines. Student affairs staff could take the extra step of researching possible venues in the region to host an academic working group and then set up the first meeting for students in the region.

Student organization involvement. When envisioning students involved in a student organization, you may imagine groups of students meeting in a conference room. However, digital technology has changed how students engage with student organizations when on campus, a change that makes it possible for online learners to participate with on-campus student organizations. According to Magda and Aslanian (2018), almost every online learners owns a mobile device. In 2018, 79% of participants completed some of their coursework through mobile devices, with 20% completing all of their coursework through mobile devices (Magda & Aslanian, 2018). This trend is consistent with Pew Research Center data on smartphone ownership: 52% of participants owned smartphones in the 2011 study compared to 85% in 2015 (Smith, 2011, 2013, 2015).

With 76% of online learners visiting campus at least once a year and 45% visiting three or more times a year (Magda & Aslanian, 2018), online learners can choose to travel to campus for larger events executed by student organizations. The involvement fair is a fixture of new student orientation programs, allowing students an opportunity to get involved. However, student affairs professionals should consider how to engage online learners in these fairs so they can become active and contributing members of student organizations. Virtual student activity fairs can be added as a part of online learner orientation programming. If enough students in a specific region demonstrate interest in a student organization, it is possible a "chapter" of a student organization could be formed in Atlanta, for example, when the physical campus is in Washington, D.C.

Alumni association events. Clinefelter and Aslanian (2017) reported the primary reason students pursue online coursework is to advance in their careers, and, as a result, Clinefelter and Aslanian recommended networking and making connections between online learners and alumni to assist with online learners' career advancement. Furthermore, some larger higher education institutions have well established regional alumni chapters (e.g., University at Buffalo, The George Washington University). Alumni events that take place in a specific region are a prime opportunity to engage with online learners who live in the same area.

Thompson and Burnett (2019) found students who engaged in a leadership and extended orientation program at Louisiana State University demonstrated greater participation and giving as new alumni. In addition, connecting alumni to student life creates opportunities for networking between alumni and current students, and "collaborative programs, events, and activities that bring together students, faculty, staff, and alumni, and friends builds institutional pride and loyalty" (Rissmeyer, 2010, p. 22). Extending this collaborative relationship to online learners will serve to further enhance institutional pride for both constituents. In addition, online learners who are engaged with the alumni association may be encouraged to continue engagement following graduation.

Student affairs professionals partnering with alumni affairs to engage online learners at alumni events (e.g., socials, speakers) can result in positive outcomes for both students and alumni. Since regional alumni chapter events already have existing budgets, the cost of inviting online learners is minimal while providing a great potential for return on investment.

Athletic events. Athletic events provide another opportunity to engage in person with online learners. Larger institutions with extensive athletics programs have organizations and websites dedicated to alumni engagement at away games. Athletics websites often provide information on tailgating opportunities in addition to viewing parties and attendance at games (e.g., Cal Alumni Association [University of California, Berkeley], Nebraska Alumni Association, Northwestern Alumni Association, Penn State Alumni Association). Smaller higher education institutions with Division III athletics programs also promote opportunities for fans to attend away games.

Institutions that want to engage online learners could invite them to both away games and home games. Two of the main reasons online learners do not engage in cocurricular activities is simply not knowing about them, or they are concerned they may not have enough time to attend; but, as previously mentioned, less than 5% of online learners shared they have no interest (Burton et al., 2018). This suggests online learners will attend events and programs if they are made aware of cocurricular opportunities, and if the opportunities are convenient. Extending invitations to online learners to attend both home and away games will assist with building institutional affinity for online learners and connecting online learners with students from different courses and programs.

Tips for Getting Started

- Incentivize online learners' attendance at athletic events.
- Have conversations with both the athletics department and alumni affairs. It is important to engage these campus partners in any efforts to engage online learners.
- Offer online learners discounted or free tickets to athletic events.
- Plan tailgating opportunities specifically for online learners. For away games, be sure to review the institutional policies where the games are taking place prior to making plans for tailgating activities.
- Design giveaways (e.g., T-shirts, hats) to promote your institution and online programs.

Facilitating online learner attendance at regional athletic events for small institutions may have particular promise, because there is little additional cost for the institution to invite online learners, and events near their home will be convenient to attend. Enrollment patterns have put significant financial pressures on small, private liberal arts institutions (Marcy, 2017). As a result, departments need to be creative in sharing resources (Rissmeyer, 2010). A quick review of NCAA Division III athletics conferences demonstrates higher education institutions within these conferences were often within several hundred miles of each other. For example, the Middle Atlantic Conference (2019) has 17 member institutions where the farthest distance between two institutions is about 270 miles, while many are within 150 miles of each other. The New England Small College Athletic Conference (2019) has 11 member institutions where the farthest distance between two institutions is about 400 miles, while many are within 250 miles. Given 72% of online learners take coursework at an institution whose campus is within 100 miles of where they live (Clinefelter & Aslanian, 2017), students could easily take advantage of these opportunities at almost no additional cost to the institution.

On-Campus Engagement of Online Learners

Online learners are coming to campus, and institutions must engage with them effectively to ensure they are treated as full members of the community. In 2011, I was given the responsibility of seeking opportunities to engage with online learners, and I discovered some online learners were coming to campus for research conferences or career fairs. Those students were not able to access campus facilities and had challenges accessing WiFi. Ensuring online learners access to services and facilities can help them feel a part of the institutional community. There are a number of strategies student affairs professionals should consider for helping online learners feel like students and not visitors when they engage with the campus.

Student ID cards. Online learners should be provided a college or university ID card. With an ID, students are full members of the campus community. Although an ID card does not build community on its own, students who are not permitted to obtain an ID card may feel they are not as legitimate of a member of the community as a student who takes courses on campus.

A review of websites of several institutions with online academic programs (i.e., Berkeley College, The University of Southern Mississippi, Boston University, The George Washington University, Chestnut Hill College, and West Chester University) revealed three general stances related to online learners' ability to obtain an institution ID card: (a) there was no information about obtaining an ID card, (b) online learners could receive an ID card without a photo that would not grant them access to campus facilities, and (c) online learners could obtain a photo ID card and replace it with one that grants access to facilities when they visit the campus.

According to The George Washington University (2019) website, there is a process for online learners to submit a photo to obtain a university ID card without ever needing to step foot on campus. When students do visit campus, they can trade in that ID card for one that will allow them access to various facilities on campus. In situations when institutional policies do not permit online learners to access campus facilities, colleges and universities should allow students to have an institutional ID card that provides access. As some online learners may never visit campus, institutions should consider how they can provide photo ID cards to those individuals. Perhaps higher education institutions could ask students to use a notary service, coupled with video technology, to verify a student's identity and provide the individual with a photo ID card.

With an institution ID card, an online learner can demonstrate they are a student and take advantage of the many opportunities available to them. In addition, students can receive benefits from local businesses that provide discounts for students with an institution ID card; there are over 200 businesses across 13 industries that provide students with discounts (Lewis, 2019).

Policies, protocols, and fees. Institutions of higher education have a variety of tuition and fee structures. Tuition is sometimes inclusive of certain services on campus, while other services are covered by separate fees. How those fees are administered, and policies related to the services covered by those fees, can impact online learners' experiences when they visit campus. For example, students may pay a campus recreation fee, which gives them access to the gym and recreation facilities. If online learners are not paying the campus recreation fee, the policy may not permit them to use that service. There could be similar issues for online learners when considering a library fee. Will online learners have access to the library when they are on campus? Some other fees on-campus students pay but online learners often do not are activities and technology fees. It makes sense to differentiate these fees, since online learners are not going to access those services in the same way on-campus students will; however, this could impact online learners' ability to access events on campus or login to the campus WiFi network.

Online learners are visiting campus (Clinefelter & Aslanian, 2017; Magda & Aslanian, 2018), and, when they do, it is important for colleges and universities to do what they can to ensure these students feel as welcome as students who take courses on campus. Although charging online learners the same fees as on-campus students would unfairly burden online learners, higher education institutions should consider differential fees or one-day/multiday visit fees. Colleges and universities could also consider whether to include the limited access online learners will need into the cost of their tuition. Institutions of higher education should consider online learners in their policies, protocols, and fees.

Larger institutional events. Online learners should be invited to large events on campus (e.g., career fairs, graduation). These larger events can enhance the connection between the institution and online learners, ensuring they feel like they matter as members of the campus community. Invitations to career fairs will also meet an existing need of online learners.

Career services are important to online learners (Clinefelter & Aslanian, 2017; Magda & Aslanian, 2018). In fact, 77% of online learners use career services available at their institution (Clinefelter & Aslanian, 2017). In addition, Clinefelter and Aslanian (2017) stated, "The primary reason online students go to school is for career advancement" (p. 31). Furthermore, almost three quarters of online learners sign up to take online coursework because they are motivated by career needs, and 35% of online learners already attend their school's career fair (Magda & Aslanian, 2018). Since career services are so important to online learners, institutions should take the steps necessary to make career fairs and services available to them. Career

Potential Challenges and Practical Solutions

Online learners are visiting the physical campus. Many policies, protocols, and fee structures may unintentionally exclude online learners when they are on campus. This has the potential to reduce online learners' sense of belonging at the institution. To overcome this, the following potential challenges and practical solutions are offered.

Potential Challenge: Many institutions use fee structures to cover the cost of student services, which may then exclude online learners.

Practical Solution: When online learners are not included in current fee structures, consider the implementation of single day use or visitation fees for online learners.

Potential Challenge: A differential fee could cause an online learner to still feel like an outsider when on campus.

Practical Solution: Online program administrators should consider including student services fees in the cost of online learner tuition.

Potential Challenge: Policies and protocols may not consider the needs and possibly exclude the online learners.

Practical Solution: Ensure you engage with academic colleagues who are responsible for students in online programs, when developing or reviewing institutional policies.

fairs and services should be resourced to allow online learners to engage fully in these opportunities. For example, travel and lodging assistance would serve to encourage engagement with these services for online learners.

Conclusion

The number of students enrolling in online programs continues to increase, even as overall college and university enrollment numbers decrease (Clinefelter & Aslanian, 2017; Magda & Aslanian, 2018). This chapter demonstrated engaging online learners in the region where they live and on campus is not only possible but also beneficial to both online learners and the campus community. Student affairs administrators, partnering with other departments on campus, should work to enhance the engagement of online learners.

Social media, academic working groups, student organizations, alumni associations, and athletic events are ways to engage with online learners where they live at minimal additional cost to the institution. Dedicating a staff person to build collaborative efforts between departments will facilitate these opportunities. In addition, exploring how online learners engage could lead to additional opportunities for regional connections with these students.

It is important to ensure online learners feel part of the community when they visit campus. Reviewing existing policies and protocols, ensuring access to institution photo ID cards, and inviting online learners to campus events are good starting points to integrate these students into the fabric of the institution. College and university administrators should continue to assess the on-campus experience for students who take courses online.

? Questions for Reflection

- Does your institution have a comprehensive list of online learners, or are lists maintained by individual colleges and academic programs? Is there a way to gather this information centrally? Who owns this information at your institution?

- Are there student organizations on the physical campus that lend themselves to online connection more than others (e.g., a gaming group)?

- How can you use video conferencing technologies (e.g., Zoom) or social media tools to facilitate opportunities for online learners to meet and then connect in person?

- Athletics and alumni events are opportunities to engage online learners regionally. Are there other regional activities in which online learners could be included?

- Promotion for on-campus events is already online, and online learners are likely learning about these events. How can you ensure your event advertising includes outreach to online learners?

References

Allen, I. E., & Seaman, J. (2017). *Digital learning compass: Distance education enrollment report 2017.* Retrieved from Online Learning Consortium website: https://onlinelearningconsortium.org/read/digital-learning-compass-distance-education-enrollment-report-2017

Astin, A. (1984). Student involvement: A developmental theory for higher education. *Journal of College Student Personnel, 25,* 297–307.

Baker, C., & Taylor, S. L. (2010). The importance of teaching presence in an online course. In M. Bart (Ed.), *Online student engagement tools and strategies* (pp. 6–8). Retrieved from https://www.facultyfocus.com/free-reports/online-teaching-strategies-free-reports/online-student-engagement-tools-and-strategies

Budhai, S. S., & Skipwith, K. B. (2017). *Best practices in engaging online learners through active and experiential learning strategies.* New York, NY: Routledge.

Burton, T., Chicone, R., & Ferebee, S. (2018). Enhancing online student engagement with extracurricular activities. *Issues in Information Systems, 19,* 202-211. Retrieved from http://www.iacis.org/

Campbell, C. M., & Cabrera, A. F. (2011). How sound is NSSE? Investigating the psychometric properties of NSSE at a public, research-extensive institution. *Review of Higher Education, 35,* 77–103. doi:10.1353/rhe.2011.0035

Cassuto, L. (2018). On the value of dissertation-writing groups. *The Chronicle of Higher Education.* Retrieved from www.chronicle.com/article/On-the-Value-of/245184

Clinefelter, D. L., & Aslanian, C. B. (2017). *Online college students 2017: Comprehensive data on demands and preferences.* Louisville, KY: The Learning House.

Das, S. (2010). Increasing instructor visibility in online courses through mini-videos and screencasting. In M. Bart (Ed.), *Online student engagement tools and strategies* (pp. 8–9). Retrieved from https://www.facultyfocus.com/free-reports/online-teaching-strategies-free-reports/online-student-engagement-tools-and-strategies

Dixson, M. D. (2015). Measuring student engagement in the online course: The Online Student Engagement Scale (OSE). *Online Learning, 19*(4). doi:10.24059/olj.v19i4.561

Driver, H. (2018, December 27). How to alleviate loneliness when you study online. *OnlineLearningTips.com.* Retrieved from https://onlinelearningtips.com/2018/12/alleviate-loneliness

The George Washington University. (2019). GWorld card. Retrieved from http://online.gwu.edu/gworld-card

Glazier, R. A. (2016). Building rapport to improve retention and success in online classes. *Journal of Political Science Education, 12,* 437–456. doi:10.1080/15512169.2016.1155994

Goretsky, A. M. (2016). *Student engagement of traditional-aged undergraduates using portable Internet devices* (Doctoral dissertation). Retrieved from ProQuest Dissertation and Theses database. (Order No. 10076079)

Harrington, S. J., & Floyd, K. S. (2009). Enhancing engagement and the value of the course to the student through course organization and active learning. In M. Bart (Ed.), *Online student engagement tools and strategies* (pp. 15–17). Retrieved from https://www.facultyfocus.com/free-reports/online-teaching-strategies-free-reports/online-student-engagement-tools-and-strategies

Hew, K. F. (2016). Promoting engagement in online courses: What strategies can we learn from three highly rated MOOCS. *British Journal of Educational Technology, 47,* 320–341. doi:10.1111/bjet.12235

Hunter, J. H. (2017). On dissertating. *Inside Higher Ed.* Retrieved from https://www.insidehighered.com/advice/2017/10/05/how-survive-dissertation-process-essay

Hutchinson, A. (2019, February 13). LinkedIn announces new group features, catering to increased group engagement. *SocialMediaToday.* Retrieved from https://www.socialmediatoday.com/news/linkedin-announces-new-groups-features-catering-to-increased-group-engagem/54827

Kelly, R. (2010). Tips from the pros: 4 ways to engage students. In M. Bart (Ed.), *Online student engagement tools and strategies* (p. 10). Retrieved from https://www.facultyfocus.com/free-reports/online-teaching-strategies-free-reports/online-student-engagement-tools-and-strategies

Kowalik, E. (2011). Engaging alumni and prospective students through social media. In L. A. Wankel (Ed.), *Higher education administration with social media* (Cutting-Edge Technologies in Higher Education, Vol. 2, pp. 211–227). Bingley, United Kingdom: Emerald Group.

Kuh, G. D. (1993). In their own words: What students learn outside the classroom. *American Educational Research Journal, 30*, 277–304. doi:10.3102/00028312030002277

Kuh, G. D. (2003). What we're learning about student engagement from NSSE: Benchmarks for effective educational practices. *Change: The Magazine of Higher Learning, 35*, 24–32. doi:10.1080/00091380309604090

Kuh, G. D. (2009). What student affairs professionals need to know about student engagement. *Journal of College Student Development, 50*, 683–706. doi:10.1353/csd.0.0099

Lederman, D. (2018, November 7). New data: Online enrollments grow, and share of overall enrollment grows faster. *Inside Higher Ed*. Retrieved from https://www.insidehighered.com/digital-learning/article/2018/11/07/new-data-online-enrollments-grow-and-share-overall-enrollment

Lee, S., & Golde, C. (2019). *Starting an effective dissertation writing group* (Hume Writing Center Graduate Student Workshop). Stanford, CA: Stanford University.

Lewis, E. (2019). Student discounts guide: The ultimate list of stores. *Dealhack*. Retrieved from dealhack.com/blog/student-discounts-guide

Magda, A. J., & Aslanian, C. B. (2018). *Online college students 2018: Comprehensive data on demands and preferences.* Retrieved from Learning House website: https://www.learninghouse.com/knowledge-center/research-reports/ocs2018

Mandernach, B. J. (2010). Indicators of engagement in the online classroom. In M. Bart (Ed.), *Online student engagement tools and strategies* (pp. 10–12). Retrieved from https://www.facultyfocus.com/free-reports/online-teaching-strategies-free-reports/online-student-engagement-tools-and-strategies

Marcy, M. B. (2017, May 9). *The small college imperative: From survival to transformation.* Retrieved from Associate of Governing Boards of Universities and Colleges website: http://agb.org/reports-and-statements/the-small-college-imperative-from-survival-to-transformation

Middle Atlantic Conference. (2019). Members. Retrieved from http://gomacsports.com

New England Small College Athletic Conference. (2019). NESCAC member institutions. Retrieved from http://www.nescac.com/about/members

Rissmeyer, P. A. (2010). Student affairs and alumni relations. In T. E. Miller (Ed.), *Advancement work in student affairs: The challenges and strategies* (New Directions for Student Services, No. 130, pp. 19–29). San Francisco, CA: Jossey-Bass. doi:10.1002/ss.357

Scheuermann, M. (2010). Engaging students with synchronous methods in online courses. In M. Bart (Ed.), *Online student engagement tools and strategies* (pp. 4–5). Retrieved from https://www.facultyfocus.com/free-reports/online-teaching-strategies-free-reports/online-student-engagement-tools-and-strategies

Smith, A. (2011). *Smartphone adoption and usage July, 2011.* Retrieved from Pew Research Center website: http://www.pewinternet.org/2011/07/11/smartphone-adoption-and-usage

Smith, A. (2013). *Smartphone ownership 2013.* Retrieved from Pew Research Center website: http://pewinternet.org/Reports/2013/Smartphone-ownership-2013/Findings.aspx

Smith, A. (2015). *U.S. smartphone use in 2015.* Retrieved from Pew Research Center website: http://www.pewinternet.org/files/2015/03/PI_Smartphones_0401151.pdf

Sood, I. (2018). An overview of 4 popular learning management systems for higher education. *eLearning Industry*. Retrieved from https://elearningindustry.com/learning- management-systems-for-higher-education-overview-popular

Sternberg, D. (1981). *How to complete and survive the doctoral dissertation.* New York, NY: St. Martin's Griffin.

Thompson, B. B., & Burnett, F. M. (2019). Impact of the S.T.R.I.P.E.S. leadership and extended orientation program on philanthropic giving. *Philanthropy & Education, 2,* 53–74. doi:10.2979/phileduc.2.2.03

Wei, H.-C., Peng, H., & Chou, C. (2015). Can more interactivity improve learning achievement in an online course? Effects of college students' perception and actual use of a course-management system on their learning achievement. *Computers & Education, 83,* 10–21 doi:10.1016/j.compedu.2014.12.013

CHAPTER 8

Mental Health Services for Online Learners

Christopher Corbett, Monica Osburn, and Kathryn P. Alessandria

IN THE 1930s landmark document, *The Student Personnel Point of View,* the American Council on Education (ACE, 1937, 1949) asserted students are more than their academic and vocational pursuits. In *The Student Personnel Point of View*, ACE (1949) posited a holistic view of students and stated it is the responsibility of higher education to attend to the emotional health and well-being of students as well as their social, physical, spiritual, and intellectual domains. This emphasis on the development of the whole student and not just their academic and vocational pursuits was groundbreaking and paved the way for modern day college counseling (Paladino, Alessandria, & Denino, 2020).

College counseling "developed from the merging of several movements: vocational guidance, mental health, and student personnel work" (Dean & Meadows, 1995, p. 139). Given the intersection of these movements, practitioners arrive in the college counseling setting through a variety of disciplines, all of which influence the models used in delivering counseling services. Other influences on the delivery of college counseling services include: (a) social and historical contexts, (b) wars, (c) political movements, (d) large-scale crises (human-made and natural disasters), (e) evolving student needs and changing demographics (e.g., decreased stigma of seeking counseling services, increased diversity among students), and (f) the accessibility of higher education through online learning (Paladino et al., 2020). The main focus of this chapter is the intersection of college counseling and the accessibility of higher education through Internet mediated distance learning. It is beyond the scope of this chapter to discuss the role of technology in students presenting issues.

The ubiquity of high-speed Internet, WiFi, smartphones, and other wireless-enabled devices has greatly influenced higher education. Specifically, the emergence of these technological tools and resources has contributed to the prevalence of online learning in the 21st century. As technology makes education more accessible, convenient, and customizable to students' locations and schedules, students' expect other campus resources and support services to be available in this format. One such support usually available to students at brick-and-mortar campuses is counseling (Paladino et al., 2020). Institutions range from being fully online to offering selected programs online or just a few courses. Depending on the online education options on campus, students may be on campus or relatively local while taking online courses or could be in another state or time zone completing their degree. Once an institution decides to engage online learners, it must consider how to support these students in a way that is equitable to those who are on campus and can access the brick and mortar support services on campus.

In the 21st century, it is no longer a given students will set foot on campus to complete coursework. Students can now take classes from the comfort of their own home and, in some cases, at their own pace. It is time for institutions of higher education and college counseling centers to consider how to provide online learners with access to the same high-quality counseling and wellness services brick-and-mortar students receive. Given this need, one of the aims of the chapter is to provide models, frameworks, and resources to help student affairs practitioners provide mental health and wellness services to their online learners. In the subsequent sections we will discuss the comprehensive counseling model, stepped care model, and integrated care model of services as they might look in an online environment. The unique ethical, legal, and logistical considerations for college counseling in an online environment will be reviewed as well as the institution's responsibility in providing these services. Finally, practical considerations for how to implement these services will be addressed.

Counseling for Online Learners

There are many different terms used to describe counseling services delivered from a distance. These terms include *distance counseling, telemental health, telepsychology, e-therapy, e-counseling,* and *telepsychiatry,* to name a few (Zur, n.d.b)[1]. Regardless of the terminology one uses, the premise is generally the same: a mental health professional provides counseling or therapeutic services to a person who is not present in person with the provider through the use of telecommunications technology,

---

[1] Throughout this chapter, the term *telemental health* is used as a general term that encompasses all mental health disciplines involved in college counseling. At the time of this writing, it is the prevalent term used in the literature to refer to mental health services delivered from a distance through telecommunication technology. As technology evolves, so too does the vocabulary.

such as telephone, text message, chat, e-mail, and video conference (Zur, n.d.b). These technologies may occur synchronously or asynchronously. In synchronous services, the provider and recipient are communicating in real time, though they are not in the same location, such as with Internet-based video conference programs, telephone conversations, or instant messaging/chat functions. In contrast, asynchronous communication incorporates a delay in the communication process, such as with e-mails, voicemails, and text messages.

Telemental health (TMH) services generally are provided through an Internet-connected device, such as a computer, smartphone, tablet, or telephone (Dart, Whipple, Pasqua, & Furlow, 2016). The TMH format can be used to bring a specialist in for consultation with the client, with or without the therapist in the room (e.g., psychiatrist), while the client is onsite at the college counseling center. However, this is not how we are defining TMH in this chapter. It is more likely the client will be at a distance from the institution seeking support services mediated by technology, and the clinician will be at the brick-and-mortar campus counseling center. There are a variety of possibilities for where the counselor could be located, particularly if an institution is contracting with a third-party provider. Alternately, as the security of technology evolves, it is possible TMH providers could be located at off-campus sites, or even working from home. However, the formats discussed here assume there is a brick-and-mortar counseling center at which the TMH provider is located, or at least making the decisions about contracts for TMH services that will be offered to students.

TMH services may be delivered by individual practitioners and through third-party platforms. Some third-party TMH providers operate by matching clients with providers who are credentialed in the client's location and offer an array of service options and/or packages. Other third-party TMH providers offer products and a range of services that may include online psychoeducation and self-help tools to promote wellness and prevention, and provide therapy with a distance provider, through their proprietary platforms, thus combining synchronous and asynchronous services (Higher Education Mental Health Alliance [HEMHA], 2018).

Envisioning College Counseling in an Online Learning Environment: Models and Frameworks

In traditional brick-and-mortar institutions, it is common to implement a particular model for college counseling services. The model selected by the counseling center leadership, or in many cases, the institution's leadership, often dictates the type of service provided to students. A college counseling model can also be particularly helpful for an online environment, and it is important to consider which model or framework might work best in a virtual environment. In this section, we discuss three models to demonstrate the potential applicability of each for distance counseling.

Comprehensive Counseling Model

The comprehensive counseling model (CCM; Brunner, Wallace, Keyes, & Polychronis, 2017) focuses on four foundational pillars deemed necessary for a thriving college counseling center: (a) clinical services, (b) consultation and collaborative services, (c) outreach and prevention programming, and (d) training and education. One of the strengths of the CCM is how it is integrated into the larger university community. Designed to achieve contact with as many students as possible while using the most appropriate resources, this model has mental health clinicians interacting with a large section of the university population. Each of these four pillars will be explained in more detail.

Clinical services

Clinical services focus on the direct therapeutic work with students through individual and group counseling (Brunner et al., 2017). In most settings, clinical services also include crisis intervention and psychiatric care. Other services in this area may include career counseling and psychological assessment, but this varies by institution. For the e-learning environment, providing individual counseling, crisis response, and assessment services can be achieved by using some of the platforms discussed in the Technology and Innovative Tools sidebox. There are many options for online or distance counseling, but special consideration needs to be given to confidentiality, legal and ethical issues, and evidence-based practice, which will be discussed later in this chapter.

Consultation and collaborative services

Consultation and collaborative services are an important part of the relationship with the greater university. Often times, situations arise which require specific knowledge related to mental health concerns. Having a resource students, faculty, and staff can contact to gain further insight on a particular challenge can often prevent crises from occurring as well as positively impact academic success. Consultation services are offered to students, parents, staff, and faculty when clinical expertise is needed, whether that is in a crisis or routine setting (Brunner et al., 2017). While there is high availability of on-call type services, it is more likely a response from the counseling center is designed for crisis response and not consultation or collaboration. At times, it may be difficult to secure accurate consultation if a situation is nuanced to your campus environment. Specifically, using an outside consultant who is not familiar with the campus culture adds an additional layer of complexity to the consultation. The counseling center on campus is encouraged to work collaboratively with online teaching faculty and other university student service departments to learn what the needs for collaboration and consultation are, how university culture may impact that, and how to implement the best supports to increase positive outcomes.

Outreach and prevention programming

Students learning about specific mental health conditions and the coping skills to manage them is an essential element to wellness and student success. Outreach and prevention programming focuses on: intentional skill building, psychological and emotional well-being screenings, coaching and campus community development, and teaching students and the community vital interventions to support and intervene with themselves and others in distress (Brunner et al., 2017). This area lends itself well to the online environment. There are many programs that incorporate psychoeducation into both interactive and self-guided learning. A few evidence-based examples are included in the Technology and Innovative Tools sidebox.

Training and education

As the fourth pillar for this model, counseling centers make training and education a priority through being a site for clinical internships to not only train future mental health clinicians, but also to be involved in teaching, staff development, and continuing education for current staff working in the counseling center and greater university (Brunner et al., 2017). A byproduct of training future counseling professionals is keeping permanent staff up to date and clinically sound. Continuing education for mental health clinicians is easily achievable in online trainings; however, integrating clinical training and internships would require more technology support. For example, many counseling centers hire interns to provide clinical care to the student population. These interns need immediate access to licensed clinicians and consistent supervision. Having a model that could be used to manage the need for immediate response in crisis situations may provide increased challenges, but it is possible.

Figure 8.1. Stepped Care Model

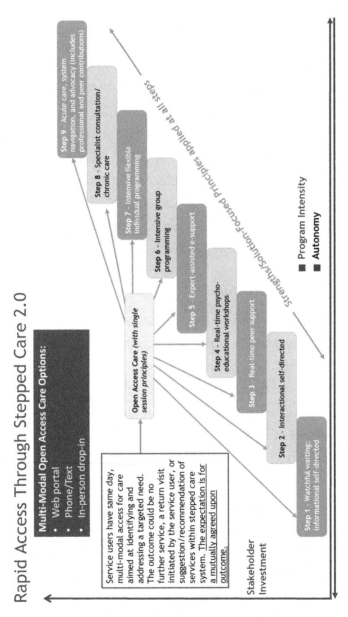

Note. Reprinted from "What is Stepped Care 2.0," by Stepped Care 2.0, 2019 (https://steppedcaretwopoint0.ca/what-is-stepped-care-2-0). Copyright © 2019 by Peter Cornish. Reprinted with permission.

Stepped Care Model

The stepped care model is based on a model focused on family medical practice. This model, developed by Cornish et al. (2017), is specific to the university campus environment. It outlines a range of evidence-based mental health programs along a continuum of treatment intensity (see Figure 8.1.). It is designed to meet a student where they are under the assumption not everyone needs individual therapy. This model includes many online experiences embedded within the framework. There are several other versions of stepped care models, but this model is one of the more widely used.

The stepped care model may be the easiest to implement for students at a distance. All nine of these steps are readily available in an online format (see examples in the Technology and Innovative Tools sidebox). Minor adjustments would need to be accounted for, such as changing the action of "walking in" within Step 1 in a counseling services model to a phone call or video chat option. In addition to the logistical and practical changes to service delivery to ensure quality care that meets best practice standards, a significant challenge for implementation would likely be a financial one, as having a comprehensive services model that adequately covers student needs in an online environment can be quite expensive.

Technology and Innovative Tools

There are many new online products designed to address mental health. The key is finding products that are evidence based, easy to use, and focused on college students. Some are very comprehensive and offer a wide variety of services, and some specialize in one particular area. Each will have their pros and cons. Here are a few you may want to research further.

* **WellTrack**

    https://welltrack.com

    WellTrack is a hands-on tool that uses aspects of cognitive behavioral therapy to help users identify, understand, and address issues they are having in their lives. This system is data driven and user friendly. It includes:

    * Online assessment to evaluate and track stress levels, anxiety and depression
    * MoodCheck for instant feedback on daily moods
    * Self-help focus for self-paced training and practice on one's own
    * Video chat ability for quick check-ins or remote counseling sessions
    * Customizable resources for access to everything needed on campus all in one place
    * Personal data tracking

* **Talkspace**

    https://www.talkspace.com

    Talkspace is a telebehavioral health care company with a network of over 5,000 licensed mental health therapists. Users can communicate with dedicated therapists through text, video, picture and audio messages. Depending on the program selected, contact with the therapist may occur five days per week with unlimited engagement. Talkspace also provides psychiatry services and couples counseling along with individual therapy.

* **SilverCloud**

    https://www.silvercloudhealth.com

    SilverCloud is designed to help you learn about and reduce symptoms of anxiety, depression, and stress. Each program consists of articles, video clips, interactive activities, and short quizzes. Clients work through weekly activities with the support of a trained clinician who reviews progress and provides feedback and encouragement.

* **iHope Network**

    http://www.ihopenetwork.com

    iHope Network is a network of therapists providing counseling securely in an online format. Therapists are licensed in multiple states, which assists with many of the challenges of practicing across state lines. Therapeutic interventions are similar to face-to-face counseling, but all counseling takes place through video.

Integrated Care Model

Integrated care, according to the Substance Abuse and Mental Health Services Administration (SAMHSA; 2020), is the systematic coordination of general and behavioral healthcare, including mental health, substance abuse, and primary care services for people with multiple healthcare needs. The integrated care model is often implemented to improve communication between physical and behavioral health units. When applied to higher education settings, most recent data show there is not a significant difference in treatment outcomes based on the level of integration between health centers and counseling centers, especially as it relates to medical records (Center for Collegiate Mental Health, 2018).

An integrated or collaborative model would be most difficult in an online environment. The most common implementation of this model is with primary care or in a student health setting. In a white paper, Mitchell, Oakley, and Dunkle (2019) cautioned against mental health care being merged into a medical framework. Instead, they proposed both medical and mental health professionals giving attention to a student's unique developmental and contextual needs. Although there are some good advice-type medical hotlines, there is not a strong blueprint for medical care online. A more common approach is to have counseling and psychiatric care available virtually and medical care continue to be a brick-and-mortar service.

Things to Consider Before Getting Started

There are several things to consider before an institution should move forward with offering distance counseling services. In this next section, we will briefly review the variables to consider. Should your institution choose to move forward with distance counseling services, your awareness of these variables will contribute significantly to your success. These variables are models of care and ethical, legal, and liability considerations.

Models of Care

Earlier in this chapter, we discussed models of care. Prior to selecting and implementing a distance counseling model, stakeholders should consider several questions to make an informed decision. Some questions to consider include: Have you determined what your model of care is? How will distance counseling be a part of this? While distance counseling is often considered a way to extend services to online learners, it is important to determine if services will be made available to all students and not just online learners. How about students who are studying abroad, students who are away at internships, or students involved in other off-campus extended learning opportunities? Will there be limitations on eligibility for services based on the nature or severity of students' presenting concerns? Will students in crisis who need a high level of care be eligible for services at a distance? Additionally, will the school be providing services directly or working with a third-party servicer, or both? Answers to these questions will help campuses structure services for students.

Ethical, Legal, and Liability Considerations

Another central set of factors to consider are ethical, legal, and liability matters. It is critically important all state and federal laws, ethics, and standards of practice are upheld in the provision of services (Barnett & Kolmes, 2016). The following sections will break these areas down into their individual components for further discussion.

Ethical Considerations

While many states often adopt the ethics of a given mental health profession into their legal code, this is not always the case. Therefore, it is critical the institution and clinicians providing the services are aware of the relevant ethical standards, particularly those codes that relate to distance based and/or services provided through technological means. Some examples of these relevant professional organizations are the American Counseling Association (2014), the American Psychological Association (2017), and the National Association of Social Workers (2017). Zur (n.d.a) provides a consolidated list of professional associations' ethical codes related to TMH. It is important to review and note if there are any conflicts between the ethical standards and legal codes. If so, it is generally recommended the legal code is followed.

Legal Considerations

Currently, all 50 states require clinicians to be licensed to provide mental health services. While there have been some conversations and efforts for license compacts between states, there is no current national license option. Therefore, at a minimum, a practitioner is highly encouraged to be licensed in both the location of the counselor and the location of the client (Kramer, Kinn, & Mishkind, 2015). Prior to the emergence of technology, it was assumed a client receiving services was in the same state as the provider. Now this is often not the case, as technological advances have made it possible for people to connect at great distances from each other. For this reason and others, it is very important for institutions to be aware of state laws regulating clinical practice and in particular any specific guidelines that may exist for offering distance-based services (Turvey et al., 2013).

Is it also critical to determine whether states and/or professional organizations have specific training requirements for clinicians who offer these services. While state laws are not explicitly clear in some cases, it is generally assumed anyone providing distance counseling is licensed, at a minimum, in the state in which they are practicing and in the state where the client is located. This can present certain costs and logistical issues for the institution, so it is critically important to know state laws. Once the laws concerning TMH services are identified, it is critical all legal requirements are followed as they would be for in-person services. While the logistics will be discussed in greater detail in the section "How Tos for Implementing Telemental Health Services," among the things to have in place are documents of informed consent, releases for local providers, crisis plan agreements to be used between provider and client, and policies on limitations of and eligibility for TMH services.

When reviewing the provision of services in higher education, three federal laws will quickly stand out: (a) the Health Insurance Portability and Accountability Act (HIPAA), (b) Family Educational Rights and Privacy Act (FERPA), and (c) the Health Information Technology for Economic and Clinical Health (HITECH) Act of 2009 (HEMHA, 2018). While these may not be the only examples of privacy and technology laws and standards, they are examples of the laws and regulations institutions are required to follow. Because of the strict and comprehensive nature of these laws, the institution needs to determine if the department providing services is considered a "HIPAA-covered entity" (HEMHA, 2018). HIPAA is a federal law on the handling of electronic personal health information. FERPA is a federal law on the protection and privacy of educational records. FERPA also has guidelines on the access and sharing of educational records and includes a section on "treatment records" and how they can be excluded from some FERPA requirements, with deference given to HIPAA (see FERPA, 2009, 34 CFR § 99.3). However, according to HIPAA, any records maintained by the school are excluded from HIPAA. For a more direct explanation of this, refer to the HIPAA regulations and review the exception at paragraph (2)(i) and (2)(ii) for what is considered protected health information at 45 CFR § 160.103.

Even with these laws in place, things can get complicated, and questions may arise. For example, if you are not a HIPAA-covered entity and FERPA does not apply, then what are your guidelines? An institution would fall back on any state laws and regulations governing the practice of mental health services. Lastly, HITECH became federal law in 2009 as part of the American Recovery and Reinvestment Act and provides specific guidelines on the regulation of healthcare informatics. It often complements HIPAA while providing additional specifics. Awareness and ability to be in compliance with these and all federal laws is a must. Again, this highlights the importance of understanding and knowing the opinion of your university legal counsel in advance of offering counseling services in an online environment.

Liability Considerations

The practice of using TMH services is also fraught with risk and liability (HEMHA, 2018). While some of these risks and liabilities are not exclusive to distance-based services, many are further highlighted by it. Due to this increased risk, some policies do not provide coverage of TMH services or may restrict their coverage to certain types of services. Therefore, it is vitally important the institution and providers know, before providing services, what the rules are and what the coverage is for their liability insurance. If these services are not covered, can the institution acquire a secondary policy or change policy providers? For a more complete discussion on risk management related to TMH services, see Kramer et al. (2015).

Finally, there are likely many different reasons and explanations for why your institution is considering distance counseling. The risks and benefits are not the same for each institution, so it is highly recommended you conduct a thorough risk-and-benefit analysis. We will not take the space in this chapter to discuss this in detail but recommend a review of a comprehensive risk-and-benefit analysis found within the HEMHA (2018) guide, *College Counseling From a Distance: Deciding Whether and When to Engage in Telemental Health Services.* This interdisciplinary resource is free and provides a framework for institutions to use to proactively and intentionally make decisions on whether and under what circumstances to offer distance counseling services.

Tips for Getting Started

It is easy to start providing services once you have decided to provide them. In this chapter we have discussed several of the important areas to cover, such as models of care, legal and ethical issues, and logistics. Your ability to answer the following questions will be key to implementing a successful distance counseling service:

• Determine which service model you will be providing and which students are eligible for the services. This includes considering the boundaries of services and the goals of the services.

• Establish what need is going to be met if distance counseling services are offered and if these services will be in addition to or instead of existing services offered.

• Confirm what the legal and ethical standards are for distance counseling in your state. Also verify the opinion of your institution's legal counsel office on your TMH implementation plan.

• Verify the counseling center staff are trained and equipped to provide distance counseling in accordance with ethical codes, state licensing regulations, and best practices. For the counseling center staff that do not have distance counseling and/or TMH training, decide who will be responsible for the cost of training and how it will be accessed.

• Ensure the school liability insurance covers distance counseling services.

• Guarantee the institution is prepared and committed to providing these services, as they will take additional financial, material, and staffing resources.

• Determine if you have the necessary technology and equipment available, and whether it meets all privacy and confidentiality requirements. Identify who will be responsible for equipment maintenance and monitoring digital security best practices. See HIPAA and HITECH.

• Ask for the opinion of your counseling center staff and achieve buy in with them.

• Gather all stakeholders who will be responsible for and involved with delivering these services to confirm buy-in.

How Tos for Implementing Telemental Health Services

So far in this chapter we have discussed a number of important areas to cover when considering the possibility of offering TMH services, including ethical and legal considerations, as well as your model of care. In this section, we will focus more on how to implement TMH services on campus. This section centers around the areas of institutional resources, logistics, institutional responsibility, and accessibility.

Institutional Resources

Now that your institution is considering TMH services, there are several important aspects to consider. In addition to the ethical, legal, and liability concerns, it is important to assess the available institutional resources. The greatest of these are the clinicians. The demand for mental health services continues to rise despite underfunding and many centers are not adequately staffed to meet the demand (HEMHA, 2018). Understanding the existing resource limitations in serving students through face to face services, it is important to set and hold realistic expectations about the objective in adding distance counseling services. Higher education institutions should be clear as to whether the goal is to increase the number of students served or to provide equitable access to all enrolled students. Clarity on the existing resources (or shortages of resources) will also assist with creating clear goals by which to measure and assess the effectiveness of new service delivery formats. Campus decision makers should answer the following questions prior to offering TMH services:

1. What type of TMH services do we plan to offer?
2. What is our goal for offering these services?
3. Since offering TMH services requires clinical staff, will additional clinical staff be recruited? If not, what other services will be decreased or cut as a result?

4. What are the state's requirements for offering TMH, and do we have enough, if any, of these credentialed clinicians? If clinicians do not have this training, then how will training be acquired and implemented?

It is imperative you know your risk and liability with offering these services (Kramer et al., 2015; Palomares, Bufka, & Baker, 2016). It is also critical to know your institution's legal counsel's opinion (HEMHA, 2018). If this is not their area of specialty, then it is important to consult with additional legal counsel. Does the school's liability insurance cover TMH services, and, if not, do you need to purchase additional coverages?

Logistics

The next area to consider to provide TMH services effectively is logistics. While these needs can vary depending on the type of services you will provide, there are a couple standard technology needs: (a) fast and consistent Internet connection with good bandwidth, (b) a consistent phone line, (c) available and up-to-date software and devices, (d) data security practices aligned with current legal and industry standards, and (e) a good relationship with your institution's information technology (IT) experts. This is even more important when considering how to provide services for online learners. You will be relying on your IT team for their technical know-how and their expertise with data security and IT infrastructure. Similarly, they will be relying on you for your knowledge of privacy and confidentiality needs. Your combined experience and expertise are a central part of your TMH system. IT will assist with determining how data are collected, stored, and protected. Your IT team will likely also assist with the technology training needs of your clinical staff. It is important to discuss these training needs with IT staff first so appropriate expectations are set. When you encounter technical difficulties, your IT experts will be a critical part of the team.

Your next area of logistics is clinical service logistics. This area will also be highly impacted by the other types of clinical services you are offering on your campus. One of the most important initial questions to answer is: Who is eligible for services? This question is closely followed by "What are the limitations to these services?" and "What is your plan for clients in crisis?" Since these services will be offered via technology, what is your plan if/when services are interrupted and not able to be restored? Are there plans in place in the event of natural or manmade disasters that could disrupt communication services?

While it was discussed briefly during the technical logistics section, it is necessary to discuss documentation and clinical record keeping. It is likely your center has a clinical documentation policy and system for all records. Since offering TMH services provides a new dimension to your services, it is very important to reassess your standards and documentation practices. Will there be any differences in documentation of TMH services, and will there be any difference in how these records are accessed? Remember to plan for clinical administrative logistics like hours of operation, costs of providing services, the physical location of the service providers, and the staging of the office environment.

Potential Challenges and Practical Solutions

Once you have decided to provide TMH services, keep in mind the following potential challenges and practical solutions.

Potential Challenge: Coordinating administrative logistics, including costs, technology infrastructure and maintenance, data security/encryption, hours of availability, service disruption contingency plans, and training standards and requirements for staff providing services.

> **Practical Solution:** Be proactive, research all your options, identify student needs and institutional resources, and then select the best model for your population. Identify limitations and/or parameters for the virtual services offered.

Potential Challenge: Determining how and where services will be provided and who will be responsible for monitoring.

> **Practical Solution:** Work with key stakeholders on campus to proactively identify answers to the challenges identified above. There are no one-size-fits-all answers. Policies and standards must be in place to maintain the privacy of services, during and after they are provided.

Potential Challenge: Preparing counseling center trainees to be supervised in their TMH service delivery, and determining if sessions will be recorded and secured.

> **Practical Solution:** Invest in the necessary training and resource upgrades and maintenance plans prior to implementation.

Institutional Responsibility

Institutions should consider several factors prior to implementing TMH services for all students, including those who learn online. First is the institution's obligations and responsibilities to external bodies (i.e., accreditation organizations). Most, if not all accrediting bodies, have requirements related to the provision of services for online learners, so it is important these are reviewed on a continual basis. Second, but just as important, is a series of questions related to the school's identity and student population. Important questions to ask are: How are we serving the needs of online learners? What are the expectations from students and the institution for providing counseling services to online learners? Where are our distance learners located (i.e., local to our brick-and-mortar center or at a significant distance)? Is there an unmet need that requires counseling services delivered online? The answers to these questions may best be understood through an internal self-study to understand the demographics and needs of online learners. HEMHA (2018) has published an interdisciplinary resource to guide stakeholders in making informed decisions.

Another important and related consideration is to determine who you are trying to serve with distance counseling services. This is an area where the concept of equity becomes important. On one hand, if online learners tend to be local students on campus who are taking one or two classes online, their needs may already be met by existing brick-and-mortar resources. On the other hand, if online learners are individuals who never set foot on campus and do not have access to the same support services as other students, we must ask ourselves why. And, what might be the consequences of this disparity (e.g., differences in retention rates, average GPAs)? When answering these questions, it is pertinent to consider how counseling services are funded on campus and whether there are students paying these student fees who do not have access to the services. It is common practice to charge online learners an additional technology fee. Administrators should consider whether these technology dollars are being used to support counseling services. If the answer is yes, then we have a moral obligation to provide reasonable access to student support services for which online learners are paying. Similarly, administrators should consider whether online learners pay health services fees used to fund student counseling services. If it is determined students are paying for these services, reasonable access should be offered.

Accessibility

Offering TMH services can improve access to mental health services not just for online learners but also for students who may have mobility support needs, limited access to transportation, or whose mental health concerns may make it difficult to attend counseling on campus (e.g., agoraphobia, PTSD, social anxiety; HEMHA, 2018). These services may also improve access to services for students who live in remote areas. Severe weather that disrupts infrastructure is on the rise; distance counseling services may also provide access to students who may be temporarily cut off from their institution due to weather disruptions (e.g., blizzards, hurricanes, floods).

Access to services can be viewed through the lens of social justice. Minoritized and underrepresented students may benefit from access to TMH services. Online learners may benefit from the convenience of access from their home by limiting time in transit to and from appointments, limiting lost pay from missed work, and possibly reducing child care expenses while traveling to campus for services. Eliminating some of these barriers may make counseling services easier to integrate into busy students' schedules (HEMHA, 2018). Students who are hearing impaired or non-native English speakers who need a translator or a counselor fluent in their language may need access to practitioners or specialists with these skills who might not be accessible through the staff on campus. TMH services can expand access to these underserved populations by providing the opportunity to find practitioners and/or translators who are fluent in various languages. This particularly applies to contracts through third-party platforms.

Conclusion

The decision to provide TMH services to students is one that should be made intentionally to ensure: (a) the mental health staff are prepared, (b) the technology is in place, (c) risk mitigation plans are established, (d) the institution is following all best practices with respect to legal and ethical responsibilities, and (e) policies have been developed to determine student eligibility for services and crisis contingency plans. All stakeholders should be involved in the decision-making process to ensure the institution is well prepared to put TMH services in place and assess their effectiveness in meeting the needs of students, staff, and the institution. These areas are critical to the success of providing TMH options for students.

? Questions for Reflection

- How can online learners at your institution access student support services?
- How can student support services be made equitable for all students enrolled at your institution?
- What are the mental health and wellness needs of online learners at your institution? How can you meet these needs?
- What are the ethical guidelines and concerns you must consider to implement services to best meet students' needs and be sustainable?
- What are the training and qualifications of counseling center and IT staff?
- What is the status of technology infrastructure at your institution in support of TMH services? What additional training/infrastructure investments are necessary to provide services in accordance with legal and ethical standards?
- What resources are available to help you make informed decisions on how to implement TMH services for online learners?

References

American Council on Education. (1937). *The student personnel point of view*. Washington, DC: Author.

American Council on Education. (1949). *The student personnel point of view* (Rev. ed.). Washington, DC: Author.

American Counseling Association. (2014). *ACA code of ethics*. Alexandria, VA: Author.

American Psychological Association. (2017). Ethical principles of psychologists and code of conduct. Retrieved from https://www.apa.org/ethics/code

Barnett, J. E., & Kolmes, K. (2016). The practice of tele-mental health: Ethical, legal, and clinical issues for practitioners. *Practice Innovations, 1*, 53–66. doi:10.1037/pri0000014

Brunner, J. L., Wallace, D., Keyes, L. N., & Polychronis, P. D. (2017). The comprehensive counseling center model. *Journal of College Student Psychotherapy, 31*, 297–305, doi:10.1080/87568225.2017.1366167

Center for Collegiate Mental Health. (2018). *Center for collegiate mental health 2018 annual report*. Retrieved from https://sites.psu.edu/ccmh/files/2019/01/2018-Annual-Report-1-15-2018-12mzsn0.pdf

Cornish, P. A., Berry, G., Benton, S., Barros Gomes, P., Johnson, D., Ginsburg, R., . . . Romano, V. (2017). Meeting the needs of today's college student: "Reinventing services through stepped care 2.0." *Psychological Services, 14*, 428–442. doi:10.1037/ser0000158

Dart, E. H., Whipple, H. M., Pasqua, J. L., & Furlow, C. M. (2016). Legal, regulatory, and ethical issues in telehealth technology. In J. K. Luiselli & A. J. Fischer (Eds.), *Computer-assisted and web-based innovations in psychology, special education, and health* (pp. 339–363). Boston, MA: Academic Press.

Dean, L. A., & Meadows, M. E. (1995). College counseling: Union and intersection. *Journal of Counseling & Development, 74*, 139–142. doi:10.1002/j.1556-6676.1995.tb01838.x

Higher Education Mental Health Alliance. (2018). *College counseling from a distance: Deciding whether and when to engage in telemental health services*. Retrieved from http://hemha.org/wp-content/uploads/2018/04/HEMHA-Distance-Counseling_FINAL.pdf

Kramer, G. M., Kinn, J. T., & Mishkind, M. C. (2015). Legal, regulatory, and risk management issues in the use of technology to deliver mental health care. *Cognitive and Behavioral Practice, 22*, 258–268. doi:10.1016/j.cbpra.2014.04.008

Mitchell, S. L., Oakley, D. R., & Dunkle, J. H. (2019). White paper: A multidimensional understanding of effective university and college counseling center organizational structures. *Journal of College Student Psychotherapy, 33*, 89–106. doi:10.1080/87568225.2019.1578941

National Association of Social Workers. (2017). NASW code of ethics. Retrieved from https://www.socialworkers.org/About/Ethics/Code-of-Ethics/Code-of-Ethics-English

Paladino, D. A., Alessandria, K. P., & Denino, D. J. (2020). History and evolution of college counseling. In D. A. Paladino, L. M. Gonzalez, & J. C. Watson (Eds.), *College counseling and student development services: Addressing the needs of the contemporary college student*. Alexandria, VA: American Counseling Association.

Palomares, R. S., Bufka, L. F., & Baker, D. C. (2016). Critical concerns when incorporating telepractice in outpatient settings and private practice. *Journal of Child and Adolescent Psychopharmacology, 26*, 252–259. doi:10.1089/cap.2015.0013

Substance Abuse and Mental Health Services Administration. (2020). *What is integrated care?* Retrieved from https://www.integration.samhsa.gov/about-us/what-is-integrated-care

Stepped Care 2.0. (2019). What is stepped care 2.0. Retrieved from https://steppedcaretwopoint0.ca/what-is-stepped-care-2-0

Turvey, C., Coleman, M., Dennison, O., Drude, K., Goldenson, M., Hirsch, P., . . . Bernard, J. (2013). ATA practice guidelines for video-based online mental health services. *Telemedicine and E-Health, 19*, 722–730. doi:10.1089/tmj.2013.9989

Zur, O. (n.d.a). *Professional association codes of ethics and guidelines on telemental health, e-therapy, digital ethics, & social media*. Retrieved from https://www.zurinstitute.com/ethics-of-telehealth

Zur, O. (n.d.b). *Telemental health definitions*. Retrieved from https://www.zurinstitute.com/telehealth-define

CHAPTER 9

Reaching Beyond the Screen:
A Case Study for Linking
Online Learners to Virtual
Career Resources

J.L. Wyatt and Jasmine Posey

THE ABILITY TO ACCESS college coursework online has captured the attention of traditional and post-traditional learners, and, over the past 30 years, distance learning has grown to serve countless numbers of college students (Perry & Pilati, 2011). Online learning made its mark in 1982 when National Technological University began offering continuing education and graduate courses by using satellite transmission to obtain course materials from higher education institutions and then redistributing content (Casey, 2008). This change in how students received information soon caught the attention of institutions across the country, and, in 1989, the University of Phoenix began meeting the demands of growing numbers of students who wanted to pursue an education online. The attraction to obtaining an education online has increased exponentially; according to the National Center for Education Statistics (NCES; n.d.), in 2017, 15.42% of students were enrolled in fully online programs (academic programs with 100% of required program courses offered online), while 17.64% of students were enrolled in some online programs, an increase of 2.19% respectively, from online enrollment in 2016. Approximately 33% of students attending college are enrolled in at least one online course (Lederman, 2018).

The increase in virtual learners has created a growing need for student affairs departments to provide students with guidance that extends beyond the classroom, particularly those in need of career resources. According to Arnold (2018), Generation Z students (those born in 1995 to the present) have entered postsecondary education with the expectation they will have instant access to information. Due to this shift and the growing numbers of online learners, the need to meet students where they are has become even more critical. The purpose of this chapter is to examine the integration of virtual career readiness programs into a preexisting catalogue of career services programs and resources at a four-year, public university. The instruments, tools, and programs used, along with key players in the integration process, are noted. Results of e-mail campaigns and a needs assessment are shared with the intent of informing career services professionals in other settings of the nuances of integrating virtual career readiness programs into their current resources.

The Need for Virtual Career Resources

The newest generation of learners entering postsecondary education includes students who work full time and are enrolled in online classes. In fact, a 2017 report of college student employment rates showed 43% of full-time and 81% of part-time students were employed (NCES, 2019). Institutions across the country have started to enhance their career services through social media and video conferencing to provide customized services to each student's unique development (Dey & Cruzvergara, 2014).

Usefulness of Online Career Toolkits

Virtual resources have gained popularity, and online toolkits are now used within career services departments at several institutions. Toolkits include virtual learning resources embedded in the academic course shell of online classes. Loyola University Chicago, Colgate University, Cal Poly, and the University of Illinois Springfield are examples of institutions that include such toolkits for students, some of which are located on separate webpages specifically for online and alumni students. While each institution varies in how toolkits are presented, information on self-assessment tools, job and internship strategies, search engine navigation tips, interviewing skills, and professional social media accounts (e.g., LinkedIn) is consistently reviewed across each toolkit. The most informative toolkits contain handouts and career guides on how to build a résumé, expand professional networks, write documents, negotiate salary, and they have access to links for special populations (online learners, students with disabilities, minority students, and international students). Toolkits typically are listed on the career website under student resources with a brief description of the resource and a variety of links to further assist students in the career planning process. According to the University of Illinois Springfield, Center for Online Learning, Research and Service (2019), the institution was the first to offer virtual career services 24/7, and the center employees certified distance career counselors to provide career counseling to those students not within the state.

Development of Core Career Readiness Skills

Career resources are essential to enhancing and developing core career readiness skills (critical thinking/problem solving, oral/written communication, teamwork/collaboration, digital technology, leadership, professionalism/work ethic, career management, and global/intercultural fluency) deemed necessary by the National Association of Colleges and Employers (2019). As Chin, Blackburn Cohen, and Hora (2018) stated, "Campus administrators widely view career services centers (CSCs) as central in helping students prepare for and compete in a rapidly changing global economy" (para. 1). This movement toward expanding virtual education has left faculty and student affairs staff members with the challenge of connecting with online learners, and, according to Venable (2010), online career resources offer students the ability to balance both life and work.

Virtual Career Programming

The importance of online career resources now extends beyond career services centers. Although research implicates the promise of virtual career programming to students, on average, 77% of students express concerns about their preparedness for potential jobs (Bauer-Wolf, 2019). Student concerns are confounded by employers using online methods to screen and select candidates through the use of websites, social media, and virtual interviews. Researchers have shown virtual recruiting allows employers to reach significantly more students than they would during traditional on-campus visits (Hudak, Kile, Grodziak, & Keptner, 2019). As such, students not only need access to resources online, but also they must be prepared to establish a professional presence virtually and learn strategies to engage and communicate with employers online.

According to Hudak et al. (2019), employers recognize recent graduates demonstrate deficiencies in the area of communication. To assess and enhance students' virtual interview performance, Hudak et al. instructed students to complete mock virtual interviews using an online resource called InterviewStream. Prior to the virtual interviews, students engaged in instruction via short lectures, class discussions, a tell-me-about-yourself student worksheet, and an employment interview scenario simulation (Hudak et al., 2019). At the conclusion of the interview, students reported feeling more confident in their interviewing skills. Hudak et al. shared while students stated they were discouraged after the first set of interviews, their self-assessment of the virtual interview process had a significant impact on their experience.

Creating and Connecting Online Learners to Virtual Career Resources: A Case Study

In an effort to contribute to the career growth and development of online learners, the career services department at a public research university in the Southwestern region of the United States conducted a case study of an institution with an enrollment of less than 15,000 students. The institution serves approximately 11,155 undergraduate students and 2,598 graduate students, 1,780 of whom are currently enrolled in fully online degree programs, which was an 18% increase from Spring 2018 online enrollment. The university presently offers fully online programming for five undergraduate degrees, 15 graduate degrees, seven specialist degrees, and four doctorate degrees. In addition, nine undergraduate degrees and one specialist degree are offered in a hybrid format at the institution. As online programs continue to increase in popularity among the institution's students, the need to establish a strong online presence of digital career resources for distance learners has become a priority for career services. Career services implements programming in the Division of Student Affairs and Enrollment Management. Alongside student affairs departments, such as counseling, university recreation, housing and residence life, the Center for Student Involvement, health services, and student conduct, career services focuses on engaging at-risk students and assisting in retention efforts. Each of these student affairs departments either reports to the assistant vice president of student affairs or the dean of students. Career services falls under the leadership of the assistant vice president of student affairs. Leadership in career services is comprised of a director, two associate directors, and one assistant director.

The Liaison Model

The career services team's overall mission includes providing students with the comprehensive resources they need to attain their professional career goals, and the department achieves this through campus, employer, and community partnerships. The team also facilitates career development through career counseling, student employment, and experiential learning. The team, comprised of full-time staff members working in three separate functional areas, including career development, experiential learning, and employer relations, uses a liaison model where staff within career development are assigned to specific academic colleges for programming, career counseling, and overall collaboration with a focus on fostering intentional partnerships. For example, each career counselor (reporting to the associate director of career development) is assigned two academic colleges, and they are responsible for programming for students enrolled in those academic programs. The liaison model extends into career counseling within career services, where students are assigned appointments with career counselors based on the student's major and the academic college for which the counselor serves as a liaison. The use of the liaison model allows staff members to individually support two colleges. Doing so provides streamlined communication between departments and fosters personal relationships among staff, students, and faculty members. These cross-divisional partnerships between student affairs and academic affairs lead to innovative programming tailored to the needs of a broad range of student learners.

Use of Virtual Career Services

While career services offers a variety of programs, materials, and content students can easily access virtually, participation among online learners is lower than participation among on-campus students. The School of Nursing at the university adopted the career services toolkits as an online resource embedded in academic courses, which is a promising example of a collaborative approach to guiding students to career readiness content between career services and academic affairs staff. The university uses CourseDen, a virtual learning management system, to administer online courses for credit. By 2019, career services had embedded online career readiness toolkits in CourseDen for students enrolled in all online nursing coursework. Although the overall number of online learners enrolled in credit courses/programs has increased, the overall number of online learners engaged in career services programming at the university has not increased proportionately.

As with most student support programming, predictors of student participation, engagement, learning, and the efficacy of programming is limited to units of measurement, including immediate post-program evaluation or longitudinal measurement of a student's ability to apply skills learned through the initial program. Hutchings (2010) asserted faculty involvement in assessment is critical to positive student outcomes. Given this, career services employed a needs assessment to gauge faculty perceptions and solicit recommendations for virtual career readiness resources for students. This chapter provides an overview of steps taken by career services to introduce virtual career readiness programs to the university.

Expanding Virtual Career Services Resources

Career services offers several online resources beyond assistance with résumé and cover letter writing, such as career counseling and exploration, graduate school preparation, and salary negotiation. Providing these services has helped students in the job and internship search process, academic major exploration, and interview preparation. Resources such as Vault, an online tool for students to research job and internship opportunities, and Buzzfile, an online tool that lists available employers in each industry, provide students with unique job exploration strategies. In addition, resources such as What Can I Do With This Major and Focus 2 give students the opportunity to make meaningful connections between who they are and available career opportunities. These resources were used by students at increasing rates from 2017–2018, which demonstrates growing student engagement in online resources. For example, in 2017, 28% of undergraduate students who were enrolled in 60 credit hours took the Focus 2 assessment compared to 34% of this population who completed the assessment in 2018.

The success of several events for on-campus students, such as a Student Professional Wardrobe Program (a clothing closet for students in need of professional attire for an interview or first day of work), a Government and Public Service Panel (a program highlighting an array of careers across the public sector), a Nonprofit and History Panel (a program specific to industries that allow students to gain knowledge about their areas of interest), 100 Days of Graduation (a series of workshops to provide postgraduation career readiness strategies to graduating seniors), and multiple career fairs initiated the question, How can career services reach online learners to ensure they are afforded the same career opportunities and guidance as on campus students? Since the number of online learners continues to rise, online career toolkits were created, and the effectiveness of these online toolkits on distance learner engagement was examined. For the School of Nursing, which adopted the toolkit model, career services engagement among students enrolled in the school's programs has increased. Collaboration between career services and the School of Nursing has also increased to include a close partnership for working to enhance the postgraduation outcomes of nursing students.

Currently, one college within the university uses the virtual career readiness toolkit in all online classes for students. This implementation is fostered continuously through a healthy partnership between career services leadership and the leadership within the academic college. Leadership from both areas convene to discuss student usage, administration of the toolkit, and other functional properties. The career services liaison manages the project, ensures the vision for the toolkit is reached, and oversees communication to students about the resource. The toolkit was created as a Google Doc, and the link was uploaded to the Resources tab in every online course offered for the college. Each year, leadership from career services along with the dean and lead faculty from the academic program communicate to discuss toolkit updates and enhancements needed in preparation for the upcoming year. The toolkit is designed in compliance with Quality Matters course standards. These standards serve as the university's guidelines for the content, placement, and implementation of items located within online courses. In the spring 2019 semester, approximately 86 undergraduate and 125 graduate students were enrolled in one or more online courses that contained the career readiness toolkit as a resource. This enrollment constitutes approximately 10% of the total enrollment for the academic college. Table 9.1 illustrates the content included in the toolkit.

Table 9.1. Virtual Career Readiness ToolKit Table of Contents

Section	Title/Content	Section	Title/Content
1	Welcome	8	InterviewStream
2	Purpose	9	Dressing for Your In-Person or Online Interview
3	Developing Your "In Field" Résumé	10	Professional Presence on Social Media
4	Conducting Your Job Search	11	LinkedIn Quick Stats
5	"In Field" Employment Resources	12	When Connecting With Recruiters or Alumni
6	Preparation for an Interview	13	Office of Career Services
7	Practice Interview Services	14	Quality Matters Course Standards

Technology and Innovative Tools

Focus 2	Offers customized major exploration and career planning in conjunction with the institution's academic program offerings. Provides simple assessments on interests and careers and provides an individualized student report to foster career development discussions. *https://www.focus2career.com*
Handshake	A platform to connect students to employment opportunities among several institutions in the United States. *https://www.joinhandshake.com*
InterviewStream	Offers students the opportunity to assess their skills while also receiving additional feedback from career services staff. The online resources used within career services allow students to play an active role in their own career development. *https://interviewstream.com*
Symplicity	Used to connect students to employers, manage job opportunities and internships, house students' professional profiles, showcase career services events, and secure event attendance and registration data. *https://www.symplicity.com*
Vault	Provides students with detailed descriptions of career and industry trends. Offers rankings and reviews of thousands of jobs and companies. Students, employers and career professionals can receive résumé, interview, and other career development-related advice and guidance through the online platform. *https://access.vault.com*
What Can I Do With This Major	Provides students with resources on available job and internship opportunities. Proven to be effective in conjunction with career counseling as students can continue their career outside of career counseling appointments. *https://whatcanidowiththismajor.com/major/majors*

Taking the First Step in Creating
Virtual Career Resources

Beginning in the spring 2019 semester, career services inventoried the number of online degree programs offered and the number of active students enrolled in courses in these programs. Online courses offered through academic programs that are not fully online were not included in the study. Academic deans and department chairs for each fully online program were asked to participate in a survey about their ideas related to virtual career readiness programs for students. Once responses were received, career services began to implement the development of virtual toolkits for other academic colleges. Student feedback was collected through focus groups, and feedback was incorporated into the design of a comprehensive toolkit with skills students and faculty deemed essential.

During the spring semester, a group of seven students, from first to fourth year, were asked to participate in a focus group on the virtual career readiness resources they perceived were needed on campus. Convenience sampling was used, and students employed as student assistants within career services participated. These students gave time during their work schedule for the focus group discussion and then developed a presentation to showcase their recommendations to career services staff.

A needs assessment was distributed during the spring 2019 semester to both full- and part-time faculty. The online instrument for faculty included five questions; three were Likert scale questions, one was a short-answer question, and one was a yes or no question. The 4-point Likert scale questions allowed participants to select *highly likely*, *likely*, *unlikely*, and *highly unlikely*. An option to select *neutral* was intentionally omitted so overall responses could be categorized as either *likely* or *unlikely*. The survey was distributed to the faculty e-mail list. Nonteaching staff were not invited to participate in the survey since the focus of career services was on implementing virtual career readiness resources in academic courses. The needs assessment was prefaced by a brief introduction that included contact information for questions or clarifications. The introduction read as follows:

> Thank you for your participation is this survey. The Office of Career Services is interested in learning more about the need for career readiness resources to prepare online students for employment. Please take a moment to complete the survey below regarding career readiness resources for online students. As faculty, your feedback is critical to increasing variety among the types of programs offered to students (both undergraduate and graduate). Should you have any questions, or wish to share additional feedback, please contact [Career Services Director, Name, E-mail, Phone Number]

In addition to distributing the needs assessment, career services used divisional e-mail distribution lists to promote the use of InterviewStream during the month of March, in connection with an annual InterviewStream March Madness contest hosted by the online interview platform for colleges and universities that use the platform. During the first week of March, three unique e-mail messages were distributed campuswide using three e-mail distribution lists (see Table 9.2).

Table 9.2. March Madness Email Distribution Lists

E-mail Frequency During Month	Distribution List	Approximate Number of Recipients
2	Student Affairs and Enrollment Management Division	240
1	Academic Affairs Division	400
1	All Staff	1,830

In the e-mail message, faculty and staff were asked to encourage students to complete a virtual interview in March. Ideas were pitched such as offering a mock interview as an extra-credit assignment to students and promoting mock interviews to students currently employed in on-campus positions. The e-mail also included a link that could be shared with students to complete an already established virtual interview. At the conclusion of the e-mail campaign, students completed 97 mock interviews for the month of March.

The potential for this virtual interviewing resource to help online learners at the university in career development and job preparation is immense. Currently, there are more than 1,800 students employed on campus, of which only 3% are enrolled in only online courses. This cohort of 1,800 student employees represents just over 10% of the total student population. This student population is also spread across all academic colleges and programs. While 3% of online learners working on campus is miniscule, the opportunity to use InterviewStream to engage online learners and foster communication skills remains.

Tips for Getting Started

* **Acknowledge each student is unique, and develop programming and resources tailored to each student.** Forty-three percent of online learners are working full time, while 81% are working part time. Career services professionals should consider when students are most likely to engage and access content in toolkits.
* **Develop a structured process to solicit feedback from students.** Staff should consider sending surveys (see chapter 5 for suggested tools) to gain a deeper understanding of what resources students are using and what they would like to see improved. These surveys can also be used to evaluate online webinars or live events the department chooses to broadcast.
* **Engage faculty in the planning process.** Career services staff should work to identify faculty members who have an interest in careers and postgraduation outcomes. Consider creating an award to recognize the faculty member who provided the greatest amount of support to career services throughout the year. The selected winner can have their photo taken and receive a career services gift. An institutionwide e-mail should be sent to ensure the faculty members are acknowledged campuswide.
* **Identify an implementation strategy.** Decide as a staff which resources suit the needs of online learners. Are online learners requesting help with interviewing or salary negotiation? The focus of the initial toolkits should be on resources students are currently using. If online learners are not using any of the available resources, use student feedback and develop student focus groups to identify which resources should be placed online.

Needs Assessment Results and Next Steps

The needs assessment survey response rate was 5%. Overall, faculty responses to the needs assessment indicated the perception students would be most receptive to learning about their inherent skills and interests to narrow down a list of relevant career options. This question was presented as a yes or no question, and 83.3% of respondents thought students would be interested in skills and interest inventories offered online. Ironically, career services currently offers Focus 2, Myers-Briggs Type Indicator, and other online assessments with participation from less than 20% of the student population. Of the respondents, roughly 5% represented the academic college where the career readiness toolkit was already in use. Overwhelmingly, responses from faculty in this area indicated receptiveness to all forms of virtual career readiness resources for online learners.

In the needs assessment survey, participants were asked, "How likely would students enrolled in online courses be to participate in an online mentor program?" Fifty percent of participants responded *likely*, and 33.3% selected *unlikely*. Both *highly likely* and *highly unlikely* received 8.3%, respectively. Survey participants were also asked, "How likely would students enrolled in online courses be able to participate in a virtual career fair?" Of the responses, 83.3% were divided between *highly likely* and *likely*. Only 17% of the respondents thought students would be either *highly unlikely* or *unlikely* to participate.

There was an overwhelmingly positive response to the needs assessment question that indirectly referenced the existing online career readiness toolkit. The question was, "How likely are instructors who teach online courses to add customized career readiness resources for students to their online course sections? (These resources would be developed by career services.)" This question yielded a 100% response rate divided between *highly likely* and *likely*. Of the five questions contained within the survey, this was the only question that directly inquired about faculty participation and behavior related to online career readiness resources.

Potential Challenges and Practical Solutions

Career services staff often have limited personal interactions with online learners. Creating and maintaining meaningful relationships with students who may not visit campus requires staff to become more innovative and intentional with each student appointment. In addition, ensuring students have the same opportunities to learn about career services in the classroom setting as on-campus students also becomes increasingly difficult when faculty may not fully support the mission of career services. The following are some of the potential challenges and solutions career services departments may encounter:

Potential Challenge: Career services lacks faculty engagement and strong collaboration with colleges.

> **Practical Solution:** Create faculty buy-in through annual meetings that provide updates on student successes related to the use of career services.

> **Practical Solution:** Provide resources faculty can implement in the classroom setting that can later be reviewed by a career services professional

Potential Challenge: Developing useful content for an online toolkit.

> **Practical Solution:** Benchmark career services toolkits created by other institutions.

> **Practical Solution:** Assess online learner needs at your institution.

> **Practical Solution:** Establish the focus of the toolkit, how students will access materials, and the overall appearance of toolkits.

Potential Challenge: Creating effective ways to market to online learners.

> **Practical Solution:** E-mail students through listservs or the institution's communication or advising platform to students.

> **Practical Solution:** Embed marketing materials in the career services management system.

> **Practical Solution:** Include a separate webpage for online learners within the career services website

Reflections and Implications

Responses to the needs assessment indicate communication of the existing virtual career readiness resources to students needs to be a more concerted effort, one made by both faculty and staff who can offer similar messages of importance. The majority of respondents indicated online learners would be interested in the skills and interest assessments; however, participation among online learners remains relatively low at the university. Information sharing with faculty also appears to be a divisional need to influence faculty perceptions of which virtual resources students would use the most. The success of the toolkit in realizing a high level of student engagement and participation is indicative of the progress realized through partnering around shared goals. Additionally, learning outcomes and online resources that comply with preexisting academic practices appear to be better received than other types of programs.

Responses also illustrate faculty support of programs with descriptions using familiar career-related terminology such as 'résumé,' 'interview,' and 'job,' and programs that add value to their academic content may be more welcomed as information to share with students. Terms such as *virtual career fair* and others that are easily defined are more likely to be welcomed and received by faculty tasked with implementing and/or explaining career-related programs, services, and resources to students. For example, faculty are more likely to promote a 'virtual career fair' than a 'reverse career fair' due to their understanding of the term virtual and its association with online learners. Given this, career services intends to identify faculty within the remaining six academic colleges with whom resources can be shared to help demystify the role of career services. A review of the existing online toolkit will be scheduled with these faculty with the goal of collaboration and planning to introduce the resource to online learners. In addition, the department is working to host its inaugural virtual career fair, with faculty communication to students as an integral part of the planning.

Conclusion

Over 5.5 million students were enrolled in at least one online course at a postsecondary institution in 2013 (Dumford & Miller, 2018). As this number continues to grow, higher education institutions and career services departments will need to uncover the most effective way to deliver content to online learners. Students decide to pursue an online education for various reasons, and their need to access career resources and guidance if they so choose is critical. This chapter provided insight on the value students place on access to online resources, evidenced by the majority of respondents expressing an interest in the availability of online resources and inventories. This interest can be gleaned as a bit of opportunity for career services departments to continuously work on improving the understanding among academic professionals of how career development services are delivered to students. As career services programming continues to evolve beyond résumé assistance and career fairs, open lines of communication between student affairs and academic affairs must be maintained. Showcasing the value virtual career services programming adds to the academic experience of online learners should remain at the forefront of conversations about student success, so equity in access to career development programming and resources is afforded to all learners.

Questions for Reflection

Results from the needs assessment provided career services with an opportunity to develop additional questions on how to impact online learners in meaningful ways. The following questions were posed at the conclusion of the study:

- How can career services collaborate with faculty to incorporate career resources into online curriculums?

- In what ways can toolkits be revamped to include resources online learners may find more appealing, such as webinars and online videos?

- What marketing strategies will prove to be most effective in informing online learners of available resources?

- Should online learners be considered a "special population" included within the liaison model? Why or why not?

References

Arnold, W. W. (2018). Strengthening college support services to improve student transitioning to careers. *Journal of College Teaching & Learning, 15*, 5–26. Retrieved from https://files.eric.ed.gov/fulltext/EJ1186161.pdf

Bauer-Wolf, J. (2019). Survey: Employers want soft skills from graduates. *Inside Higher Ed.* Retrieved from https://www.insidehighered.com/quicktakes/2019/01/17/survey-employers-want-soft-skills-graduates

Casey, D. (2008). A journey to legitimacy: The historical development of distance education through technology. *TechTrends, 52*, 45–51. doi:10.1007/s11528-008-0135-z

Chin, M. Y., Blackburn Cohen, C. A., & Hora, M. T. (2018). *The role of career services programs and sociocultural factors in student career development* (WCER Working Paper No. 2018-8). Retrieved from University of Wisconsin–Madison, Wisconsin Center for Education Research website: https://wcer.wisc.edu/publications/working-papers

Dey, F., & Cruzvergara, C. Y. (2014). Evolution of career services in higher education. In K. K. Smith (Ed.), *Strategic directions for career services within the university setting* (New Directions for Student Services, No. 148, pp. 5–18). San Francisco, CA: Jossey-Bass. doi:10.1002/ss.20105

Dumford, A. D., & Miller, A. L. (2018). Online learning in higher education: Exploring advantages and disadvantages for engagement. *Journal of Computing in Higher Education, 30*, 452–465. doi:10.1007/s12528-018-9179-z

Hudak, K., Kile, A., Grodziak, E., & Keptner, E. (2019). Advancing student interview skills: Incorporating virtual interview technology into the basic communication course. *International Journal for the Scholarship of Teaching and Learning, 13*(1), Article 3. doi:10.20429/ijsotl.2019.130103

Hutchings, P. (2010). *Opening doors to faculty involvement in assessment.* Retrieved from National Institute for Learning Outcomes Assessment website: https://www.learningoutcomeassessment.org/documents/PatHutchings_000.pdf

Lederman, D. (2018). Online education ascends. *Inside Higher Ed.* Retrieved from https://www.insidehighered.com/digital-learning/article/2018/11/07/new-data-online-enrollments-grow-and-share-overall-enrollment

National Association of Colleges and Employers. (2019, February 19). *Are college graduates "career ready"?* Retrieved from https://www.naceweb.org/career-readiness/competencies/are-college-graduates-career-ready

National Center for Education Statistics. (n.d.). Fast facts: Distance learning. Retrieved from https://nces.ed.gov/fastfacts/display.asp?id=80

National Center for Education Statistics. (2019). *The condition of education: College student employment.* Retrieved from https://nces.ed.gov/programs/coe/indicator_ssa.asp

Perry, E. H., & Pilati, M. L. (2011). Online learning. In W. Buskist & J. E. Groccia (Eds.), *Evidence-based teaching* (New Directions for Teaching and Learning, No. 128, pp. 95–104). San Francisco, CA: Jossey-Bass. doi:10.1002/tl.472

University of Illinois Springfield, Center for Online Learning, Research and Service. (2019). *The Career Development Center offers services to online students and alumni.* Retrieved from https://www.uis.edu/colrs/students/newsletter/career-development-center

Venable, M. A. (2010). Using technology to deliver career development services: Supporting today's students in higher education. *Career Development Quarterly, 59,* 87–96. doi:10.1002/j.2161-0045.2010.tb00132.x

CHAPTER 10

A Comparison of Online and On-Campus Orientation:
Understanding the Differences to Improve Student Services for Online Learners

Andrew S. Herridge, Jon McNaughtan, and Lisa J. James

THE RISE OF ONLINE learning has been coupled with an increase in online student support services, such as advising, technical support, student organizations, and orientation (Cho, 2012). This chapter serves as a resource for practitioners who oversee online orientation programs. It provides new insight for future research in this area by comparing the experiences of students who use online orientation to those students who participate in traditional on-campus orientation. A structural equation model that highlights the relationships between engagement, belonging, and knowledge of institutional resources is presented with the goal of informing student affairs practitioners of the differences that may exist for students who participate in online orientation versus those who engage in traditional face-to-face orientation. The analysis presented in this chapter gives insight into how online learners' knowledge of services offered at their institution is associated with desirable outcomes, such as in-class engagement and sense of belonging.

This chapter is organized in three parts. First, a review of the current literature on the role of online orientation and its relationship to student success, sense of belonging, and collegiate engagement generally is provided as context. Second, data from the Survey of Entering Student Engagement (SENSE), which is conducted at U.S. community colleges, are used to conduct a descriptive analysis of perceptions and knowledge of student support services for online orientation students compared to traditional on-campus orientation students. In addition, this descriptive analysis highlights the resources focused on in this chapter. Finally, SENSE data and structural equation modeling (SEM) are presented to highlight how knowledge of advising and student support services are associated with in-class engagement and student sense of belonging when comparing online orientation and traditional on-campus orientation students. Understanding these differences can help student affairs professionals prepare effective virtual orientation programs for online learners and increase awareness of potential challenges for online orientation students with engaging campus resources in comparison to those faced by traditional face-to-face students.

Online Learner Satisfaction and the Need for Virtual Orientation Programs

Current empirical work on student satisfaction with online education courses delivers mixed results (Salimi & Kornelus, 2018). Similar challenges may exist in online orientation: A recent survey of undergraduates found 63% of respondents reported they did not take advantage of the distance orientation sessions provided (Caliskan, Suzek, & Ozcan, 2017). With 6.6 million students taking at least one online course in fall 2017 (around 33% of all higher education enrollments), many students are left in need of support (National Center for Education Statistics, 2017). For decades, online education has served as an academic option for students; however, more information is needed to effectively and efficiently develop online programs to meet students' needs, both academically and emotionally.

Students' experiences in online environments are often not positive, which may lead to lack of participation (Eom, Wen, & Ashill, 2006; Roddy et al., 2017; Salimi & Kornelus, 2018). Roddy et al. (2017) and Veletsianos (2016) reported dropout rates in online courses are at an all-time high, which threatens student retention and consequently affects higher education revenue and students' ability to secure high paying positions in the workforce. In response to this dilemma, Arhin and Wang'eri (2018) and Bailey and Brown (2016) recommended developing and designing more effective online orientation courses to aid students in the transition from secondary to postsecondary-level course work. Research identifies four overarching issues for students in online learning environments: (a) feelings of isolation, (b) problems with technology, (c) time management, and (d) how instructors will address students' diverse learning styles (Arhin & Wang'eri, 2018; Roddy et al., 2017; Veletsianos, 2016).

The work of Braxton and McClendon (2002) supported findings from Pascarella, Terenzini, and Wolfle (1986) who argued students benefit from orientation sessions, and participation in orientation programs promote "social integration and a positive direct effect on persistence" (Braxton & McClendon, 2002, p. 65). As recently as 2017, Caliskan et al.'s survey of undergraduate students revealed 63.3% of survey respondents reported they did not take advantage of orientation sessions. This lack of understanding illustrates the need for student affairs units that organize orientation to be in communication with academic units to ensure online course technology and expectations are clearly articulated early on in a student's academic career. In addition to orientation, at some institutions, student affairs divisions and academic units should see this as an opportunity to support students in their online courses.

Online learning environments and orientation programs vary in design to meet the needs of students' different learning styles. However, online orientation programs differ vastly and must go beyond simply presenting students with links to online student support services. Instead, orientation for online learners should be complex, including multiple mandatory modules or sections, as Jones (2013) suggested.

Interaction with other students and instructors is vital to success as students need to learn how to interact with others to be successful in online activities (Cho, 2012; Cho, Kim, & Choi, 2017; Kauffman, 2015; Yilmaz, 2017). Cho (2012) suggested systemic design and development using instructional systems design as a framework for the development process in four key phases: (a) analysis, (b) design, (c) development, and (d) evaluation (Dick & Carey, 1996; Hirumi, Savenye, & Allen, 1994; McKenney, Nieveen, & van den Akker, 2002). Results from Cho's study revealed for students to be successful in online learning environments, students must understand online learning, have basic technology skills, develop self-awareness (time management skills, awareness of time commitment necessary for online learning), and possess self-efficacy. Many of these areas are within the scope and purview of the various functional areas within student affairs. For example, student involvement units can use similar online tools to those academic units use to deliver courses. On some campuses, student clubs use the campus learning management system (LMS) to post club documents, announce events, and maintain their calendar. Other student affairs units, such as career services and academic support, also have the opportunity to help students develop these skills. In addition, online orientation developers may consider factors such as learning contexts, time, resources, and client needs (Gaytan, 2015; Richey & Klein, 2005).

Technology and Innovative Tools

Enhancing online orientation

YouTube videos can be used to customize online student orientation tutorials and are economical, relatively easy to produce, and can be accessed at the learner's convenience. Student affairs professionals can use YouTube to archive and share tutorials.

Webpages dedicated to online orientation can help centralize resources for online learners. Here are examples from two different institutions:

* Andrews University
  https://www.andrews.edu/distance/students/orient-success

* Marquette University
  https://www.marquette.edu/online-programs/online-student-orientation.php

Mobile apps allow learners to quickly access data, course materials, and participate in dialogue with peers. College students report preference accessing courses on their mobile devices (Magda & Aslanian, 2018). Student affairs professionals can use mobile apps to better reach and engage with students.

Artificial intelligence (AI) is often missing global voices and cultural data. If AI-powered bots learn from people, then people influencing bots should include more diverse perspectives by leveraging a network of international researchers, storytellers, and locals to train voice-enabled bots to better respond to cultural inquiries and share stories that are more authentic to cultural traditions (Avedisian & Matsumoto, 2018). Student affairs professionals can use AI to better respond to inquiries from students.

Method of Inquiry

This investigation was guided by the following overarching questions. First, is there a difference in knowledge of student services between students who participate in an online orientation and students who engage in traditional face-to-face orientation? Is there a relationship between knowledge of student services and students' engagement or sense of belonging at their institution? These questions were analyzed through the use of a t test difference of the means and employing an SEM focused on the components of four main constructs (see Figure 10.1) the analysis presented illustrates key differences in the experiences of students using online orientation programs compared to students in traditional face-to-face orientation programs. The results of this analysis will help student affairs practitioners to understand the experiences of students who engage in online and face-to-face orientations. This information can then be used to develop and adjust current orientation programming. For example, if online learners have significantly lower understanding of academic advising understanding, online orientations could focus more on relationships and connections with advisors.

Developing a Conceptual Model

To develop our conceptual model we created four main constructs through the use of student responses to the Survey of Entering Student Engagement (SENSE), which will be discussed later. First a latent construct for knowledge of institutional support services was created, which includes student organizations, career counseling, tutoring services, and others. This construct was designed to measure how aware these students were of these services. Similarly, the second construct included was students' awareness of academic advising support, which includes the student's awareness that advisors are there to help with major selection, academic goals, and course taking. The third construct was students' in-class engagement, which accounts for student's contributions to class, class collaboration, and faculty interaction. The final construct was centered on students' sense of belonging, including students' perception of feeling welcome, getting to know other students, and other students getting to know them.

Figure 10.1. Hypothesized Conceptual SEM Model

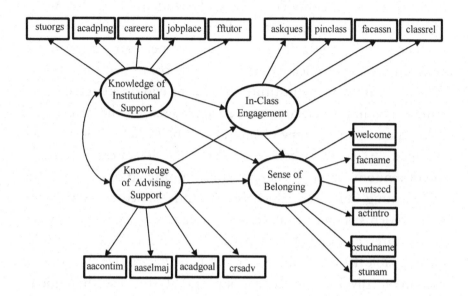

Use of the Survey of Entering Student Engagement

The data used for analysis in this chapter come from the Survey of Entering Student Engagement (SENSE), which is administered by the Center for Community College Student Engagement. The SENSE is a research-based tool used to measure institutional practices and student behaviors at community colleges (Center for Community College Student Engagement, 2018) and is administered during the fall term with participants randomly selected from participating institutions. Of the more than 30 items on the SENSE instrument, participants are asked about their first impressions, the admissions and registration process, assessment, orientation, financial aid, level of engagement with courses and peers, and their relationships with faculty and advisors (Center for Community College Student Engagement, 2018). The total number of respondents was 17,124 with $n = 13,852$ for on-campus orientation and $n = 3,272$ for online orientation.

The SENSE is ideal for this exploratory analysis for two reasons. First, the survey is conducted during the students' first three weeks of enrollment, so we are better able to associate their knowledge of student services, engagement, and sense of belonging to their orientation experience. Second, the survey is comprised of responses from students at many institutions, thus providing a large national sample. It is important to note the sample used for this analysis is a 25% random sample drawn from the complete 2014 cohort, which included 261 different colleges in 36 of the 50 states. Despite the use of random sampling, surveys are administered in classrooms at participating campuses, which is inherently biased to sample full-time students; however, a sampling weight was applied to ensure broad representation (M. Bohlig, personal communication, April 10, 2015). Table 10.1 includes a series of basic descriptive statistics for the sample, divided into three groups: (a) all students, (b) students who participated in online orientation, and (c) students who participated in traditional face-to-face orientation.

Latent constructs and the specific components separated into two groups of students (those who participated in online orientations and face-to-face orientations) can be found in Table 10.2. Each of the components of the individual latent constructs are from participant responses to specific question items contained within the SENSE data (see Table 10.2).

Table 10.1. Select Descriptive Statistics for All Students, Domestic Students, and International Students

		All Students to Attend Orientation	On-Campus Orientation	Online Orientation
Sex	Male	0.421	0.421	0.421
	Female	0.547	0.547	0.546
	missing	0.031	0.032	0.032
Race	American Indian	0.019	0.020	0.016
	Asian/Pacific Islander	0.031	0.028	0.039
	Native Hawaiian	0.001	0.001	0.001
	Black	0.153	0.152	0.161
	White	0.513	0.511	0.521
	Hispanic	0.213	0.218	0.189
	Other	0.041	0.040	0.042
	missing	0.029	0.029	0.031
Age	< 20	0.727	0.745	0.654
	20-29	0.176	0.165	0.229
	30-39	0.043	0.041	0.055
	40-50	0.022	0.021	0.029
	> 50	0.012	0.011	0.014
	missing	0.018	0.018	0.019
High Intent	Certificate	0.022	0.022	0.022
	Associates	0.177	0.175	0.185
	Transfer	0.768	0.771	0.758
	missing	0.033	0.032	0.035
Avg. HS GPA	4.0	0.066	0.066	0.069
	3.5	0.309	0.310	0.306
	3.0	0.232	0.231	0.238
	2.5	0.254	0.256	0.248
	2.0	0.083	0.083	0.080
	< 2.0	0.031	0.030	0.031
	missing	0.024	0.023	0.028
		N = 17,124	*n* = 13,852	*n* = 3,272

Table 10.2. Variable List, Descriptive Data for Latent Constructs, and T-Test Results

Latent Variable/Observed Variables (Indicator)	Possible Responses	On-Campus Orientation (*n* = 13,852)		Online Orientation (*n* = 3,272)		
Knowledge of Institutional Support (α = .64)	1 = Yes 2 = No	%		%		
Did you know about the academic advising/ planning services? (acadplng)		81%		80%		
Did you know about the career counseling services? (careerc)		55%		53%		
Did you know about the student organizations on campus? (stuorgs)		67%		58%		**
Did you know about the job placement services? (jobplace)		38%		35%		*
Did you know about the tutoring services? (fftutor)		81%		78%		**
Academic Advising Support (α = .83)	1 = Strongly Disagree 2 = Disagree 3 = Neutral 4 = Agree 5 = Strongly Agree	M	SD	M	SD	
I was able to meet with an academic advisor at times convenient for me (aacontim)		3.81	0.98	3.79	0.99	
An advisor helped me to select a course of study, program, or major (aaselmaj)		3.73	1.15	3.68	1.18	*
An advisor helped me to set academic goals and to create a plan for achieving them (acadgoal)		3.33	1.16	3.33	1.18	
An advisor helped me to identify the courses I needed to take during my first semester/ quarter (crsadv)		3.97	1.03	3.92	1.07	*
In Class Engagement (α = .61)	1 = Never 2 = Once 3 = Two or Three Times 4 = Four or More Times	M	SD	M	SD	
Ask questions in class or contribute to class discussions (askques)		2.85	0.86	2.87	0.86	
Work with other students on a project or assignment during class (pinclass)		2.55	0.96	2.50	0.98	*
Discuss an assignment or grade with as instructor (facassn)		2.08	0.93	2.13	0.93	**
Ask for help from an instructor regarding questions or problems (classrel)		2.36	0.96	2.40	0.96	*
Sense of Belonging (α = .73)	1 = Strongly Disagree 2 = Disagree 3 = Neutral 4 = Agree 5 = Strongly Agree	M	SD	M	SD	
The very first time I came to this college I felt welcome (welcome)		4.08	0.78	4.06	0.81	**
The instructors at this college want me to succeed (wntsccd)		4.31	0.68	4.28	0.69	*
All instructors had activities to introduce students to one another (actintro)		3.36	1.18	3.25	1.20	**
At least one instructor learned my name (facname)		4.32	0.83	4.28	0.88	*
At least one other student whom I didn't know learned my name (ostunam)		4.24	0.90	4.17	0.95	**
I learned the name of at least one other student in most of my classes (stunam)		4.32	0.83	4.26	0.89	**

Note. Statistically significant results from the *t*-test analyses are signified by * $p < 0.05$, ** $p < 0.01$

Onboarding Online Learners

Figure 10.2 maps how knowledge of academic support and student support services are associated with out-of-class engagement and student enrollment satisfaction. The data suggest the relationship between knowledge of institutional support and in-class engagement is stronger for students who attend online orientation than for students who participate in face-to-face orientation. Similarly, online orientation students show a stronger relationship between knowledge of institutional support and sense of belonging. While the coefficients for online and face-to-face orientation students are similar, these differences highlight online orientation students may require a stronger sense of institutional support to engage and develop a sense of belonging on their campus. This is an area where student affairs can develop and promote virtual resources for online learners to engage with the campus environment. Maintaining online environments where online learners have the ability to participate in student organizations or interact with other online learners would promote student engagement and higher levels of sense of belonging.

The Difference in Knowledge of Student Services from Online Orientation

Both online and traditional face-to-face students reported higher levels of engagement with student services when they were made aware of the services available to them (see Table 10.2). However, students who engaged in traditional face-to-face orientations reported higher levels of knowledge of the support services available to them at their institution. The difference was statistically significant for knowledge of job placement support and tutoring services.

Figure 10.2. Standardized Coefficients and Final SEM Model for Students Who Participated In an On-Campus or Online Orientation

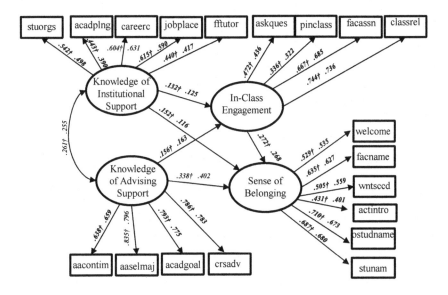

Note. All values reported are significant at the *p* > .01 level. †Online Orientation Students; *NS = Not significant*

Increased student engagement. Having awareness of student services increased the levels of engagement by students for both traditional face-to-face students and online learners. Given the finding traditional face-to-face students reported higher levels of awareness of job placement services and tutoring services, student affairs practitioners would benefit from reviewing the orientation process and presentations for these resources and develop an online component to better market these particular services. However, it is important to consider the ability of an online learner to engage with support services that do not have an online component. For example, if student organizations are solely on campus and do not have an online component, online learners would be prevented from engaging with the service and would not benefit from a presentation on student organizations during orientation. When assessing support services, student affairs practitioners must determine if all services are offered in a manner that allows for online learners to engage with them. For example, tutoring services may be offered through online video messaging services that allow tutors to communicate and share their screen and resources in real time. By using technology, support services can improve resources to online learners and gear their orientation presentations to highlight and market these resources appropriately during online orientation sessions.

Academic advising familiarity. When comparing online and traditional face-to-face orientation students, the traditional orientation students reported higher levels of knowledge of academic advising. The differences between online and traditional face-to-face orientation students were significant for two aspects of academic advising: (a) having an advisor help students select a program or major, and (b) using an advisor to help identify the courses students needed to take during their first semester.

When considering the differences in levels of knowledge or awareness of different support services, student affairs professionals should consider the availability of each support service in an online format. There was a significant difference between face-to-face students and online learners in knowledge about academic advisors' role in selecting a major. An emphasis should be made to highlight the multiple roles of advisors that are inclusive to online learners.

Additionally, when considering the higher level of awareness by students who attended face-to-face orientation, the structure of the online orientation could factor into how much time a student spends focused on and retaining the information presented to them. Student affairs practitioners should consider the format and structure used for online orientation sessions. Differences in audience and needs must be taken into account when developing online orientation sessions. Online orientations should avoid simply replicating face-to-face orientation sessions, but rather be intentionally developed for the students who are more likely to use the online format. Online orientation sessions should use technology so students can interact with the content by navigating online to learn more about particular services or take short quizzes to test their knowledge of important information about essential resources.

While mandatory orientation for online learners is suggested in the literature, it is unknown what the best approach is or what components should be included (Salimi & Kornelus, 2018). Given the association between knowledge of institutional support and out-of-class engagement, there is significant evidence online orientations need to be strengthened to focus on institutional support mechanisms. The development of online orientation should follow a similar development process to an online course. Song, Singleton, Hill, and Koh (2004) explained to be effective and to promote student success, goals and objectives should be outlined, and all components should be appropriate for the technology being used.

Relationship Between Knowledge of Student Services and Sense of Belonging

Students who attended online orientation reported higher levels of sense of belonging when they had a higher level of knowledge of institutional support available to them. Additionally, students who were engaged in-class reported higher levels of sense of belonging regardless of orientation format. This important finding aligns with Brown's (2001) findings that suggest students are more likely to engage when they are familiar with what is available.

Similar to the finding that students who are aware of available support services are more likely to be engaged, students who are aware of available support services and who are engaged are more likely to report a higher perceived sense of belonging. In an effort to increase students' sense of belonging, it is important for student affairs practitioners to ensure students are engaged with the campus community. Online learners have a unique opportunity to connect with their classmates and faculty through online video communication to create a personal connection. The inclusion of these technological resources during online orientation sessions will inform online learners of resources available to them and opportunities to engage with their faculty and classmates in a digital environment to establish a sense of community.

 Tips for Getting Started

• **Take a holistic approach.** When developing online orientation sessions, student affairs practitioners must be intentional and student centered. However, topics presented must be relevant and clear. Institutional services and programs that use online technology and resources should be highlighted and discussed throughout the session. Additionally, institutional components that are not relevant to online learners should be excluded as this information can lead to decreased engagement.

• **Set and measure goals.** To improve retention of information, student affairs practitioners need to establish clear and measurable goals and outcomes. Without a clear map of what students need to obtain, online orientation sessions cannot be effective. Following the completion of orientation sessions, assessment of student learning and retention of the information should be conducted.

• **Create an environment conducive to students' needs.** It is important to consider both the environment and needs of students who will be completing online orientation sessions. Student affairs practitioners must ensure materials are relevant and accessible. Effective online orientation sessions should complement various learning styles. Rather than using the same approach as traditional face-to-face orientations, incorporate various forms of technology, such as videos, links, or interactive assessments to engage students.

Considering levels of in-class engagement, traditional face-to-face students who attended on-campus orientation reported lower levels of engagement than students who attended online orientation. Similarly, traditional face-to-face students who attended on-campus orientation reported lower levels of belonging than students who attended online orientation. This finding supports the literature (Brown, 2001; Cho et al., 2017; Kauffman, 2015; Yilmaz, 2017) that suggests students who are more engaged are more likely to report higher levels of sense of belonging. Additionally, when it comes to student engagement, it is students' responsibility to use available resources and be successful (Eom et al., 2006). Students who attended online orientation engaged out of class at higher levels than students who attended face-to-face orientation. Bandura (1977, 1997), Eom et al. (2006), and Yukselturk and Bulut (2007) would suggest students who report higher levels of engagement are more likely to have strong self-efficacy, self-regulatory skills, and self-confidence. Student affairs practitioners would benefit from promoting available technology and encouraging faculty and students to use these technologies to promote student engagement.

Potential Challenges and Practical Solutions

The goals and objectives of orientation programming are articulated differently by institutions of higher education. Many institutions struggle to innovate their online orientation programming and may seek to recreate face-to-face programming when a new approach may be needed. To overcome this, the following potential challenges and practical solutions are offered:

Potential Challenge: Developing online orientation sessions that meet the needs and interests of online learners.

> **Practical Solution:** Student affairs professionals need to better understand the motivation and interests of students who are seeking online orientation. These may or may not align with the reason students engage in online course taking. When clarifying these motivations, the structure of the online programming should be adjusted to best support students.

Potential Challenge: Ensuring online orientation sessions meet institutional needs and goals.

> **Practical Solution:** Objectives of online orientation programming need to be articulated. These objectives may be the same as those for traditional face-to-face on-campus orientation; but, without first clarifying the intent of the programming, it will be difficult to identify the mechanisms for program development. After objectives are identified, aligning specific program components to the objectives is critical to success.

Potential Challenge: Ensuring online orientation sessions are meeting established objectives while also remaining relevant to the population of students and format being used.

> **Practical Solution:** Using clearly defined objectives, and after connecting specific program components to the stated objectives, it is critical to discuss and evaluate how these components might be received by different student populations.

Potential Challenge: Developing online orientation sessions that present information in an engaging and relevant manner.

> **Practical Solution:** Student affairs professionals should ensure best practices for online learning are used in the creation of content. For example, short video clips should be used as opposed to the traditional longer lecture format that can be effective in traditional face-to-face settings.

Implications for Student Services
Supporting Online Learners

With the rise of online learning and the increase in online learner support services (Cho, 2012; Seaman, Allen, & Seaman, 2018), it is important to understand the experiences of online learners using these services compared to students on campus. Researchers investigating students' satisfaction with courses delivered at a distance discovered many students do not understand how to access or use online resources to their advantage (Caliskan et al., 2017). In an attempt to support students in learning through online courses, there has been an upsurge in online orientation programs incorporated into online learning environments. As student affairs professionals, it is important to understand the knowledge level and experiences of the incoming class of students with regard to the online educational environment to appropriately develop an online orientation most beneficial to students' different learning styles and knowledge levels. This study serves as a resource for student affairs professionals charged with creating virtual orientation experiences for online learners. Additionally, it provides insight into the experiences and needs of community college students using online support services, such as online learner orientation.

Three main implications arise from this study. First, when determining what components to include in online orientation, institutions must be intentional and understand their online learner population. The study at hand highlights for students completing online orientation, having a strong sense of institutional support is more critical than it may be for traditional face-to-face orientation students. This may be due to online learners who complete orientation virtually not having a chance to physically engage with advisors, faculty, and students. As institutions develop online orientations, strengthening students' sense of support will be crucial to enhancing engagement and sense of belonging.

Second, this study highlights in all cases, enhancing levels of institutional support—advising or institutional—is associated with positive results in out-of-class engagement and sense of belonging for students who complete online or traditional face-to-face orientation. This study also provides evidence for the continued use of orientation and the development of additional ways to enhance student knowledge of institutional and advising support.

Finally, this study provides student affairs practitioners with one way to evaluate and compare institutional orientation programming. As the availability of data increases, and as the number of online programs grows, institutions should seek to understand what is associated with desired constructs such as perception of institutional support and sense of belonging. Increased research and scrutiny of orientation could help to increase the impact of these important programs.

Conclusion

To ensure students' satisfaction in the online environment and to introduce students to an institution's support services, orientations should be offered to all online learners. Additionally, Roddy et al. (2017) and Veletsianos (2016) explained orientations should be mandatory for all students who enroll in an online format. This could provide a more holistic approach and positive experience for online learners (Bailey & Brown, 2016). One key finding from this study was the difference in the level of knowledge of available student services by students who participated in online orientation versus those who participated in traditional face-to-face orientations. However, both groups of students reported higher levels of engagement with student services when they were made aware of what services were available to them at their institution.

Orientation sessions can be designed to help students address concerns about technology issues, course goals and objectives, effectively and efficiently communicating with course instructors, and interacting collaboratively with peers in online groups (Bailey & Brown,

2016), but, through orientation sessions, students should also learn where to go for counseling and wellness, career development, and diversity and inclusion programming. Students in online learning environments experience four overarching issues: (a) feelings of isolation, (b) problems with technology, (c) time management, and (d) how instructors will address students' diverse learning styles (Roddy et al., 2017; Veletsianos, 2016). Connecting students to services beyond their coursework can help ameliorate some of this.

There was a correlation between students' knowledge of student services and students' level of engagement and their sense of belonging at their institution. Students who were engaged out of class reported higher levels of sense of belonging. Bailey and Brown (2016) supported offering orientation and claimed it "could provide a more holistic approach and positive experience for online learners" (p. 454). Student affairs practitioners must be cognizant of the population and format they use and deliver online orientation sessions relevant to online learners, use technology to promote engagement and interaction, and be purposeful and student centered.

? Questions for Reflection

- How are practitioners at your institution evaluating orientation programs (online and face to face) to ensure the best student outcomes?
- What are the orientation programming objectives, and how can those objectives be met in different ways online and face to face?
- What are some forms of technology your institution can incorporate into online orientation programs to enhance student engagement?
- Using the forms of technology you identified in response to the previous question, how can students develop stronger connections with students, faculty, and staff through online orientation?
- How can practitioners at your institution promote student engagement and knowledge of services in their online orientation programs while remaining pertinent to online learners yet equitable to traditional face-to-face orientation programs?

References

Arhin, V., & Wang'eri, T. (2018). Orientation programs and student retention in distance learning: The case of University of Cape Coast. *Journal of Educators Online.* doi:10.9743/JEO2018.15.1.6

Avedisian, A., & Matsumoto, E. (2018). 3 emerging technologies that will reshape education in 2019. *EdSurge News.* Retrieved from https://www.edsurge.com/news/2018-12-29-3-emerging-technologies-that-will-reshape-education-in-2019

Bailey, T. L., & Brown, A. (2016). Online student services: Current practices and recommendations for implementation. *Journal of Educational Technology, 44,* 450–462. doi:10.1177/0047239515616956

Bandura, A. (1977). Self-efficacy: Toward a unified theory of behavioral change. *Psychological Review, 84,* 191–215. doi:10.1037/0033-295X.84.2.191

Bandura, A. (1997). *Self-efficacy: The exercise of control.* New York, NY: W. H. Freeman and Company.

Braxton, J. M., & McClendon, S. A., (2002). The fostering of social integration and retention through institutional practice. *Journal of College Student Retention, 3,* 57–71. doi:10.2190/RGXJ-U08C-06VB-JK7D

Brown, R. (2001). The process of community-building in distance learning classes. *Journal of Asynchronous Learning Networks, 5,* 18–34. doi:10.24059/olj.v5i2.1876

Caliskan, S., Suzek, S., & Ozcan, D. (2017). Determining student satisfaction in distance education courses. *Procedia Computer Science, 120,* 529–538. doi:10.1016/j.procs.2017.11.275

Center for Community College Student Engagement. (2018). About the survey of entering student engagement (SENSE). Retrieved from https://www.ccsse.org/sense/aboutsense/index.cfm

Cho, M., (2012). Online student orientation in higher education: A development study. *Education Tech Research Development, 60,* 1051–1069. doi:10.1007/s11423-012-9271-4

Cho, M., Kim, Y., & Choi, D. (2017). The effect of self-regulated learning on college students' perceptions of community of inquiry and affective outcomes in online learning. *The Internet and Higher Education, 34,* 10–17. doi:10.1016/j.iheduc.2017.04.001

Dick, W., & Carey, L. (1996). *The systematic design of instruction* (4th ed.). New York, NY: Harper Collins.

Eom, S. B., Wen, H. J., & Ashill, N. (2006). The determinants of students' perceived learning outcomes and satisfaction in university online education: An empirical investigation. *Decision Sciences Journal of Innovative Education, 4,* 215–235. doi:10.1111/j.1540-4609.2006.00114.x

Gaytan, J., (2015). Comparing faculty and student perceptions regarding factors that affect student retention in online education. *American Journal of Distance Education, 29,* 56–66. doi:10.1080/08923647.2015.994365

Hirumi, A., Savenye, W., & Allen, B. (1994). Designing interactive videodisc-based museum exhibits: A case study. *Educational Technology Research and Development, 42,* 47–55. doi:10.1007/BF02298170

Jones, K. R. (2013). Developing and implementing a mandatory online student orientation. *Journal of Asynchronous Learning Networks, 17,* 43–45. doi:10.24059/olj.v17i1.312

Kauffman, H. (2015). A review of predictive factors of student success in and satisfaction with online learning. *Research in Learning Technology, 23.* doi:10.3402/rlt.v23.26507

Magda, A. J., & Aslanian, C. B. (2018). *Online college students 2018: Comprehensive data on demands and preferences.* Louisville, KY: The Learning House, Inc.

McKenney, S., Nieveen, N., & van den Akker, J. (2002). Computer support for curriculum developers: CASCADE. *Educational Technology Research and Development, 50,* 25–35. doi:10.1007/BF02504982

National Center for Education Statistics. (2017). *Enrollment and employees in postsecondary institutions, fall 2017; and financial statistics and academic libraries, fiscal year 2017: First look (provisional data).* Retrieved from https://nces.ed.gov/pubsearch/pubsinfo.asp?pubid=2019021REV

Pascarella, E. T., Terenzini, P. T., & Wolfle, L. M. (1986). Orientation in college and freshman year persistence/withdrawal decisions. *Journal of Higher Education, 57*, 155–175. doi:10.2307/1981479

Richey, R. C., & Klein, J. D. (2005). Developmental research methods: Creating knowledge from instructional design and development practice. *Journal of Computing in Higher Education, 16*, 23–38. doi:10.1007/BF02961473

Roddy, C., Amiet, D. L., Chung, J., Holt, C., Shaw, L., McKenzie, S., Garivaldis, F., Lodge, J. M., & Mundy, M. E. (2017). Applying best practice online learning, teaching, and support to intensive online environments: An integrative review. *Frontiers in Education, 2*, Article 59. doi:10.3389/feduc.2017.00059

Salimi, A. Y., & Kornelus, A. (2018). An investigation of student satisfaction with distance education courses based on student characteristics. *Journal of Business and Educational Leadership, 7*, 146–155. Retrieved from http://asbbs.org/files/2018/JBEL7.1.pdf

Seaman, J. E., Allen, I. E., & Seaman, J. (2018). *Grade increase: Tracking distance education in the United States*. Retrieved from Online Learning Consortium website: https://onlinelearningconsortium.org/read/grade-increase-tracking-distance-education-united-states

Song, L., Singleton, E. S., Hill, J. R., & Koh, M. H. (2004). Improving online learning: Student perceptions of useful and challenging characteristics. *The Internet and Higher Education, 7*, 59–70. doi:10.1016/j.iheduc.2003.11.003

Veletsianos, G. (2016). Defining characteristics of emerging technologies and emerging practices. In G. Veletsianos (Ed.), *Emergence and innovation in digital learning: foundations and applications* (pp. 3–16). doi:10.15215/aupress/9781771991490.01

Yilmaz, R. (2017). Exploring the role of e-learning readiness on student satisfaction and motivation in flipped classroom. *Computers in Human Behavior, 70*, 251–260. doi:10.1016/j.chb.2016.12.085

Yukselturk, E., & Bulut, S. (2007). Predictors for student success in an online course. *International Forum of Educational Technology & Society, 10*, 71–83. Retrieved from https://www.learntechlib.org/p/75304

CHAPTER 11

Supporting Online Learners Through Flipped Advising Practices

Kristin Sowden

AS A YOUNG graduate student, I had grandiose visions of a future in academic advising. I imagined welcoming students into my cozy office, ushering them over to comfortable seating, and leisurely asking them questions about their college experience—carefully probing to ensure they were developing holistically through curricular and cocurricular involvement on campus (He & Hutson, 2016). Flash forward: I am now six years into what I would consider a highly fulfilling career in professional academic advising at a traditional brick-and-mortar institution—but "leisurely" is not an adjective I would use to describe any part of my day.

Alternatively, while I do have the true pleasure of problem solving and planning alongside my students, it is rare I connect with them exclusively in person as I originally imagined. Most of my advisees seek advice through a variety of technologically enabled tools; in fact, many of my students prefer to interact only via e-mail, video call, or other web-based platforms. This chapter presents flipped advising as a way to support online learners. Aspects of flipped advising practices are considered along with aspects of institutional structures that may be required to implement them. Finally, technological tools that can assist with carrying out flipped advising, as well as other strategies, resources, and ideas, are included.

Doing More With Less

Academic advisors who find themselves supporting students enrolled in exclusively online learning programs are in a unique situation. At the forefront of their practice, advisors in e-learning environments are tasked with building student confidence and competence—in many cases, without ever actually meeting the advisee in person. Thus, advising needs manifest differently for online learners than they do for face-to-face learners, and two issues at the forefront of virtual advising are meeting the needs of older students, students working full time, and/or students with families; and student reten-tion—factors advisors of online learners must carefully balance all while supporting students from afar.

Students enrolled in distance education have different kinds of educational needs than traditional 18- to 22-year-old students. Among these needs are educational options related to modality, institutional flexibility in curricular and cocurricular support ser-vices, academic and motivational advising support for life and career goals, and acknowledgement and integration of previous learning and work experience (Council for Adult and Experiential Learning, 2000). Online learners may also find themselves in unique personal life situations where they are engaging with degree programs primarily for career-related outcomes, all while juggling other major roles and responsibilities (Iloh, 2017; Moore & Kearsley, 2011), such as working full time, caring for both younger and elderly family members, or earning college credit while on active deployment (Chen, 2017; Soares, 2013).

These personal and professional complexities can affect an online learner's ability to persist through their education. Markle (2015) highlighted the inner conflicts post-traditional students face as a result of holding a variety of personal and professional responsibilities, adding to the complexity of issues advisors face when working with this population of learners. This function is as important with online learners as it is with on-campus students. Researchers have shown low retention rates in online programs are an issue (Chiyaka, Sithole, Manyanga, McCarthy, & Bucklein, 2016), and lack of proficient student support can influence a student's decision to leave a degree program (Dahl, 2004; Tinto, 1987). Comprehensive, holistic advising may be the solution in online learning contexts to combat competing conflicts online learners may face in their educational journey. Just as university instructional faculty have responded to the technological revolution with new ways to support online learners, student support functions such as advising must follow.

The Importance of Advising for Online Learners

In its own right, advising is a form of teaching (Appleby, 2008; Crookston, 1972). Tinto (1993) suggested quality academic advising is essential to effective student success initiatives and reflects a college's commitment to its students. From helping students to persist through graduation requirements and connecting students with faculty members who share their scholarly interests to getting involved in meaningful cocurricular engagement, advisors act as a guide for students during their college experience, cheering them on to achieve their highest potential.

Why Not Flip It?

One effective way to engage online learners in academic advising is by "flipping" the advising practice. The University of Florida Center for Instructional Technology and Training (2018) defined *flipped advising* as "a pedagogical approach that emphasizes creating meaningful discussions and relationships during the advising session, while housing advising-related tasks in a learning management system. Research on effective advising emphasizes establishing advising as a teaching practice" (para. 1).

The Benefits of Flipped Advising

Steele (2016) highlighted several advantages to flipped advising. First, students and advisors can work to customize academic planning in a way that works for the student's multiple roles in life. Second, the use of an online learning platform for advising allows meetings to be conducted during flexible hours and in locations preferable to both the student and the advisor. Third, any analytics collected by the learning platform on student use can potentially be used for program evaluation and assessment. Resources provided in an online space can be easily curated by the advisor and searched by the student. Finally, online advising can be more cost effective than other forms of advising.

Flipped advising perpetuates the philosophy of advising as teaching given advisors increasingly support their advisees by giving them additional levels of autonomy over their academic and career choices and by assisting them in developing self-authorship. Baxter Magolda (2008) defined *self-authorship* as "the internal capacity to define one's beliefs, identity and social relations" (p. 269). Furthermore, Amini et al. (2018) asserted flipped advising allows advising to become a 24/7 model where mentor and mentee can work together on achieving goals.

The best skill academic advisors can teach their students is how to find answers to questions—not answer the questions for them—an act that will undoubtedly serve them throughout their entire professional career. As Larson, Johnson, Aiken-Wisniewski, and Barkemeyer (2018) asserted, academic advising as a profession is designed to "empower students and campus and community members to successfully navigate academic interactions related to higher education" (p. 86), which, thanks to the flipped advising approach, can take place in the manner and modality in which a student feels most empowered.

 Technology and Innovative Tools

Using an LMS for flipped advising

- **Teach students how to update their LMS notification preferences.** In the LMS Canvas, for example, notifications can be sent immediately as something is added to the course—daily, weekly, or not at all. Some LMSs can push notifications via e-mail and/or text and can be synced with Google Docs, Dropbox, LinkedIn, and Twitter. Work with students to determine which applications they find most beneficial.

- **Offer an app.** See if your institution's LMS has an app version. Students love the feature of viewing resources and receiving notifications on the go.

- **Explore LMS alternatives.** Not in love with your institution's LMS? Experiment with alternative options such as Google for Education. It offers many of the same features as other LMSs with the accessibility of being a Google product, and it is usually low cost or free.

Seeing the Forest for the Trees

Before getting started with flipped advising practices, consider whether this model fits the needs of your institution's online learners. Flipped advising can be highly beneficial for advisors, especially those with large caseloads and complex advising policies and procedures to follow.

Fit With Online Learners

For online learners, flipped advising may be a way to ensure comprehensive amounts of content are provided to them in an interesting way. Even though online learners should already have regular access to the Internet, ensure they are familiar with the functions of your institution's technology platforms and that technical supports are in place to assist students if/when issues arise. For example, an online learner may have trouble accessing certain websites or have a limited amount of time to dedicate to their studies, and they may become frustrated with technical issues, which may limit their access to advising content. I found my students were already using the LMS Canvas for their courses, so adding a course on academic advising to their dashboard was a simple extension of what they were already doing. Advising professionals should think about using technology familiar to students as they consider flipped advising practices.

Institutional and Departmental Support

Advisors serve many functions within the institution, and one of the most important may be in promoting retention and student success. If student success and retention is the case at your institution, consider the culture and climate of your college and whether your advising practice requires a more intrusive approach before investing time and intellectual capital into a flipped advising system. Another thing to consider is whether advisors will be willing to adopt a flipped advising philosophy. Unless the caseload of online learners is small, advisors would need to change how they advise so all online learners benefit. Having the support of faculty, academic departments, unit heads, and deans who rely on academic advisors to disperse information should also feel comfortable with this model. It is important to consider if there are any other institutional factors that may inhibit the success of a flipped advising system and ensure efforts are not duplicated in any way. For example, if the registrar's office uses a blog to communicate dates and deadlines, do they mind if resources are incorporated in this new way?

Access to Technological Assistance

New technologies can be enthralling—and also a bit terrifying, especially at the beginning. Before digging into a flipped advising model, make sure the technological capabilities exist to implement the new strategy. Confirm the technology the institution uses is capable of functioning in a manner that is most useful for online learners. Know who supports the use of technology on campus and work with them to develop a plan for supporting online learners. For example, instructional designers often work with faculty members on course design, and they may be able to work with you in a similar capacity and bring their expertise to flipped advising practices.

Determine Implementation Start

It is challenging to be an academic advisor from both a time and resource perspective. Consider when there will be time during the academic year to design a master plan of a flipped advising approach, and then build the system from there. The work required to create a flipped advising system can be frontloaded, meaning advisors can use the first part of a semester to curate materials into a common repository for students to use throughout their entire term. Flipped advising will be most difficult at the beginning—and, while there will be routine updating of resources required, the work invested likely will be very different from the day-to-day work of a traditional on-campus advisor.

Consider using two to three weeks in the summer to design and build the flipped advising tool before the new academic year begins. A plan should also be in place for when the tool will be modified throughout the year. It may make sense to block some time out for this project daily or weekly. Finally, ongoing monitoring and assessment of the project should be planned to confirm flipped advising is working for both advisors and online learners. Have a plan for how assessment data will be collected and how and to whom it will be distributed.

Tips for Getting Started

Once the big picture questions have been asked and answered by all stakeholders who have a vested interested in supporting flipped advising at your institution, put pen to paper and start actually creating your flipped advising resources.

• **Create a vision.** If you had an unlimited amount of time and resources, what would your ideal flipped advising practice look like? Who would be a part of it? How many and what types of resources would be available? Once you have considered this, think about scaling to something that is realistic given your situation.

• **Have conversations.** What do other advisors, either inside or outside of your institution, deem as important? How can you incorporate those things into your flipped advising model?

• **Locate technological tools.** Choose which tools will be used to build your institution's flipped advising approach. These tools can include websites, blogs, e-newsletters, or interactive e-mails, videos, and social media.

• **Look for samples.** See if there is anyone else who is also practicing flipped advising that you would be interested in learning from or modeling after.

Building a Roadmap

Developing and implementing a new system often requires building from the ground up. Committing to building a new communication pattern with online learners is more than just creating a system of resources. Flipped advising is about embracing a process through which online learners must take a level of ownership and responsibility in their academic pursuits that may be new to them. There is a good chance when pioneering this new system on campus, people will have questions. Be willing to teach others, share resources, and open the door for students, staff, and faculty to provide feedback and ideas for improvement. Once you have considered this practice, creating a roadmap for implementation of a flipped advising approach can guide the process. This roadmap includes identifying flipped advising objectives; locating technological tools; engaging a coalition of change agents; and building, reviewing, revising, and resubmitting. These components of a flipped advising roadmap are discussed in the following sections.

Identify Flipped Advising Objectives

Determine the goals of the institution's advising practices and craft an outline of core objectives. When creating online modules with content for advisees to access, advising objectives will guide the process and can be consulted as needed to assess if online learners met stated learning outcomes. Here are a few example objectives of student learning outcomes:

- As a result of completing the fall 2019 enrollment module, first-year geographic science students at James Madison University will be able to list the four basic requirements for graduation: 120 credits, Bachelor of Arts/Bachelor of Science requirements, general education requirements, and major/minor requirements.

- As a result of completing the internship module, second-year geographic science students at James Madison University will be able to recall the process of obtaining an internship within the department, including identifying and communicating with a faculty sponsor, filling out appropriate paperwork, and enrolling in GEOG 495 in MyMadison (the university's course enrollment system).

- As a result of completing the Graduation Application enrollment module, eligible graduating geographic science students at James Madison University will be able to correctly fill out their graduation applications for advisor approval.

A communication strategy should also be identified. How often will advisors reach out to online learners? Can other tools and technologies be incorporated into advising practices that may help connect advisors to online learners? How should advisees connect with advisors and in what manner? How will advisors communicate their communication strategies with online learners? Be transparent about the communication strategy so students can be guided appropriately as new information is released throughout the semester.

Locate Technological Tools

Once a roadmap has been created to guide the structure of your flipped advising practices, it is time to choose the technological tools with which to build this new approach. These tools can include websites, blogs, e-newsletters or interactive e-mails, videos, and social media. An LMS is a logical place to house flipped advising resources, as these systems are often already in place at most institutions, and typically there is technical support available from the college's information technology or teaching and learning office. More importantly, online learners should already be familiar with how to use the institution's LMS and may easily integrate advising into their academics, making it a one-stop shop for them.

Other technological tools to consider include those with screencasting capabilities, infographics and visual design templates, and virtual bulletin board features. While there are many tools that do these things, the following examples include an option for each:

- **Screencast-O-Matic:** To record videos or content to review during an advising session, consider the free tool Screencast-O-Matic. A variety of videos can be recorded, including weekly announcements to review what online learners should be thinking about during the given week, enrollment videos on how to use various technological tools, and fun videos that can be used to wish first-year students a good first week of classes or good luck on finals. This adds a personal touch to my advising so students feel they are interacting with me.

- **Canva.** Canva can be used to make posters, infographics, or other aesthetically pleasing designs. The website is quick and easy to use, and students will likely be more drawn to a colorful display of information than one made in Microsoft Word.

- **Padlet.** To display information on a virtual bulletin board, consider Padlet. One great feature of Padlet is it is interactive, so it can be used to solicit questions about an upcoming enrollment period, identify learning resources across campus for students, or collect "what I wish I would have known" messages from seniors before they graduate.

Engage a Coalition of Change Agents

Change cannot occur without change agents (Armenakis, Harris, & Mossholder, 1993). To produce successful organizational change, coalitions of willing supporters must be identified and engaged in the process. The most important change agents for executing a flipped advising approach are your institutional leaders and online learners—especially at the beginning. Schedule regular times to check in with the appropriate institutional leaders during the design and implementation process and brainstorm means of advocacy that may be required along the way. Consider putting together online learner focus groups or advisory councils (of three to four students) to solicit feedback to make the new advising practices more effective.

Build, Review, Revise, Resubmit

Similar to the cyclical nature of higher education and academic advising, advising tools and technologies will need to be routinely updated. Schedule time every week (or maybe even 15 minutes every day) to add announcements, monitor discussion boards, post updates, or view student activity. Then, during a slow time of year (perhaps summer), schedule two to three days to update, overhaul, and redesign flipped advising practices for the following year. Make the tool, routinely refine it, and eventually it will run with less maintenance.

A Word About FERPA

How advisors interact with advisees can and will change with technological trends, but a commitment to student confidentiality should not. The Family Educational Rights and Privacy Act (FERPA) requires strict adherence to protecting student information as soon as a student enrolls in an institution. Academic advisors frequently have access to private student information that must be carefully guarded for both on-campus and online learners.

As new ways to use technology to enhance advising practices are considered, a method should be developed to protect student information. If there are questions or concerns related to FERPA, reach out to your institution's registrar or legal counsel for clarification.

Potential Challenges and Practical Solutions

There will be challenges to implementing flipped advising. These bumps in the road can be categorized into cultural challenges and technological challenges.

Potential Challenge: Your institution may not be prepared to change the advising structure.

Practical Solution: Make sure you have done your due diligence in introducing this new practice to your institution, as outlined earlier in the chapter.

Potential Challenge: Technological issues may surface.

Practical Solution: Persist through technological issues by recognizing this process mirrors the persistence you are hoping to teach your students.

Potential Challenge: Getting stuck with one advising model.

Practical Solution: Remember to be agile in your practice. If you ultimately decide flipped advising does not work for you or your online learners, then modify, transform, or abandon the practice by moving to another approach you feel works better.

Troubleshooting Flipped Advising

While it can be exciting to flip advising practices to support online learners, the institutional leaders on your campus may not immediately be on board with this new model of advising. Be transparent about the reasons for changing the practice and how the change will benefit students, faculty, the department, and the institution. Be sure to share how it will likely help the institution save time and money. Find and highlight other success stories and best practices at other institutions. Help the campus leaders in your area to visualize what implementation of a flipped advising approach could look like and the impact it could have on students.

Additionally, take baby steps. Instead of starting out with a full flipped advising system, create one video to answer one question frequently asked in advising. When that single video saves a significant amount of time and energy, create another one, or build a standardized messaging database for questions on events or activities that happen every year, like graduation. Keep the faith. It may take a few semesters or even years for the system to really take hold. Stay strong and know the efforts are best for both advisors and online learners.

Learn from setbacks, because mistakes happen! Always save everything in more than one place. If the platform that hosts advising videos goes down, be sure they are saved to a cloud system, such as Google Drive, so efforts are not lost. Recognize the cyclical nature of technology use—there is always something bigger, better, or in need of modification. Also remember there may be a break-in period. The going may be tough at the beginning of the implementation—that is normal. Try to get through an entire semester before making decisions on whether or not to abandon a current advising approach. Pick and choose the most useful resources—just because a suite of technological options has worked for another advisor does not mean it will work for every advisor. Keep what works best for advisors and students!

Conclusion

Flipped advising is not about just using technology to make life easier for advisors and online learners, although that is definitely part of the charm. It is about empowering online learners to fully use their resources. Higher education is changing, and academic advising practices are changing at the same pace. Advisors who work with students in any type of modality, but especially in online learning environments, should consider leveraging technologies already in place to institute a flipped advising model that fosters transformation, independence, and critical consumption of information. Flipped advising is the 2.0 version professionals seek to provide online learners with the tools they need to be successful in their personal and professional lives.

? Questions for Reflection

Flipped advising is more than just a technological choice over content delivery; it is a philosophy of advising that must be carefully presented to stakeholders as a cultural shift in student support services. The following questions should be reviewed at individual, departmental, and institutional levels to ensure this method aligns with institutional goals and priorities.

- How does a flipped advising model fit the needs of your institution's online learners?
- In what ways does a flipped advising model fit your institution?
- What level of supervisor and/or colleague support do you have?
- Do you have access to technology and/or technological assistance?
- When is the right time in your academic year to begin flipped advising?
- What do you need to prepare for the complexity of creating culture change surrounding the current state of academic advising at your institution?

References

Amini, R., Laughlin, B. S., Smith, K. W., Siwik, V. P., Adamas-Rappaport, W. J., & Fantry, G. T. (2018). "Flipped classroom" for academic and career advising: An innovative technique for medical student advising. *Advances in Medical Education and Practice, 9*, 371–376. doi:10.2147/AMEP.S162504

Appleby, D. (2008). Advising as teaching and learning. In V. N. Gordon, W. R. Habley, & T. J. Grites (Eds.), *Academic advising: A comprehensive handbook* (2nd ed., pp. 85–102). San Francisco, CA: Jossey-Bass

Armenakis, A. A., Harris, S. G., & Mossholder, K. W. (1993). Creating readiness for organizational change. *Human Relations, 46*, 681–703. doi:10.1177/001872679304600601

Baxter Magolda, M. B. (2008). Three elements of self-authorship. *Journal of College Student Development, 49*, 269–284. doi:10.1353/csd.0.0016

Chen, J. C. (2017). Nontraditional adult learners: The neglected diversity in postsecondary education. *SAGE Open, 7*(1). doi:10.1177/2158244017697161

Chiyaka, E. T., Sithole, A., Manyanga, F., McCarthy, P., & Bucklein, B. K. (2016). Institutional characteristics and student retention: What integrated postsecondary education data reveals about online learning. *Online Journal of Distance Learning Administration, 19*(2). Retrieved from https://www.westga.edu/~distance/ojdla

Council for Adult and Experiential Learning. (2000). *Serving adult learners in higher education: Principles of effectiveness* [Executive summary]. Chicago, IL: Author.

Crookston, B. B. (1972). A developmental view of academic advising as teaching. *NACADA Journal, 29*, 78–82. doi:10.12930/0271-9517-29.1.78

Dahl, J. (2004). Strategies for 100% retention: Feedback, interaction. *Distance Education Report, 8*, 5–7.

He, Y., & Hutson, B. (2016). Appreciative assessment in academic advising. *Review of Higher Education, 39*, 213–240. doi:10.1353/rhe.2016.0003

Iloh, C. (2018). Not non-traditional, the new normal: Adult learners and the role of student affairs in supporting older college students. *Journal of Student Affairs, 27*, 25–30.

Larson, J., Johnson, A., Aiken-Wisniewski, S. A., & Barkemeyer, J. (2018). What is academic advising? An application of analytic induction. *NACADA Journal, 38*, 81–93. doi:10.12930/0271-9517-38.2.81

Markle, G. (2015). Factors influencing persistence among nontraditional university students. *Adult Education Quarterly, 35*, 267–285.

Moore, M. G., & Kearsley, G. (2011). *Distance education: A systems view of online learning*. Belmont, CA: Cengage Learning.

Soares, L. (2013). *Post-traditional learners and the transformation of postsecondary education: A manifesto for college leaders*. Washington, DC: American Council on Education.

Steele, G. (2016). Creating a flipped advising approach. *NACADA Clearinghouse of Academic Advising Resources*. Retrieved from https://www.nacada.ksu.edu/Resources/Clearinghouse/View-Articles/Creating-a-Flipped-Advising-Approach.aspx

Tinto, V. (1987). *Leaving college: Rethinking the causes and cures of student attrition*. Chicago, IL: University of Chicago Press.

Tinto, V. (1993). Building community. *Liberal Education, 79*, 16–21.

University of Florida Center for Instructional Technology and Training. (2018). *Blended learning and the flipper classroom*. Retrieved from http://citt.ufl.edu/showcase/flipped-hybrid/flipped-advising

Leveraging Ubiquitous Technologies:
Advancing the Work of Student Affairs Practitioners for Online Learners

CHAPTER 12

Bringing the Student Experience Into the Online Ecosystem

Bonnie Peters and Anita Crawley

THERE IS NO QUESTION technology has revolutionized higher education in the United States and the rest of the world (Johnson et al., 2016). For almost three decades, online education has steadily grown in both credibility and student enrollments (Allen & Seaman, 2016). In Fall 2018, a report from the U.S. Department of Education's National Center for Education Statistics revealed in 2016–2017, the number of U.S. students who took at least some of their courses online grew by more than 350,000 (McFarland et al., 2018). In California alone, community college online learner enrollment totaled 860,283 students, accounting for 28% of the total unduplicated enrolled students that year (California Community Colleges Chancellor's Office [CCCCO], 2017). Both California Community Colleges system and U.S. Department of Education data are demonstrating online education has established its place in the higher education landscape. Additionally, with the focus on completion and success, online learning has shown its effectiveness as a viable learning modality. It is now accepted as a practical and valued option for potential students who are not able to attend college because of circumstances that limit their access to face-to-face classes (Shea & Bidjerano, 2018)

The Need for Students Services for Online Learners

In spite of these advancements, the history of online education is still being written. While online class enrollments continue to grow with the emphasis being placed on integrating technology to support course management and course delivery, the lack of advancement in smart and effective integration of online student support services is still glaringly apparent (Peters, Crawley, & Brindley, 2017). In the results of the National eLearning Survey of Community Colleges, the Instructional Technology Council (2018) identified "adequate student services for distance education students" (p. 9) as one of the top three administrative challenges. In that same survey, two of the top three challenges were noted as "orientation/student readiness for taking online classes [and] providing equivalent virtual student services" (Instructional Technology Council, 2018, p. 9). These student support strategies are recommended to address these challenges: (a) analytics to identify at-risk students, (b) mandatory student orientation, and (c) hiring a retention specialist to address the needs of online learners.

With so many college students engaged in online learning, and with today's technological advancements making all things possible in the online environment, higher education is being challenged to meet the needs of online learners. Because of how students engage with technology in their social, personal, and academic lives, students, when selecting a college or university, are beginning to designate the quality of online student services as a critical factor in their decision making (Johnson et al., 2016). Students expect to be able to take advantage of comprehensive online student services. Those expectations are not only reasonable but a required ingredient for success in online education.

Additionally, students may have a preference for taking face-to-face courses but prefer their student support online because of scheduling and convenience. This then identifies a new category of students—the "hybrid student." The hybrid student is defined as a student who has the opportunity to attend in-person classes but has a preference and/or need for online support services after traditional business hours of on-campus student services. This student now shares a need with their traditional online counterparts when it comes to receiving support services in the online environment. Both categories of students have a desire and/or need to participate in remotely delivered student services.

For institutions to effectively serve today's online learners, it is necessary to use tomorrow's technologies. This chapter addresses the importance of preparing online learners for success and describe strategies for developing and delivering effective online student services. The California Virtual Campus–Online Education Initiative (CVC-OEI) is used as a case study to demonstrate how collaboration across a large system can provide cost savings and resource efficiencies when negotiating contracts with technology providers and developing online support services shared by multiple institutions.

Preparing Online Learners for Success

Subscribing to the early view that the only preparation students need to succeed in online classes is learning how to navigate a learning or course management system (LMS or CMS, used synonymously) can contribute to the discrepancy between success rates of students in online and face-to-face courses (Palloff & Pratt, 1999). Put simply, online learners require all the same services students need to take courses on campus, along with a few unique services. As with on-campus student services, a one-size-fits-all approach to delivering online student services will not meet the needs of all students (Crawley & Howe, 2016). It can be further argued the need for deliberate attention and support in the online arena is even more critical to a student's success because of the potentially isolating impact of the online learning environment. Therefore, rather than thinking exclusively about the difference in the scope of services needed by online learners, it is important to also think about different methods and appropriate technologies needed to deliver comparable online services.

Ideally, the goal is to decrease or eliminate the gap between student success and course completion in online and traditional courses. Institutions that provide interactive online student support services technologies fully integrated into every department across an institution contribute to these improved outcomes for online learners. While the delivery of online student services may not follow the organizational structure of the institution, when effectively designed with students' needs at the center of the online support experience, the result will be a higher percentage of students completing their academic goals.

More importantly, elevating online student services to the next level to truly meet the needs of online learners calls for a shift in mindset and design by colleges. The shift in the design must include both high tech and high touch. High touch speaks to the human element—that is, trained college personnel, such as counselors, advisors, tutors, and admissions and financial aid personnel, who use online technology to facilitate communication and interactivity among students. High tech speaks to the incorporation of innovative leading-edge technologies to serve as the platforms to conduct such business. On-campus student services professionals work in various functional areas to assist students by helping them develop in the areas of cognitive, psychosocial, and social domains. The importance of interaction between remotely located students and these professionals is no less important for their retention and academic success.

Solving the Problem

In 2002, the Western Interstate Commission for Higher Education Cooperative for Educational Technologies (WCET) published *Guidelines for Creating Online Student Services* (Shea & Armitage, 2002). In this publication, Shea and Armitage (2002) identified and categorized key online student support services. To better conceptualize the scope of online student services offered by colleges and universities, Shea and Armitage (2002) identified the following categories:

- Administrative Suite represents business transactions students are accustomed to completing online.

- Academic Suite includes online libraries, bookstore services, technical support, online academic advising, online tutoring, and online assessment and testing.

- Personal Services Suite includes career and placement information and personal counseling, health and wellness services, ethical and legal services and plagiarism, student authentication, and other academic honesty services.

- Communications Suite provides remotely delivered faculty-to-student, institution-to-student, and student-to-student engagement and relationship building. Social networking and other web- and cloud-based technologies have altered the way institutions communicate with all stakeholders.

- Student Communities Suite contains student activities, an essential component of the college experience for many traditional students and other population segments. With isolation being a key contributor of students not succeeding in their online courses, online clubs, student government, college newspapers, mentorship, and support groups are particularly important to consider

Shea and Armitage's (2002) approach to organizing online student services in suites focused on students' needs is only one example that highlights the importance of not providing services that reflect institutional organizational structures but rather presenting services and resources in a way that supports student success. Perhaps a clearer way to conceive of the scope of online services Shea and Armitage (2002) described is to aggregate those services into two categories: (a) access services, and (b) continued support services. Access services refer to matriculation-related student support activities, such as, but not limited to, admissions, orientation and student readiness, matriculation, financial aid, and the bookstore, while continued support services focus on support services students use throughout their enrollment. These can include tutoring, counseling, peer mentoring, writing centers, library services, and others.

Even when online student services are developed with student needs in mind, not all online services are created equal. The now-defunct Center for Transforming Student Services (CENTSS), whose focus was to help institutions of higher education use technology to develop improved online student services, introduced an audit tool to provide institutions with a systematic process for examining 31 remotely delivered student services. The CENTSS audit tool was a collaborative effort among WCET, the Minnesota State Colleges and Universities, and Seward, Inc. It provided a mechanism for institutions to assess their online student services and plan for improvements. The CENTSS tool described ways of delivering critical components of each service online. Each response described a delivery mechanism that was increasingly more interactive and more personalized to the individual student. These responses correlated to generational scores in the resulting reports. Generational scores were defined as follows:

- Generation 1: Service is not provided on the website
- Generation 2: Informational, internal focus on the institution
- Generation 3: Informational, audience focused (e.g., prospective students link, continuing students link)
- Generation 4: Process-oriented – customized community, personalized, portal
- Generation 5: Virtual mentor – process orientation and decision-making guide

Although the CENTSS audit tool is no longer available, it is offered as an example of how institutions might use a tool with similar features to evaluate and improve online student services. Using this sort of analysis can help institutions identify gaps that exist between their current online student services and what they deem to be important improvements, with the overarching goal being to provide students a useful online experience that improves their chances for academic success.

For the most part, colleges and universities have invested heavily in technology to support online access services, but the outcome of such an investment typically yields CENTSS generational scores of 3 and 4—that is, websites that are largely text based and information focused (Johnson et al., 2016). Providing access to student information systems allows students to submit admissions applications, check and review grades, and passively view some portion of their academic record. Many institutions deliver these services via web portals but still have not maximized their full potential. As a result, the student experience is not greatly improved.

Colleges and universities that have started to explore the possibilities of active engagement through continued support services are doing so with the right intent. However, without a shift in mindset, changes will be incremental and student success improvements insufficient. Incremental improvements include periodically revising institution websites and adding portal technology with limited functionality. Significant improvements require using the right technology, identifying effective practices, and developing common online student support services based on industry standards governing design and delivery.

Unfortunately, the examples and guidelines provided by WCET and CENTSS have not resulted in development of universal standards for delivery of online student services one can easily point to as a guide to establishing effective online support services. Even in the CENTSS example, while on the right track with Generation 5, they did not venture far enough to meet the needs of today's students. The creators of the CENTSS audit tool did not anticipate the capabilities of today's technology.

Technology and Innovative Tools	
Platforms used by CVC-OEI	
Canvas/Instructure	Common course management system with a familiar online environment for instruction and academic and student support. *https://www.instructure.com*
Cranium Café/ ConexED	Virtual meeting space designed for counseling, which includes a lobby, individual and group meeting technology, and single sign-on authentication. *https://www.conexed.com*
NameCoach	Recording and sharing of correct name pronunciation so students feel more valued and a stronger sense of belonging; demonstrates a college's commitment to inclusion. *https://cloud.name-coach.com*
Net Tutor/Link-Systems	Synchronous 24/7 online tutoring using professional tutors. *https://www.nettutor.com*
Notebowl	The Bulletin facilitates sharing external sources like videos and reflections and Discussion is a social feed; both facilitate social learning and relationship building within Canvas courses *https://notebowl.com*
Proctorio	Online exam proctoring service and identity verification to assure the student doing the work is the one who gets credit. *https://proctorio.com*
SmarterMeasure/ SmarterServices	Diagnostic assessment of student readiness for online learning based on noncognitive indicators of success; used as part of Quest for Online Success, the comprehensive readiness program. *http://www.smarterservices.com*
WorldwideWhiteboard/ Link-Systems	Platform used for tutoring and collaboration. *http://www.link-systems.com/worldwidewhiteboard*

Note. Platforms used by CVC-OEI are all FERPA and ADA compliant.

California and Online Student Support Services

In California, there are 115 community colleges serving more than 2.1 million students, providing a wide variety of career and educational programs. More importantly, with one of five community college students in the nation attending a California community college, and one of three California community college students taking at least one online course, the discussion around the quality and structure of available online student support services needs to be front and center (CCCCO, 2017). In 2014, California established the CVC-OEI. The multi-million-dollar project, state-funded through the CCCCO, represents a comprehensive and collaborative program that leverages best practices and technology to significantly increase the opportunity for higher education degree attainment in California. As CVC-OEI continues to scale its services and resources, more and more online learners will have access to support services and tools that can improve the online learning experience.

From its inception, the CVC-OEI has focused on offering student support services to provide equitable access and opportunities for success in the online environment. The services are purposefully designed to improve student outcomes for all—in particular, for students who choose to study online.

The Online Student Services Hub— The App Experience

The CVC-OEI created an ecosystem that is an organized and directed systemwide approach, whereby all California community colleges work together to ensure online learners are fully supported. Online student support is one of four components needed to improve CCC distance education programs. As such, the key to the CVC-OEI's success has been its holistic approach to online learning. By recognizing online student services are as important as the other three components to the success of online learners, the OEI not only continues to help California community colleges expand and innovate their distance education programs but also is influential in closing the achievement gap between online and face-to-face California community college students. The benefit of the deliberate focus placed on making student support services available in the online environment is suggested by a marked reduction in the student achievement gap between face-to-face and online courses, from 14% to 4% in five years (CCCCO, 2017).

Through the assistance of the CVC-OEI, most California community colleges have access to the technology needed to redesign online student services, which is often a challenge for institutions without access to similar resources. The expected outcome is an updated and dynamic interactive approach to providing online student support services, in keeping with Generation 5 on the CENTSS audit tool. The uniqueness of the CVC-OEI's approach is the use of the common CMS as the location for each college's online student service hub. In the case of California, Canvas was selected as the common CMS. The online hub can be accessed via the common CMS, whereby all participants (students, faculty, counselors, tutors, and staff) can engage with each other in a familiar environment, regardless of their college. The platform and its functions allow for Learning Tools Interoperability (LTI) and native integrations of additional technologies to provide opportunities for a variety of interactive services. LTI and native integration allow for a seamless way to launch external tools from inside the CMS. The result is the creation of an online one-stop student services shop or hub.

With the CMS in place at most colleges by the end of 2016, the CVC-OEI began encouraging colleges to design student support hubs to include LTI integrations of an online counseling platform, online tutoring, online proctoring, library services, online mental health student support resources, and the student readiness for online learning program. To promote the concept and to provide equitable access, the CVC-OEI brokered statewide licenses with numerous partners to provide the necessary technology tools.

Designing the Hub

The number one reason students choose to take online courses is convenience. These students expect the services that support their success to be delivered in an equally convenient format online. If we start from the assumption online learners require the same services as on-campus students, plus a few additional services unique to their learning modality, institutions offering online courses and programs are faced with the immense challenge of rethinking what types of support they offer, the accessibility of these services, and how to make investments in student support that will have the greatest impact on student success.

Hub services are organized according to two basic categories: access services and continued support services. One expectation is all services will be presented in a more interactive format than is typical of Generation 2 online student services. The hub includes some services that are Generations 3 and 4 (information and process oriented) and many others that are Generation 5 and beyond (providing opportunities for goal setting and decision making). Additionally, some services are designed to be self-service, while others require students to interact with a professional or a bot. The availability of services extends beyond normal business hours to meet the needs of students located in multiple time zones who are learning around the clock.

Elevating the delivery of online student services beyond Generation 5 calls for a new concept. To fully meet the needs of online learners using current technology, institutions might consider designing online services that mimic the "app experience." For both access and continued support services, today's students require a more engaging environment than is typically provided by an institution's website or student portal. Understanding the difference between the two will help stakeholders determine the quality of the online learner experience. The traditional website experience is information driven and characterized by passive communication. With this form of delivery, the expectation is students will be proactive and seek out the help they need from an individual or campus representative. The app experience is much more dynamic and in line with how students experience technology today. It forces interactivity, requires action on the part of students, demonstrates efficacy, and focuses on accomplishing a task that will further students' progress.

This type of transformation requires student services leadership to use leading-edge technologies that are not only user friendly but user reliable—that is, capable of supporting the online learner with technologies designed or modified specifically for student services. It is important to consider, as is the case for on-campus services, a one-size-fits-all approach to online services will not meet the needs of all students. Additionally, while remotely located online learners depend on online services, on-campus students are also choosing to use online student services. All of these learners need access to services outside of traditional campus office hours and from the comfort of their home.

In an era of limited resources, efficient and effective applications of technology allow institutions to use their professional resources with students who are most in need of this level of interactivity to achieve their educational goals. In the case of online learners, those services are remotely available, which results in the playing field being closer to equitable.

Components of the Hub

Tables 12.1 and 12.2 provide examples of services, delivery methods, and platforms to be included in the online student services hub and which can be converted to deliver an app experience. Specific student services features are also components of the hub. Table 12.1 includes a few of the services viewed as critical components of the hub that are shared across the CCC system.

Table 12.1. Delivery Methods

Self-Services	Professional/Peer-Supported Services
• AI chat bots available after normal business hours • Brochure information • Interactive multimedia tutorials (e.g., readiness, library, academic support, wellness) • Smart FAQs (e.g., help desk, registration, library, tutoring) • Transactions (e.g., registration, book purchase, application, appointment scheduling, appeals submittals)	• Counseling • Disability support services • Health and wellness services • Help desk (technology) • Library • Student ambassadors • Student community • Student success coaching • Tutoring • Writing center

Table 12.2. Access and Continued Services

Access Services (During Matriculation)	Continued Services (Throughout Enrollment)
• Admissions online • Bookstore • Courses and programs • Financial aid online • Placement assessment and testing • Registration online • Schedule of classes • Student readiness and orientation	• Coaching • Counseling • Disability support services • Health and wellness services • Help desk (technology) • Library • Student ambassadors • Student community • Tutoring • Writing center

Online learner readiness orientation. The comprehensive readiness for online learning program is called Quest for Online Success (Quest). This program is composed of SmarterMeasure, a vendor product, and 11 engaging, fully accessible multimedia tutorials and four interactive tools developed under a CC-BY Creative Commons license. These tutorials are available from http://apps.3cmediasolutions.org/oei.

To meet the diverse needs of all students, the multimedia tutorials are offered in four versions: (a) fully accessible, (b) HTML-5-based multimedia presentation, (c) text-only script, and (d) an audio-only

MP3 version. The multimedia presentation is delivered from Able Player, an open-source product with many additional innovative features, such as an interactive transcript built by combining time-synchronized content from the chapters, captions, and description tracks, as well as a set of preferences dialogues to enable users to customize the appearance of closed captions and define keyboard shortcuts to operate the media player from anywhere on the webpage.

The goal for developing the multimedia tutorials in this way was to create a product that is fully accessible to students who are blind or have visual impairments; students who use audible screen readers, Braille output devices, or other assistive technologies to interact with computers; students who are deaf or hard of hearing who depend on transcripts and captions to access audio and audiovisual content; students who have physical disabilities that prevent them from using a mouse, so they operate the computer using keyboard alone, speech recognition systems, or other alternative input technologies; and students who have dyslexia or other learning or cognitive disabilities and therefore benefit from multimodal learning experiences that engage multiple senses.

Online counseling. Online counseling and advising services are important components of the student services hub, as counselors play an integral role in the personal and academic success of all students. By leveraging and partnering with a technology vendor, ConexED, whose focus is technology in student services, the CVC-OEI has supported the development of a robust online counseling program that maintains the integrity of the college counseling profession while addressing the needs of online learners. The California Community Colleges Online Counseling Network offers colleges the resources required to establish online counseling services at individual colleges. This work conforms to regulations on equity of student support services in distance education. Accomplishments that can be replicated by other student affairs professionals include:

- Established synchronous online counseling and advising services using the Cranium Café platform powered by ConexED with features such as online appointments, virtual lobby, walk-in and scheduled appointments, small and large group sessions, document collection, and sharing in a fully equipped multimedia platform.

- Counselor professional development training and materials aligned with the National Board of Certified Counselors standards for distance counseling professionals. The current offerings are: Introduction to Distance Counseling and the ConexED Platform, Distance Mental Health Counseling for Clinicians, and Distance Mental Health Counseling for Non-Clinicians.

- A uniform approach to online counseling in collaboration initially from the graduate credit-bearing online courses and then ongoing via the Online Counseling Network, resulting in a community of online counselors from participating California community colleges who are trained in working with online learners.

Wellness Central. A free health and wellness resource created collaboratively by CCC mental health professionals and the CVC-OEI is intended to make resources available to students 24/7. Organized around six dimensions of wellness, there are currently 26 topics that include basic information, an engaging multimedia tutorial, and opportunities to explore more through self-assessments and links to local resources. Wellness Central is built inside a Canvas course, CC-BY Creative Commons licensed, and available from https://ccconlineed.instructure.com/courses/1895.

Tips for Getting Started

Transforming online services into an interactive student experience is a tall order. *Quality*, in this context, is defined as providing online student services characterized as possessing a significant level of interactivity per the CENTSS generation scale. Once your project stakeholder group is in place, consider the following steps to get started.

- Determine the current quality of online student services by conducting an audit of current services available to students who do not come to campus.

- Set quality goals for each online student service by defining the degree to which interactive and transactional services can be completed remotely.

- Conduct a gap analysis by identifying discrepancies between what is currently in place and what needs to be in place to achieve the degree of interactivity defined in the previous step.

- Prioritize feature sets. Few institutions can create highly interactive online student services all at once. A more typical approach is to create a phased approach for developing an online student services hub.

- Establish a roadmap of milestones for each phase of the project, leading to completion. Project management software might assist with this step to identify priorities, dependencies, and budget limitations.

- Design with the "app experience" in mind. An app experience fully engages students in the education and career decision-making process and provides opportunities to confirm these decisions with "what-if" scenarios. Decisions are fully integrated with actual course planning and academic progress.

Evaluation

The CVC-OEI and California Community Colleges' holistic approach to designing and delivering online student support aims to significantly expand access and boost retention and success in online courses across the system. The early data show this approach is paying off. According to a report by the Research and Planning Group for the California Community Colleges:

In online course sections that piloted OEI support services at colleges during 2015–16, the average student success rate was 68.8 percent—2.9 percentage points higher than the overall online course success rate at the pilot colleges, and

3.9 percentage points higher than the average online course success rate statewide. (Nguyen & The Research and Planning Group, 2017, p. 8)

The hope of the CVC-OEI and the State of California is to expand evaluation efforts, not just on the performance of individual services but as an evaluation of the success of the entire concept. Nevertheless, measuring the effectiveness of a systematic approach to providing online support services can be challenging, because much will depend on the level of output by each college. In the early days, colleges and universities claimed quality if they merely had brochure-type information on their website describing campus-based resources and services. This is no longer good enough. Through subsidizing much of the cost of new services, part of the CVC-OEI agenda is to work with colleges to help them realize it is not always necessary to develop new services for online learners; often support already exists at the campus.

To accomplish the goal of a singular localized online student support hub, colleges lacking resources might consider leveraging already existing resources and make incremental changes first. The shift may come as part of program evaluation, whereby an environmental scan, needs assessment, or a gap analysis may be conducted within a college's student services division to prepare for transformational change. As the evaluative reports continue to reveal success with the holistic approach, another aspiration of the CVC-OEI is to take up where CENTSS left off by reestablishing industry-specific guidelines—based on research and data—for the design of quality online student support hubs. A tool that may be of assistance is the Online Learning Consortium's (2019) Quality Scorecard for Online Student Support developed by the State University System of Florida and Florida College System.

Potential Challenges and Practical Solutions

While some may argue human and financial resources are one and the same, there may be value in discussing them separately. A phased approach to developing high-quality online student services involves prioritizing those services most often used and most closely tied to student success based on research.

Human Resources

Potential Challenge: As more students use online student services, it becomes essential for student affairs professionals to incorporate the skills needed to develop and deliver services mediated through technology.

Practical Solution: Incorporate professional development (e.g., online courses, webinars) for areas relevant to remote and virtual employees, such as cybersecurity training and how to effectively work in a remote environment

Financial Resources

Potential Challenge: Transforming online student services to incorporate the highly interactive functionality described in this chapter requires the expertise of student affairs professionals as leaders and content experts, computer experts to develop the hub and connect it to current IT systems, and communication staff and administrative leadership from other stakeholder groups to bring forth the cultural change required for this type of institutional transformation.

Practical Solution: Establishing a highly functional committee of core stakeholders is essential. One measure of an institution's commitment to transforming online student services would be to hire a person specifically to lead this effort.

Conclusion

Authentic student services support can only be achieved in the online environment when students are provided just-in-time services based on their needs. Online student services hubs are designed to welcome students into an ecosystem where they can easily select from a menu of options to participate in the support services they need from the comfort of their home. While a few services may only need to be presented as static information, most will provide an engaging and interactive self-paced experience. When those self-paced resources do not sufficiently meet students' needs, students will be seamlessly led to either schedule an appointment or select a walk-in option with one of several professionals. While this type of hub is not currently available in its entirety, several components have been assembled at one college within the California Community Colleges system to be used as a prototype upon which other colleges can build. This type of collaboration has been a hallmark of the CVC-OEI, which is no small feat since California Community Colleges represents the largest educational system in the world.

Questions for Reflection

It has been suggested online learners have not been provided with equitable support services because they are somewhat invisible—"out of sight, out of mind." What indicators will your institution use to determine whether services are equitable for all?

◆ What criteria will your institution use to select the best technology to deliver each service?

◆ This chapter described two primary delivery methods for online student services: self-services and peer/professional support services. What techniques will you use to assure students can and will readily connect with peer/professional support services when needed?

References

Allen, I. E., & Seaman, J. (2016). *Online report card – Tracking online education in the United States.* Retrieved from Online Learning Consortium website: https://onlinelearningconsortium.org/read/online-report-card-tracking-online-education-united-states-2015

California Community Colleges Chancellor's Office. (2017). *Distance education report.* Retrieved from https://www.cccco.edu/About-Us/Reports

Crawley, A., & Howe, A. (2016). Supporting online students. In G. S. McClellan & J. Stringer (Eds.), *The handbook of student affairs administration* (4th ed., pp. 343–364). San Francisco, CA: Wiley.

Instructional Technology Council. (2018). National eLearning Survey of Community Colleges. Retrieved from Instructional Technology Council website: https://www.itcnetwork.org/sites/default/files/content-files/itc2017-master-final-accessible.pdf

Johnson, L., Adams Becker, S., Cummins, M., Estrada, V., Freeman, A., & Hall, C. (2016). *NMC horizon report: 2016 higher education edition.* Austin, TX: The New Media Consortium.

McFarland, J., Hussar, B., Wang, X., Zhang, J., Wang, K., Rathbun, A., & Bullock Mann, F. (2018). *The condition of education 2018* (NCES Report No. 2018-144). Retrieved from National Center for Education Statistics website: https://nces.ed.gov/pubs2018/2018144.pdf

Nguyen, A., & The Research Planning Group. (2017). *The Online Education Initiative: Access and quality of online education in California's community colleges, 2015–2016.* Retrieved from the California Community Colleges, California Virtual Campus website: http://cvc.edu/wp-content/uploads/2015/09/2015-16OEIDisseminationBriefFINAL.pdf

Online Learning Consortium. (2019). *Quality scorecard for online student support.* Retrieved from https://onlinelearningconsortium.org/consult/olc-quality-scorecard-student-support

Palloff, R. M., & Pratt, K. (1999). *Building learning communities in cyberspace* (Vol. 12). San Francisco, CA: Jossey-Bass.

Peters, B., Crawley, A., & Brindley, J. E. (2017). *Student support services for online learning re-imagined and re-invigorated: Then, now and what's to come.* Toronto, Ontario, Canada: Contact North.

Shea, P., & Armitage, S. (2002). *Beyond the administrative core: Creating web-based student services for online learners.* Boulder, CO: WCETLAAP Project.

Shea, P., & Bidjerano, T. (2018). Online course enrollment in community college and degree completion: The tipping point. *International Review of Research in Open and Distributed Learning, 19*(2). doi:10.19173/irrodl.v19i2.3460

CHAPTER 13

Making Campus Life Accessible to Online Learners:
The Technology, Innovation, and Pedagogy Method for Online Learner Engagement

Molly A. Mott and Courtney Battista Bish

ONLINE LEARNING CONTINUES to increase in its prevalence across higher education institutions. The number of students who have taken at least one online course has significantly increased in the last decade (Seaman, Allen, & Seaman, 2018). As more students seek this form of instructional delivery, online programs are becoming a more accepted part of higher education (Lederman, 2018; Wingo, Ivankova, & Moss, 2017) and an enrollment strategy of brick-and-mortar institutions (Fredericksen, 2017).

The purpose of this chapter is to share the technology, innovation, and pedagogy (TIP) method for online learner engagement and to provide specific strategies for developing relevant holistic campus experiences for online learners and decreasing their feelings of isolation. Each aspect of the TIP method is grounded in research on student engagement, teaching effectiveness, and using technology to enhance pedagogy. The use of technology to decrease transactional distance between students, peers, and the campus are discussed, and relevant applications are described. New ways of thinking related to building and strengthening student life in a virtual environment are also shared. Finally, the pedagogical principles used to scaffold student engagement are reviewed. The chapter offers creative tools and strategies for engaging online learners in student life that can be adapted to multiple institutions.

The Changing Landscape of Online Learning

The increasing normalization of online learning influences who enrolls in online education and why. Most importantly, this normalization continues to shape the expectations of online learners and their role in higher education and campus life.

The Online Learner

Similar to how the reasons students choose to enroll in an online course or program vary, online learners are increasingly diverse (Ladd, Reynolds, & Selingo, n.d.). While most online programs enroll post-traditional students (those 25 years of age and older) seeking the convenience and flexibility of online learning, increasing numbers of traditional students are enrolling in virtual classrooms or programs.

Recent trends in online education demonstrate the "typical" online learner is difficult to define and "may be a thing of the past as students of all ages and from all locations enroll in increasing numbers" (Best Colleges, 2019, p. 7). The State University of New York (SUNY) at Canton is seeing this trend as more traditional students are enrolling in its online degree programs and courses. In fall 2018, 29% of all SUNY Canton students were fully online, 39% were enrolled in face-to-face courses, and 32% were a mix of both online and traditional delivery (SUNY Canton Office of Institutional Research, 2019). This is a steady increase from 2011 in which 20% of the students were fully online, 43% were enrolled in face-to-face courses, and the rest were mixed delivery.

While students can access online programs from any location worldwide, most enrollments are local. In tracking the geography of online learners, Seaman et al. (2018) found it common for students who took at least one distance course to also be enrolled in a course on campus. Additionally, many fully online learners live in the same state as the institution in which they are enrolled in, often within 50 miles of the campus. This rate is increasing each year (Seaman et al., 2018).

Motivation for Choosing Online Learning

Students enroll in online courses and programs for various reasons. In the *2019 Online Education Trends Report*, Best Colleges (2019) found students choose the online format because of its convenience and flexibility. For students with impaired mobility or hidden disabilities (psychological or social), online instruction provides a chance for them to enhance their academic success by mitigating the stress of large classroom settings, the challenge of physical spaces, or the fixed structure of traditional classes (Terras, Leggio, & Phillips, 2015). Other students seek to shorten the time to degree completion by taking online courses offered during summer and winter sessions. Students may choose online delivery as a way to reduce the expense of attendance, specifically the expense of living on campus that is often much of the college investment (Clinefelter & Aslanian, 2015). As student perceptions of the quality and value of online learning trend in a positive direction (Best Colleges, 2019), more students are comfortable taking online programs and courses.

The Challenge of Providing Student Life to Online Learners

Regardless of the reason students choose to enroll in online offerings or whether they are traditional or post-traditional students, many are seeking a more comprehensive college experience and one of value beyond the usual links to campus resources provided to students at a distance (Blumenstyk, 2018). A SUNY Canton student best captured this sentiment: "It would be nice if the online learner were included in campus events, anything that shows we are just as important and equal to the brick-and-mortar activities to make me feel like a true student of SUNY Canton."

The challenge of engaging these students in the life of the college was first introduced by Stoller (2013) when he remarked, "Student affairs has got to stop being frozen in time when it comes to online learners" (p. 3). Westra's (2018) comment further echoed this observation:

> While many colleges and universities are offering online student services to support their online learners, the types and levels of support vary widely. Accrediting bodies have been concerned with student services for online students for some time, and a very simple tenet to follow is that whatever student services are offered for on-campus students should be offered in an equitable fashion for online students. (p. 3)

As a result of being invisible or an afterthought, many online learners feel isolated and disconnected from peers and the institution. Ali and Smith (2015) and Kebritchi, Lipschuetz, and Santiague

(2017) found isolation is the most common reason students drop out of online courses. To reduce isolation, campuses must use strategies to increase the connections online learners have with peers and the institution. Not only should institutions deliver engaging academic content, but it is also time for them to consider cocurricular opportunities in a virtual environment that are of value to traditional and nontraditional students (McKeown, 2012).

Most research on student engagement is limited to the classroom experience and focuses on student-to-teacher and student-to-student interaction via discussion board postings, group work, and other course-based activities. Described as the "forgotten frontier" by Stoller (2019), there is little research on connecting online learners to out-of-classroom experiences, except to address the need for academic support services, such as tutoring, advising, and related services. As such, the social experience of student life, and how it can reduce student isolation in a virtual environment, remains an emerging field of inquiry. Many assumptions inhibit this research, such as the belief students who study online are not interested in or do not have the time for activities outside of the classroom and/or the online environment cannot possibly replicate the cocurricular experience in a virtual setting. Yet there will always be students, on campus and online, who are not interested in student life. For online learners who do wish to engage outside the classroom, McKeown (2012) offered this reflection:

> For these students, a key factor in their choice will be the ability of online programs to provide a college experience that not only matches the academic content of a traditional college, but also includes an adequate level of the social and extracurricular components that the students desire. (p. 11)

As online offerings and programs become mainstream, it is time for colleges and universities to recognize the needs of online learners are changing and to seek innovative ways to use technology to engage online learners with the social, academic, and cocurricular components of student life. Institutions will need to explore ways to provide experiences to reduce student isolation, improve retention rates, and add value to students' college experience (Kak, 2018).

Overview of The TIP Method for Online Learner Engagement

Online learning is strategically important to the mission of the SUNY system, the largest comprehensive university system in the United States (Scalzo, 2018). As an undergraduate institution that is part of a 64-campus system, SUNY Canton enrolls a mix of on-campus, commuter, and online learners and offers many online bachelor's degree programs. Recognizing the needs of online learners are changing, SUNY Canton, in 2017, began to explore innovative ways to use technology to engage online learners with the social, academic, and cocurricular components of student life. Subsequently, the college sought funding from the state university system to develop replicable strategies and methods for engaging fully online learners in student life to improve retention and student satisfaction in the online environment.

The inspiration for the TIP method came from SUNY Canton's fully online learners. Online learners were increasingly questioning the cost of attending the college when many of the activities they read about in their campus e-mail were directed to residential students and most were unavailable virtually. At the same time students were requesting to be included in campus life, the college's online enrollments were increasing, and student retention became a focus. Both experiences were a catalyst for thinking differently about how the college serves and supports its online learners.

Student affairs professionals know engaging students outside the classroom fosters personal growth, development, and connections to others; however, it is difficult for online learners limited by geography and time to participate in campus life (Fontaine & Cook, 2014). Despite these constraints, building community and strengthening social ties to the campus are important to student satisfaction (Berry, 2019; Boston & Ice, 2011).

Is it possible online college experiences can be developed that mirror the "scope and richness" (McKeown, 2012, p. 5) of traditional campus life? Do online learners seek these experiences, and, if so, what experiences do they seek? What cocurricular opportunities do online learners believe would add value to their education? Might virtual campus experiences that address the different aspects of student life reduce student isolation and improve retention? (Ali & Smith, 2015; Rovai & Wighting, 2005).

Connecting online learners—both traditional and post-traditional—to campus life requires new ways of thinking and doing. As Fontaine and Cook (2014) stated, "Rather than trying to encourage [post-traditional] learners to engage in extra-curricular experiences designed for traditional students, consideration needs to be given to transforming co-curricular experiences to adapt to the personal and professional needs of [post-traditional] learners" (p. 7).

How do student affairs professionals create opportunities for an enriching student experience, one that includes cocurricular services such as counseling, and acknowledge online learners and on-campus students have similar socioemotional needs? Kruger and Jarrat (2018) maintained understanding what motivates students will inform how colleges and universities meet these challenges.

The TIP method for student engagement is an attempt to meet the task of providing a holistic and engaging experience for all online learners. The model is grounded in technology, innovation, and pedagogy and is mapped to the different dimensions of campus life, including social, academic, and cocurricular. Through student focus groups and surveys, SUNY Canton developed a prototype for transforming the online learner experience.

Developing the TIP Method for
Online Learner Engagement

The first phase of developing the TIP method was exploratory and was used to benchmark student interest. A student interest survey was sent electronically to all fully online learners. The survey sought students' perspectives on two primary questions: Are campus-based experiences important to fully online learners? What social, academic, and cocurricular experiences do fully online learners seek? Other survey questions asked students for suggestions on how SUNY Canton could better help online learners connect to the campus, ideas for improving the online learner experience, and how to communicate opportunities and activities to online learners.

Answers to these questions were used to create opportunities of value and interest to the online learner. Faculty seminars on effective teaching strategies for engaging online learners and developing course-based assessments were hosted. Midpoint in the semester, an e-pulse (short and targeted) survey was administered to assess how students were responding to the initiative and how well each activity was working. The formative assessment provided a mechanism for adjusting efforts as needed.

At the end of the semester, a summative survey was given to evaluate student satisfaction and participation. Students were asked if participating in the activities had an impact on their experience as a student and/or their relationship to the college. Engagement efforts for the following semester were adjusted with this feedback. A similar process was followed in subsequent semesters, and efforts were revised continuously per student feedback.

Beyond collecting feedback from students, the college administered a survey to faculty and staff to collect perspectives on connecting online learners to campus life. Questions from the survey included:

- Do you believe the campus should invest time and resources in creating opportunities for online learners to engage in campus life?

- On a scale from 1 (*not important at all*) to 10 (*essential*), how important do you think it is for the campus to provide opportunities for fully online learners to engage in campus life activities?

- Do you believe the campus is making progress in considering the needs of online learners in everyday business or when offering student life resources/providing services?

At the end of the semester, a summative survey was given to evaluate student satisfaction and participation. For the three consecutive semesters the survey was administered, 84% of faculty and staff agreed the college should invest time and resources to create opportunities for online learners to engage with campus life.

Technology and Innovative Tools

Select an engagement platform that allows online learners to interact in near real time with clubs, organizations, and departments on campus. Some options for existing engagement platforms include those from Campus Labs, Portfolium, Presence, and Ooh LaLa. These platforms, and others like them, allow students to navigate engagement opportunities across various campus offices and through student clubs and organizations. The platforms provide information about the area (i.e., office, club) and contact information, and showcase the events and programs they host.

TIP Method Dimensions

The TIP method for online learner engagement uses technology, innovation, and pedagogy to address the different aspects of campus life, including social, academic, and cocurricular dimensions. Each of these dimensions, and relevant examples, are discussed in the following sections.

Technology

Online learners value social presence and emphasize the value of belonging more frequently than on-campus students (Toufaily, Zalan, & Lee, 2018). Multiple modalities of technology broaden the diversity and create the psychological experiences of community members (Ferdman & Deane, 2014). Technology can be used to achieve this experience for students in a virtual learning environment. In the case of the TIP method, technology was used to create interactive experiences in a variety of ways, including virtual communities, the digital badge initiative, recording of campus events and speakers, online learner representation in student government, online marketing of student events, and a 24/7 online learner listserv.

Virtual communities. Online communities were organized via an engagement software platform (Campus Labs) the college named RooLife, as a kangaroo is SUNY Canton's mascot. The software platform allowed SUNY Canton to encourage student clubs and organizations to rethink how they recruited and communicated with students and managed their student organizations. The software platform provided a one-stop shop for students looking for an event to attend or a lecture, workshop, or program. More than 90% of total student clubs/ organizations created accounts for their chapter and began to evaluate their marketing, engagement, recruitment, and retention strategies. A social fraternity created an online chapter to offer fully online learners the opportunity to engage in Greek life at SUNY Canton. Beyond this, more than 30 campus departments/offices also signed on to RooLife and are using this platform to connect with students and market events for their offices.

Digital badge initiative. As a part of this work, a digital badge initiative was created to incentivize and reward student involvement beyond the classroom. Digital badging, which rewards student involvement beyond the classroom (e.g., badges in cultural competency and leadership development) is fully supported through this platform, and each event is accessible to all students, including fully online learners. Two badges were created in the 2018–2019 academic year: Cultural Competency and Leadership Development. These two badges were vetted by committees that assisted the college in developing the structure and programming to support the badges. The completed badge is reflected on the student's cocurricular transcript housed within RooLife and available on demand for students. The cocurricular transcript provides a record of student engagement opportunities in which students have participated during their tenure at SUNY Canton, including clubs/organizations, service-learning, philanthropy, and digital badging. Digital badging, coupled with the cocurricular transcript, enhances students' ability to market themselves to future employers and on graduate school applications.

Recording of campus events and speakers. Arguably the most important work in student life to grow online learner engagement has been video streaming and recording of events. The culture shift toward ensuring online learners have access to all campus life events, speakers, and presentations has been paramount to SUNY Canton's ethos of "everyone is welcome here." SUNY Canton has a strong base of commuter and post-traditional students who, along with fully online learners, are often not able to attend events in real time due to employment and family care. Through this project, 761 events have been logged in RooLife in the 2018–2019 academic year—a significant increase over the 522 events logged in 2017–2018—and more

Tips for Getting Started

- **Think differently about online learner engagement.** Use the principles of Kotter's (1996) model to initiate new ways of thinking about online learner engagement. The model offers a guide for leading transformative change across an organization. Map out opportunities for informal conversations/collision points for dialogue across your campus (retreats for out-of-the-box thinking).
- **Challenge and explore assumptions on what online learners want.** Be curious about the online learner experience. Investigate what students in online programs want by asking them. Use interest surveys to plan activities of value, and follow up with measurements on participation and satisfaction.
- **Apply research on student engagement and development to students in online environments.** Advocate that the same principles apply regardless if a student is campus-based or online.
- **Tie activities to research.** For example, understanding post-traditional students value meaningful experiences they can tie to their work (Fontaine & Cook, 2014), develop career-based engagement opportunities.
- **Engage faculty and staff.** Create mechanisms for communicating, sharing out, and engaging faculty and staff in engagement efforts (e.g., Student Online Learning Advisory Committee—a student-centered advisory structure that gives online learners opportunities to share their perspective about learning in a virtual environment and discuss ways the institution can help improve their experience).

than 2,700 students have attended these events, either in person or through recordings.

The college streamed 88 events, up from 63 the year prior. Examples of streamed events include the Leadership Lecture Series (talks given by successful alumni and partners of the college); events in the Cultural Competency badge series; and the keynote speaker for the 2019 Leadership Series badge, David Flood. Most athletic events were live streamed this year, which is a practice that has been in place for the past several years; basketball team home games are the most frequently watched.

Online learner representation in student government. Additionally, the Student Government Association added an online learner representative to its Executive Leadership Board in 2017 to provide a direct opportunity for online learners to have a hand in shaping student life and student governance at SUNY Canton. The online learner representative is present at all Executive Leadership Board meetings, including the monthly meeting held between the Student Government Association's Executive Leadership Board and the President's Executive Council. Further, the online learner representative is the direct line of communication for online learners to the Executive Leadership Board. During the Student Government Association meetings, which are live streamed, the online learner representative fields questions from and gives responses to any online learners participating via the web.

Online marketing of student events. The overwhelming positivity for the addition of RooLife and its inclusion of fully online learners has been its greatest strength. In addition to this, students' ability to seamlessly market and manage events with no cost to the organization, elicit engagement from the entire student body, and maintain an accurate membership database has been truly rewarding for student engagement. The most notable challenge has been committing to this paper-free avenue for marketing when organizations have been accustomed to less sustainable, cost-prohibitive measures, such as hanging posters and printing flyers. The latter also excludes online learners and those who do not regularly take classes on the physical campus, thereby limiting student organization outreach to these students. To overcome this obstacle, the Student Government Association has been instrumental in requiring organizations to use RooLife and assisting them in expanding their outreach to online learners. Additionally, the Student Government Association encouraged student clubs and organizations to hold a virtual club fair to allow fully online learners to familiarize themselves with club offerings on campus and to express their interest in joining.

24/7 online learners listserv. SUNY Canton created a listserv for fully online learners, and, through this endeavor, we share a weekly newsletter of tips and events geared toward online learners, managed by an online learner coordinator. Additionally, the listserv gives a venue to survey online learners to elicit feedback, ensure their needs are being met, and provide directed services and supports to them. Online learners have responded routinely to the online learner coordinator through this tool and have expressed their comfort in knowing they have direct contact with a professional staff member 24/7.

Innovation

Curiosity sparks new solutions to old problems. The TIP method encourages institutions of higher education to rethink how to offer campus-based activities in a virtual way. SUNY Canton's engagement efforts included mailing welcome and stress relief care packets; hosting virtual career, clothing, and study abroad fairs; as well as launching online learner engagement days and eSports events.

Mailed welcome kits. All first-time, fully online learners receive a welcome kit from the college, including a T-shirt, keychain, and information about support services. These mailed welcome kits are the initial point of contact with students as a way to welcome them.

Finals stress relief care packets. Helping online learners enjoy the social and informal aspects of campus life is as important as providing seamless business processes to them. Online learners receive a stress relief package during final exam times, much like what on-campus students receive. Included in this care package are small snacks, a stress ball, and study tips. Online learners are provided a form through which they can sign up to receive the stress relief package through RooLife. After the first year, the college learned we needed to cap availability as the on-campus packages were limited and supplies were costly. In the first year, 108 stress relief packages were provided; in the subsequent year, 80 packages were provided.

Virtual career fairs. Career fairs allow students to network, explore job opportunities, and practice professional behavior. As Fontaine and Cook (2014) observed, online learners value career-related activities that support their professional development. To give online learners access to this resource, SUNY Canton contracted with CareerECO, a virtual recruiting and career platform, to host the fair at $3,000. Revenue generated via the student placement fee sponsored the activity.

Virtual clothing fairs. Professional clothing can be expensive for new college graduates and can influence their negotiating power during job interviews (Kraus & Mendes, 2014). Each year, SUNY Canton hosts a clothing fair on campus. Professional clothing is donated by local campus and community members and is free to students for their first job interview. To provide online learners with access to this resource, the college moved the fair online. Shopify served as the online retail host ($31/month), and student workers sorted each donation, prepared descriptions, and photographed and labeled the clothing. Then, a SKU number was assigned and all information was uploaded to Shopify. Clothing was shipped to the online learners and postcards on support services and other engagement opportunities were included in the packages. The cost of the Virtual Clothing Fair in 2018 was $1,926.18

Virtual study abroad fairs. Study abroad experiences have a positive impact on the development of 21st-century job skills, such as global competence (Farrugia & Sanger, 2017). Once again, the technology platform CareerECO was used. Campuses across the SUNY system signed up to showcase their study abroad programs with a "room" in which program information was available for students to browse. Online learners had the opportunity to explore study abroad opportunities in 72 countries.

Online learner engagement days. Online learner engagement days were created to parallel events happening on campus for SpringFest as a way to bolster a sense of belonging and campus affinity. Each fully online learner was mailed a package with various swag—just under 1,000 packages were mailed.

Varsity eSports teams. The eSports team, mirrored to look and feel like a varsity athletics team, was an effort to engage students in competitive e-gaming and provide opportunities for post-traditional athletes to participate in campus life. Discord, a chat-based social networking platform specifically marketed to gamers, was used to recruit online learners, and an exclusive online tournament was conducted in the online video game Fortnite. Enrollments in majors related to eSports grew by 120% between 2017 and 2019. While the entirety of this growth cannot be attributed exclusively to the addition of an eSports team, through student assessment, evidence shows this factored into the decision for many when selecting a college with these similar majors.

Pedagogy

Professional development is critical to helping faculty adapt their teaching to be delivered online (Darling-Hammond, Hyler, & Gardner, 2017). Professional development can help instructors learn to connect students to activities outside the classroom (e.g., internships and academic advising), design courses that promote student interactivity and enhance learning outcomes (Knapp, 2019), use several online pedagogies to increase student engagement (Poll, Widen, & Weller, 2014), and connect students to relevant cocurricular experiences that build communities (Kahu, 2013). In addition to professional development, pedagogical practices used to encourage student engagement included funding and an advising toolkit.

Funding. The provost's office supported online learner travel to the campus to present undergraduate research and participate in the Scholarly Activity Celebration. In-state awards (maximum $500 for travel expenses) and out-of-state awards (maximum $1,000 for travel expenses) were available. Applicants were required to be enrolled in all online classes, be matriculated at SUNY Canton or a recent December graduate, and agree to present their research at the

Scholarly Activities Celebration. Students were required to complete a travel stipend application and submit a letter of recommendation from their faculty advisor.

Advising toolkit. Consolidated electronic resources on how to advise online learners on using various technologies, applications, and software platforms to form connections were created as an advising toolkit.

Potential Challenges and Practical Solutions

Potential Challenge: When trying to be innovative and creative in engaging online learners in student support services, you may get pushback from students that they do not want to be involved in the larger campus community.

Practical Solution: Explain to stakeholders what online learners do or do not want for cocurricular activities cannot be assumed.

Practical Solution: Survey students and continually seek student feedback.

Practical Solution: Dedicate a specific staff member (student life coordinator for online learners) to coordinate efforts.

Potential Challenge: Allocating resources to meet the needs of engaging online learners may require coordination with several campuses offices to ensure success.

Practical Solution: Meet with stakeholders to develop a budget model. In many cases, online learners are paying the same fees as campus-based students, and a portion of those fees could be realigned to support online learner success and engagement efforts.

Practical Solution: Work with campus offices that are providing support services to navigate how those services might best serve online learners without a tremendous increase in cost.

Practical Solution: Seek out additional funding opportunities, such as grants, to supplement the costs of providing engagement and success strategies to online learners.

Lessons Learned and Next Steps

Using the TIP method for online learner engagement, student affairs practitioners can redefine their relationship with online learners. A student engagement survey administered to online learners in fall 2017 (response rate 35%) provided insight into the needs of online learners and their engagement experiences. Students from the survey commented they felt "just as important" as face-to-face students when offered access to activities, services, and supports of value to them. The survey also revealed online learners:

- want to feel "connected."
- desire opportunities to get involved.
- may not want to participate in meetings, yet they want to know they have representation (e.g., Student Government Association Student Online Learning Advisory Board).
- value career-related activities the most.
- love swag!
- prefer to communicate through a dedicated listserv and/or learning management system announcements as opposed to social media.

Conclusion

Student affairs professionals are challenged to provide opportunities for online learners to learn outside the classroom and activities that enhance both academic and social, personal, and professional growth. This requires creatively exploring new approaches and strategies and rethinking the role of student affairs in the changing landscape of higher education. The TIP method for online learner engagement offers practitioners a way to address this challenge through the use technology, innovation, and pedagogy.

? Questions for Reflection

- Do the needs of students differ because of their instructional modality?
- What assumptions do you have about the needs of online learners? How might you explore those assumptions?
- How might you creatively provide opportunities of value to online learners?
- How do you cultivate online learners as future alumni?

References

Ali, A., & Smith, D. T. (2015). Comparing social isolation effects on students attrition in online versus face-to-face courses in computer literacy. *Issues in Informing Science and Information Technology, 12*, 11–20. Retrieved from http://iisit.org/Vol12/IISITv12p011-020Ali1784.pdf

Berry, S. (2019). Teaching to connect: Community-building strategies for the virtual classroom. *Online Learning, 23*(1). doi:10.24059/olj.v23i1.1425

Best Colleges. (2019). *2019 online education trends report.* Retrieved from https://www.bestcolleges.com/perspectives/annual-trends-in-online-education

Blumenstyk, G. (2018, June 13). What do online students want? 3 findings from a new survey offer some clues. *The Chronicle of Higher Education.* Retrieved from https://www.chronicle.com/article/what-do-online-students-want-/243653

Boston, W. E., & Ice, P. (2011). Assessing retention in online learning: An administrative perspective. *Online Journal of Distance Learning Administration, 14*(2). Retrieved from https://www.learntechlib.org/p/52638

Clinefelter, D., & Aslanian, C. (2015). *Online college students 2015.* Retrieved from Learning House website: https://www.learninghouse.com/knowledge-center/research-reports/ocs2015-report

Darling-Hammond, L., Hyler, M. E., & Gardner, M. (2017). *Effective teacher professional development.* Retrieved from the Learning Policy Institute website: https://learningpolicyinstitute.org/product/effective-teacher-professional-development-report

Farrugia, C., & Sanger, J. (2017). *Gaining an employment edge: The impact of study abroad on 21st century skills & career prospects in the United States.* New York, NY: Institute of International Education.

Ferdman, B. M., & Deane, B. (2014). *Diversity at work: The practice of inclusion.* San Francisco, CA: Jossey-Bass.

Fredericksen, E. E. (2017). A national study of online learning leaders in U.S. higher education. *Online Learning, 21*(2). doi:10.24059/olj.v21i2.1164

Fontaine, S. J., & Cook, S. M. (2014). Co-curricular engagement for non-traditional online learners. *Online Journal of Distance Learning Administration, 17*(3). Retrieved from https://www.learntechlib.org/p/152968

Kahu, R. E. (2013). Framing student engagement in higher education. *Studies in Higher Education, 38*, 758–773. doi:10.1080/03075079.2011.598505

Kak, S. (2018, January 9). Universities must prepare for a technology-enabled future. *The Conversation.* Retrieved from http://theconversation.com/universities-must-prepare-for-a-technology-enabled-future-89354

Kebritchi, M., Lipschuetz, A., & Santiague, L. (2017). Issues and challenges for teaching successful online courses in higher education. *Journal of Educational Technology Systems, 46*, 4–29. doi:10.1177/0047239516661713

Knapp, N. (2019). An interactive session on increasing peer interaction in online classes. In *Proceedings: 11th Annual Conference on Higher Education Pedagogy* (pp. 40–41). Retrieved from http://hdl.handle.net/10919/88510

Kotter, J. P. (1996). *John P. Kotter on what leaders really do*. Boston, MA: Harvard Business School Press.

Kraus, M. W., & Mendes, W. B. (2014). Supplemental material for sartorial symbols of social class elicit class-consistent behavioral and physiological responses: A dyadic approach. *Journal of Experimental Psychology: General, 143*, 2330–2340. doi:10.1037/xge0000023.supp

Kruger, K., & Jarrat, D. (2018, December 16). Student affairs goes digital: Translating student support to the world of online learning. *Diverse: Issues in Higher Education*. Retrieved from https://diverseeducation.com/article/134371

Ladd, H., Reynolds, S., & Selingo, J. J. (n.d.). *The differentiated university: Recognizing the diverse needs of today's students* (Part I). Retrieved from https://cdn.ey.com/parthenon/pdf/perspectives/4.4.2-The-Differentiated-University-Part-I-1-disclaimer.pdf

Lederman, D. (2018, November 7). Online education ascends [Blog post]. *Inside Higher Ed*. Retrieved from https://www.insidehighered.com/digital-learning/article/2018/11/07/new-data-online-enrollments-grow-and-share-overall-enrollment

McKeown, K. D. (2012). *Can online learning reproduce the full college experience?* (Center for Policy Innovation Discussion Paper No. 3). Retrieved from The Heritage Foundation website: https://www.heritage.org/education/report/can-online-learning-reproduce-the-full-college-experience

Poll, K., Widen, J., & Weller, S. (2014). Six instructional best practices for online engagement and retention. *Journal of Online Doctoral Education, 1*, 56–72. Retrieved from https://ecommons.luc.edu/english_facpubs/30

Rovai, A. P., & Wighting, M. J. (2005). Feelings of alienation and community among higher education students in a virtual classroom. *The Internet and Higher Education, 8*, 97–110. doi:10.1016/j.iheduc.2005.03.001

Scalzo, K. A. (2018). *Open SUNY 2018 annual impact report*. Retrieved from https://innovate.suny.edu/opensuny/wp-content/uploads/2019/03/Open-SUNY-Annual-Impact-Report.pdf

Seaman, J., Allen, E., & Seaman, J. (2018). *Grade increase: Tracking distance education in the United States*. Retrieved from Online Learning Consortium website: https://onlinelearningconsortium.org/read/grade-increase-tracking-distance-education-united-states

Stoller, E. (2013, March 5). Can we bridge the schism? Online learners and student affairs [Blog post]. *Inside Higher Ed*. Retrieved from https://www.insidehighered.com/blogs/student-affairs-and-technology/can-we-bridge-schism-online-learners-and-student-affairs

Stoller, E. (2019, March 28). Online education – The forgotten frontier in student affairs [Blog post]. *Inside Higher Ed*. Retrieved from https://www.insidehighered.com/blogs/student-affairs-and-technology/online-education-forgotten-frontier-student-affairs

SUNY Canton Office of Institutional Research. (2018). [Fall demographic trends.] Unpublished raw data.

Terras, K., Leggio, J., & Phillips, A. (2015). Disability accommodations in online courses: The graduate student experience. *Journal of Postsecondary Education and Disability, 28*, 329–340. Retrieved from https://www.ahead.org/professional-resources/publications/jped

Toufaily, E., Zalan, T., & Lee, D. (2018). What do learners value in online education? An emerging market perspective. e-*Journal of Business Education & Scholarship of Teaching, 12*, 24–39. Retrieved from https://files.eric.ed.gov/fulltext/EJ1193341.pdf

Westra, K. (2018, October 29). Online student services: What, where, who, when, how, and most importantly, why. *EDUCAUSE Review*. Retrieved from https://er.educause.edu/articles/2018/10/online-student-services-what-where-who-when-how-and-most-importantly-why

Wingo, N. P., Ivankova, N. V., & Moss, J. A. (2017). Faculty perceptions about teaching online: Exploring the literature using the technology acceptance model as an organizing framework. *Online Learning, 21*(1). doi:10.24059/olj.v21i1.761

CHAPTER 14

Online Learner Cocurricular Engagement:
An Integrative Learning Program Case Study

Hilary Landorf and L. Bahia Simons-Lane

INTEGRATIVE LEARNING OFTEN occurs when students address real-world problems that are "complex, difficult to describe, require a multi-perspective analysis and offer multiple solutions" (Association of American Colleges and Universities & The Carnegie Foundation for the Advancement of Teaching, 2004, p. 1). Cocurricular programs play an essential role in integrative learning, providing students with formal and informal opportunities to connect new and existing knowledge, skills, and experiences and apply them to local, national, or global issues. With one third of college students taking at least one fully online course during their undergraduate education (Gebbia, 2018), knowing how integrative learning experiences are carried out for online learners is essential.

The purpose of this chapter is to provide strategies for student affairs professionals to design cocurricular activities for online learners within the context of an integrative learning program. Through the lens of a case study on engaging fully online learners in cocurricular activities as part of an integrative learning program, the Excellence in Global Learning Medallion at Florida International University (FIU), readers will gain an understanding of the close relationship between integrative and global learning, acquire the necessary tools to adapt a face-to-face integrative learning program to the online sphere, learn about several innovative online cocurricular activities, and gain awareness of the challenges and potential solutions related to adapting integrative learning experiences for online learners.

Online and Global Learning at Florida International University

At FIU, online learning is an important mode of course delivery. The university is Miami's first and only public research institution, with a student population of over 58,000, and one of the 10 largest higher education institutions in the United States. The FIU undergraduate student is typically a first- or second-generation U.S. citizen, along with being a first-generation college student who lives at home and is responsible for caring for family members, holding a full-time job, and carrying a full course load. Students at FIU increasingly depend on online learning to further their education while they manage the other areas in their life. In spring 2019, FIU enrolled 5,252 fully online learners, which represents 10% of the total student population that semester. This was an increase of over 600 students from the previous year. Online learning is also prominent in FIU's current strategic plan, *FIUBeyondPossible2020*; whereas, in 2014, FIU delivered 25% of its courses online, the stated goal for 2020 is to increase the number of online courses delivered to 40% (FIU, 2015).

Along with FIU's commitment to providing access and success to all students by offering all modes of course delivery, the university is just as committed to global learning. The university defines global learning as "the process of diverse people collaboratively analyzing and addressing complex issues that transcend borders" (as cited in Landorf & Doscher, 2015, p. 24). FIU provides all undergraduates with multiple opportunities to engage in global learning in courses and in cocurricular activities for students to acquire knowledge of the interrelatedness of local, national, and global issues; the ability to analyze issues from multiple perspectives; and the willingness to engage in local, global, international, and intercultural problem solving. Both global learning and integrative learning depend on students' engagement in complex problem solving inside and outside the classroom. For this reason, the focus of this chapter is on creating online cocurricular activities in the context of a global learning initiative at FIU. Student affairs practitioners at other institutions who are seeking to engage their online learners could implement the strategies, ideas, and overall program structure presented in this chapter.

Online Expansion of the Global Learning Medallion

In 2014, the Office of Global Learning Initiatives (OGLI) implemented the Excellence in Global Learning Medallion (GLM), a graduation honor open to all undergraduates in all academic programs. The GLM expands FIU's commitment to students' global and integrative learning implemented by the Global Learning for Global Citizenship initiative. The GLM is nonselective and allows students to develop personalized integrative global learning pathways across curricular and cocurricular programs. Since students self-select into the GLM, and the requirements are personalized according to their interests and schedules, this program suits the customizability online learners need.

Overview

The goal of the GLM is to give students a pathway to collaborate with diverse others and in multiple environments where they can plant deep global learning roots and thrive as global citizens. The GLM is awarded to "students who have completed an extensive curriculum and cocurriculum designed to enhance global awareness, global perspective, and an attitude of global engagement" (FIU Global Learning, 2019, para. 1). Students must complete the following requirements to earn a GLM:

- Possess a minimum of a 3.0 grade point average at the time of graduation;
- Complete four global learning courses with a grade of C or above;
- Accrue 20 activity points by participating in approved global learning activities;
- Complete a global learning capstone requirement consisting of one or more of the following: a semester-long study abroad, foreign language study, a semester-long internship, or research on a globally focused topic; and
- Create an online portfolio reflecting on global learning experiences.

Enrollment

The program manager for the OGLI facilitates the GLM, guiding the students from sign-up to completion. Students' GLM progress is tracked using a customer relationship management (CRM) software tool called Zoho. CRM systems are being used in higher education to provide a consolidated view of student information (Polona & Iztok, 2018; Rigo, Pedron, Caldeira, & Silva de Araujo, 2016; Seeman & O'Hara, 2006). To virtually log their accomplishments from anywhere around the world, students use a form on the OGLI website (http://goglobal.fiu.edu) that adds their accomplishments to Zoho. If students want to view their GLM progress, the program manager pulls a report in Zoho and electronically sends it to the student.

Enrollment for the GLM is online for all students. To enroll, students fill out a form on the OGLI website. Once a student enrolls, they receive an automated e-mail welcoming them to the GLM program with links to videos that explain the process of logging the requirements. The introductory e-mail also gives the student other essential information about the GLM, such as the program manager's contact information and guidelines on how to complete each of the GLM requirements.

Expansion to Online Learners

Former program manager Eric Feldman implemented the expansion of the GLM to online learners in 2016. In an interview with the authors of this chapter, Feldman, who is now associate director of student success and academic programs at FIU's office in Washington, D.C., provided much of the content for this case study. Feldman saw the need to calibrate the GLM for fully online learners when they first started signing up for the program in 2015. It was then he realized most of the activity points entailed students physically attending events at FIU's Modesto A. Maidique campus in Miami, although online learners could already meet the other requirements. Online learners could obtain five of the activity points by holding a club leadership position, but the remaining 15 would be next to impossible to acquire if the student did not have physical access to campus events. Therefore, the bulk of the changes needed for online learners to complete the GLM addressed how online learners could acquire activity points.

Technology and Innovative Tools	
Online learning management systems	
Blackboard	*How to use:* Adopt an LMS with which your students are already familiar. Work with your institution to use the system already in place at your campus.
Canvas	
Customer relationship management systems	
Salesforce	*How to use:* Information about students' participation in programs can be tracked through customer relationship management systems.
Zoho	
E-mail marketing systems	
Campaign Monitor	*How to use:* E-mail marketing systems allow you to reach many students at the same time and track which content they are clicking on and interacting with the most.
Constant Contact	
MailChimp	
Vertical Response	
Online activity analytics	
Data from learning management systems	*How to use:* Check these sources of analytics regularly to determine how students are accessing information about programs.
Data from social media	
E-mail marketing system analytics	
Google Analytics	

Engaging in the Activity Online

Online learners earn activity points by participating in cocurricular experiences. Activities are worth one or five points, depending on the type of activity and duration. One-point activities typically consist of attending a seminar or presentation on a global issue. Five points are earned by participation in activities that represent longer term commitments, including holding a leadership role in a student club, participating in a service trip, or completing a short-term study abroad experience.

The OGLI announces cocurricular opportunities to all students, including those who are fully online, via its weekly e-newsletter. Opportunities particularly suited to online learners are highlighted to ensure students know they are part of the campus community, regardless of where they take their courses, and can participate in this cocurricular integrative learning experience. One example is of an online learner who recently returned from a fully paid Hillel-sponsored service trip to Israel she discovered via the GLM newsletter (A. Nelson, personal communication, June 20, 2019). The Paper Airplanes English Teaching program is another example of an integrative learning experience in which online learners have participated. Paper Airplanes (2019) is a nonprofit organization that uses video-conferencing technology to connect volunteer tutors with students affected by conflict. Interested online learners submit an application, and, if selected, they complete a short training prior to being matched with a student.

Online learners have also taken on club leadership roles, such as the Global Engagement Coordinator for Peace Corps Prep committee, which involves creating relationships with community partners and reaching out to students to promote involvement in Peace Corps Prep activities. In roles like this, online learners engage with community partners and the Peace Corps Prep committee using e-mail, phone, and online video calls.

The OGLI program manager must preapprove all 1-point opportunities. To accommodate fully online learners earning activity points, the program manager began to offer approved virtual events to fulfill this requirement. This includes viewing and writing reflections on videos of approved on-campus events. Preapproved events include 10 years of recordings of the Tuesday Times Roundtables facilitated by the OGLI and supported by *The New York Times*, as well as recordings of events and seminars offered by the Steven J. Green School of International and Public Affairs. To verify participation in these activities, GLM students who are on campus can sign in at the event or submit a photo of themselves at the event. Fully online learners may submit a screenshot as proof of attendance for a streaming event or submit a photo of themselves at an event they physically attend in their region.

To expand the offerings that meet the activity point component, the program manager posts online activities that meet the requirements, including webinars, Woke Wednesdays live streaming Instagram show, and Common Ground for Action Online Forums, hosted by the Kettering Foundation. Students are often surprised by how engaging an online discussion can be. Online learners also have the ability to suggest off-campus activities to meet the GLM requirements the program manager may approve. There are multiple ways to meet the activity criteria, so all students have enough opportunities to meet the requirements.

To facilitate the activity point experience for online learners, FIU uses an online learning management system (LMS), Canvas, which is the same platform used campuswide for all FIU online courses. The program manager is the instructional designer of the course, so they design content, message boards, and all other aspects of the course. The GLM program is a noncredit bearing, non-term-associated course in Canvas, so it remains live for the duration of the student's education at FIU. While activity points for online learners are logged using Canvas, all students log their other requirements using the website form that links to Zoho.

The ePortfolio and Capstone

The capstone consists of a research project, four foreign language classes, a study abroad experience lasting more than 20 days, or a globally focused internship. All of these requirements can be completed virtually or in the area where the online learner is located. Online learners can work virtually with a faculty mentor on their research project, take foreign language courses online, and find an internship near where they live. The final requirement is the creation of an online portfolio called the ePortfolio, which is due by the end of the semester the student graduates. The Go Global website provides a comprehensive guide to the ePortfolio requirements and links to the ePortfolios of all previous GLM graduates.

Students are instructed to choose the audience for the ePortfolio, select a website builder, document their experience with the GLM, reflect on their experiences, and use the ePortfolio to market themselves. If students need help with their ePortfolio, the program manager is available to provide support. Online learners connect with the program manager via e-mail or phone. The students may use any free website builder to create their ePortfolio, which should include photos and descriptions of all 5-point experiences, up to three selected 1-point experiences, sample work from global learning courses, and a written reflection on the GLM experience. The ePortfolio is an opportunity for students to market themselves to potential employers, and, as such, students are encouraged to include a résumé and contact information.

The GLM experience culminates in a special graduation award ceremony that brings together GLM students, family, friends, and community partners. In a formal ceremony, the executive director of the OGLI personally hands out the decorative medallion that is given to recognize students for their achievements. Using virtual meeting technology such as Zoom or Skype, online learners who earn the GLM can join the ceremony. Students may also designate a faculty or staff member to accept the medallion for them while they are acknowledged on the video screen.

Applying a Model of Student Engagement to an Online Integrative Learning Program

Research results clearly indicate college students' participation in cocurricular activities can strongly impact student persistence and retention(Bergen-Cico & Viscomi, 2013; Hart, 2012; Wyatt, 2011).

Availability of support and perceived connection to the institution are two key factors of persistence and retention for online learners (Calhoun, Santos-Green, & Burke, 2017). Many studies have also supported Tinto's (1997) groundbreaking work showing student involvement—often called student engagement—positively impacts student retention and success for all student groups (Bonet & Walters, 2016; Deil-Amen, 2011; Karp, Hughes, & O'Gara, 2011; Kuh, Cruce, Shoup, Kinzie, & Gonyea, 2008).

For online learners, participating in cocurricular activities is challenging due to the lack of geographic access and time constraints. However, when these activities are designed deliberately to include online learners, they too reap the benefits associated with higher levels of involvement, particularly retention and increased academic performance (DeVito, 2016; Kahu, 2013). Integrative learning programs such as the GLM are designed to create a sense of accomplishment of personal goals and mastery of specific skills, which are primary persistence factors for online learners, as identified by Hart (2012) and Yang, Baldwin, and Snelson (2017).

Adapting a Four-Pronged Model for Student Engagement

To create and sustain pathways for the success of cocurricular global learning programs like the GLM, the OGLI uses an adaptation of a four-pronged model for student engagement that was developed in 2008 by a student affairs taskforce at Nova Southeastern University (Cooper, 2009). To bring about systemic change at Nova, the taskforce knew the model would have to be robust enough for all students to claim their unique identity, and, at the same time, one that would embrace and impact all students. The model has overlapping parts: involvement, identity, reciprocal support, and recognition. What follows is a brief presentation of this model, how the OGLI has used it with online learners in its GLM program, and how other colleges and universities can adapt this model for their online learners.

Involvement. This is the entry to developing student engagement and success. Involvement entails providing students with information and opportunities to introduce them to the social and intellectual life of the university. It also includes information about integrative learning—that is, clues to making essential connections between what students are learning in the classroom, in their activities and clubs, and in their personal lives. Involvement is the lifeblood of the online GLM program. It is how students learn about the program, gain activity points, and complete their capstone.

Identity. This entails facilitating engagement with groups, classes, and activities that celebrate students' uniqueness, as well as those that promote their sense of being part of a community. Online learners have less access to groups, classes, and activities, and it can be difficult for them to feel a sense of community at their university. The OGLI has found online learners earning the GLM are seeking ways to connect with FIU, and the GLM provides it for them. For example, when an online learner joins the GLM, the program manager sends the student a T-shirt with the FIU Global Learning logo to help create a sense of community. The program manager also promotes cocurricular activities to online learners to encourage involvement, like the opportunity to participate in the Paper Airplanes English Teaching program mentioned earlier.

Reciprocal support. Reciprocal support involves giving on-campus and online learners access to essential resources that promote their well-being, such as mental and physical health resources, disability services, and conflict resolution services. All students who participate in the GLM, including those who are fully online, advocate for the program themselves. Students share events with their peers, and perhaps, more importantly, invite their peers to sign up for the GLM and participate with them. These students become true advocates for global learning. In addition to the support GLM students give to one another, the OGLI program manager, in an advisory role, meets with every online GLM student multiple times via teleconference. In these meetings, the program manager recommends activities, internships, and scholarships tailored to the passions, interests, and professional goals of the particular student. Each student's career plans and pathways are also a topic of discussion throughout their participation in the program. In effect, the program manager becomes a mentor and one of the most important people in the students' lives. Online learners especially appreciate this personal connection. As Aleta Neilson, an online GLM student, wrote before her graduation, "You have been so instrumental in including us that we can never thank you enough!"

Recognition. This involves making sure deserving students not only receive awards, but that they also are given positive verbal feedback, that significant milestones in their academic careers are celebrated, and that various media are used to give wider attention to their accomplishments.

Considerations in Adapting Integrative Learning Experiences for Online Learners

There are many challenges in adapting an on-campus integrative learning program for online learners. Student affairs professionals should consider four key areas at the onset of adapting such a program for online learners. First, it is important to evaluate the potential program and consider whether the program requirements can be adapted for online learners, particularly the cocurricular experiences, and what areas need to change to accommodate those learners. Second, student affairs professionals should consider the available technology, which is essential for online learner participation. Third, it is important to secure departmental support to ensure the program is effectively implemented for online learners. Lastly, student affairs professionals must consider the form and substance of communication with online learners.

Tips for Getting Started

Before beginning to implement an integrated cocurricular program, take these actions to determine the feasibility.

♦ **Evaluate existing programs.** Evaluate potential programs for possible adaptions of requirements for online learners, particularly cocurricular experiences and areas needed to change to accommodate these learners.

♦ **Consider available technology.** Appropriate technology is essential for online learners to participate. Take the time to evaluate the technical resources available at your institution and those used by other colleges and universities you may be able to use as well.

♦ **Solicit support from institution leaders.** Speak with key departmental stakeholders early in the process to solidify support.

♦ **Decide how you will communicate with online learners.** Consider the form and substance of how you plan to communicate with online learners.

Evaluate Adaptability

The first step is to identify prospective programs that may be adapted for online learners. One clear indicator the program might be appropriate is if an integrative learning program exists, such as the GLM at FIU. The ability to make connections between what one is learning in the classroom, in cocurricular activities, and in one's personal life is a key element of integrative learning, and students who are attracted to such programs are usually those who have that ability. Another indicator, as in the case of the GLM at FIU, is if online learners are already signing up for the program.

Next, evaluate existing programs to determine which programs are adaptable to online learners. Is it possible for students to complete the requirements online? What needs to change to allow online learners to meet the requirements? It may be helpful to review other programs that have been adapted or created for online learners. Although this research is limited, there are examples in health services (Fontaine & Cook, 2014) on how to enhance online learner engagement using cocurricular activities (Burton, Chicone, & Ferebee, 2018). While there are no other global learning programs geared toward online learners of which the authors of this chapter are aware, we hope this case study provides you with inspiration for your own programs.

Consider Technology

Technology is the doorway to involvement for online learners. Once you have identified the best program to create or adapt, consider the available technology. Both on the student-user side and on the backend, access to technology will determine how accessible your program will be to online learners. The technology you use should move integrative online learning beyond the current state of text-based discussions while limiting the use of technology types to prevent an overburden on students to learn new platforms rather than academic content and skills (Calhoun & Santos-Green, 2015). First take stock of the technology available at your university. The OGLI uses the CRM software called Zoho to track student progress, the LMS software Canvas for online learners' activity points, and e-mail and social media to communicate with students.

The OGLI uses the same LMS used campuswide to provide a space for online learners to interact with GLM requirements. Canvas is a system already available at FIU, and students are familiar with it because they use it for coursework. The OGLI chose the CRM Zoho to track all students' progress due to its affordability and ease of use. Since this is a new frontier, there may not be ideal technology available for the needs of an online program that includes cocurricular learning. FIU was not able to find any one existing platform to track GLM students' progress and activity points and give them access to view their progress.

Although the technology OGLI uses for the GLM is not perfect, FIU has made it work due to the determination and perseverance of the program manager and the students. Use the technology available at the moment of implementation, while evaluating and improving incrementally. FIU recently implemented new technology for cocurricular clubs so students can see everything they have done beyond the classroom. The OGLI is currently evaluating how to integrate the use of this new technology for students to see their GLM progress in their cocurricular activities and then how to link this technology to Zoho. This new technology would allow students to track their own progress toward completion of the GLM.

Establish Departmental Support

Departmental support and cross-department collaboration are essential components to implementing cocurricular experiences for online learners. When the GLM was implemented in 2014, full support from the OGLI was vital for its success. The OGLI provided funding for a full-time program manager and a part-time graduate assistant. As the core staff of the GLM program, the program manager and graduate assistant have been responsible for building relationships with other departments. The OGLI also provided funding for the physical medallions, Zoho, and all other program needs. When the GLM was adapted for online learners, the OGLI continued to provide the same level of support for that effort. As program adaptations are considered to accommodate online learners, ensure departmental support exists.

Adding online components to any program also requires collaboration from the department responsible for online courses and campus technology. When the online GLM was implemented, the OGLI worked with FIU Online, which oversees online learners and the technology they use, to establish the noncredit bearing, non-term-associated course online learners use to track their activity points. During the development phase, FIU Online provided essential support and guidance. The program manager worked closely with FIU Online to align the needs of the OGLI with the online course platform capabilities. In adapting a program for online learners, student affairs professionals will need to work with their institution's online department.

Potential Challenges and Practical Solutions

Implementing an online cocurricular learning program can be challenging, and you may run into difficulties. Consider the following common challenges and recommended solutions:

Potential Challenge: Creating an interactive online community. Having an online system with the ability to both collect and disseminate opportunities for students, and one in which students can communicate with one another, is quite challenging.

> **Practical Solution:** Conduct a thorough audit of information technology (IT) resources at your institution. You may have interactive online community tools of which you are not aware. Use the online tools currently in use at your institution, continuously evaluate the effectiveness of your online community tools, and adapt as you and your students learn.

Potential Challenge: Facilitating communication with students. What, where, and how students receive communication is a quickly changing landscape. To provide students with needed information, it is essential to keep up with their communication preferences.

> **Practical Solution:** Regularly poll students about their communication preferences by creating and disseminating surveys with a few key questions about the communications software students prefer to use.

Potential Challenge: Establishing interdepartment collaboration. Silos are a well-known and persistent problem at every institution of higher education. Yet, collaboration with your online learning and IT departments is essential to successfully adapt your cocurricular activities for online learners.

> **Practical Solution:** Establish communication with your online learning and IT departments early on in the process of adapting your program for online learners. If you have an advisory committee, include members of your online learning and IT departments. Keep your online learning and IT departments apprised of the progress, challenges, and changes in your program. Continuous communication is key to your success and to the success of your institution!

Facilitate Communication

Communication with online learners is another area to consider in implementing your integrated cocurricular program for online learners. Ultimately, students can only fully participate if they know what to do. Department staff facilitating programs like the GLM should ask themselves how students are engaging with their programs. Are they using the online course system used by the institution? Do they read the e-mails they receive about the program? Are they using social media to engage with the program content?

Fortunately, the tools to track the "what" and "where" of student engagement online are now quite robust. One of the primary methods the OGLI uses to communicate with students participating in the GLM is MailChimp. MailChimp is an online system for e-mail marketing used by many organizations. Similar products include Constant Contact, Vertical Response, and Campaign Monitor. These systems provide analytics about who opens an e-mail, who clicks on the links in the e-mail, and which links in the e-mail get the most clicks. The OGLI has found information on jobs, internships, and fellowships that pay get the most clicks. The analytics these systems provide will indicate the type of content most desired by your particular student population.

In addition to using e-mail analytics, the OGLI recommends using Google Analytics to track what works and to determine where students are engaging with the materials used to promote the program and its activities. It is possible to apply Google Analytics to your website and social media accounts to glean information about where the most activity is occurring. Google Analytics can provide insight into which sites students are using, whether it is a program website, Facebook, Instagram, or any other site. Since the popularity of different sites changes over time, it is imperative to monitor and constantly evaluate your communications strategy to ensure success.

Conclusion

This chapter provided an example of how an on-campus integrative learning program can be adapted to the needs of online learners. Like all students, students pursuing their education in a fully online format want to be involved and feel a part of their institution, and they deserve the same support and recognition for their accomplishments as students who are physically on campus. In a recent interview for *FIU News*, Aleta Neilson, a fully online GLM graduate, expressed the value of a successful online program:

> One of the wonderful things about online classes and global learning programs, which allow proper online communication and interaction between faculty and students like FIU does, is that you first get to know people for who they are inside, their unique personalities and minds, instead of by superficial appearances. This translates well to appreciating that we are all so much more than we can sum up at first glance and shatters many stereotypes about those who may outwardly look different from us. . . . The very values that inspired me to come here also drew me into the desire to get even deeper into global learning. (as cited in Gamarra, 2019, para. 7)

We hope this chapter has inspired you to think creatively about how programs at your institution can be adapted to serve this growing student population.

? Questions for Reflection

- What are your goals for making your program accessible to online learners?
- Is your program suitable for adaptation to online learners?
- What human, financial, physical, and information technology resources are available to you? If you do not have the adequate resources, how can you acquire them?

References

Association of American Colleges and Universities & The Carnegie Foundation for the Advancement of Teaching. (2004). *A statement on integrative learning.* Retrieved from http://gallery.carnegiefoundation.org/ilp/uploads/ilp_statement.pdf

Bonet, G., & Walters, B. (2016). High impact practices: Student engagement and retention. *College Student Journal, 50,* 224–235. Retrieved from https://academicworks.cuny.edu/cgi/viewcontent.cgi?article=1101&context=kb_pubs

Bergen-Cico, D., & Viscomi, J. (2013). Exploring the association between campus co-curricular involvement and academic achievement. *Journal of College Student Retention: Research, Theory & Practice, 14,* 329–343. doi:10.2190/CS.14.3.c

Burton, T., Chicone, R., & Ferebee, S. (2018). Enhancing online student engagement with extracurricular activities. *Issues in Information Systems, 19,* 202–211. Retrieved from http://www.iacis.org/iis/2018/3_iis_2018_202-211.pdf

Calhoun, D. W., & Santos Green, L. (2015). Utilizing online learning communities in student affairs. In M. Benjamin (Ed.), *Learning communities from start to finish* (New Directions for Student Services, No. 149, pp. 55–66). San Francisco: CA: Jossey-Bass. doi:10.1002/ss.20117

Calhoun, D. W., Santos-Green, L., & Burke, P. (2017). Online learners and technology: A gap in higher education and student affairs professional preparation. *Quarterly Review of Distance Education, 18,* 45–61.

Cooper, R. (2009). Constructing belonging in a diverse campus community. *Journal of College & Character, 10,* 1–10. doi:10.2202/1940-1639.1085

Deil-Amen, R. (2011). Socio-academic integrative moments: Rethinking academic and social integration among two-year college students in career related programs. *Journal of Higher Education, 82,* 54–91. doi:10.1080/00221546.2011.11779085

DeVito, M. (2016). *Factors influencing student engagement* (Unpublished certificate of advanced study thesis). Retrieved from http://digitalcommons.sacredheart.edu/edl/11

Florida International University. (2015). *FIU Beyond Possible2020.* Retrieved from https://stratplan.fiu.edu/docs/Strategic%20Plan.pdf

Florida International University Global Learning. (2019). Earn a prestigious global distinction. Retrieved from https://goglobal.fiu.edu/medallion

Fontaine, S. J., & Cook, S. M. (2014). Co-curricular engagement for non-traditional online learners. *Online Journal of Distance Learning Administration, 17,* 201–209. Retrieved from https://www.learntechlib.org/p/152968

Gamarra, I. (2019, May 24). Online student awarded global learning medallion and Peace Corps Prep certificate. *FIU News.* Retrieved from https://news.fiu.edu/2019/05/online-student-awarded-global-learning-medallion-peace-corps-prep-certificate

Gebbia, R. (2018, March 29). Transforming higher education for the digital age [Blog post]. *ATANEblog.* Retrieved from https://blog.ataneconsulting.com/2018/03/29/transforming-higher-education-for-the-digital-age-2

Hart, C. (2012). Factors associated with student persistence in an online program of study: A review of the literature. *Journal of Interactive Online Learning, 11,* 19–42. Retrieved from http://www.ncolr.org/jiol/issues/pdf/11.1.2.pdf

Kahu, E. R. (2013). Framing student engagement in higher education. *Studies in Higher Education, 38,* 758–773. doi:10.1080/03075079.2011.598505

Karp, M. M., Hughes, K. L., & O'Gara, L. (2011). An exploration of Tinto's integration framework for community college students. *Journal of College Student Retention: Research, Theory & Practice, 12,* 69–86. doi:10.2190/CS.12.1.e

Kuh, G. D., Cruce, T. M., Shoup, R., Kinzie, J., & Gonyea, R. M. (2008). Unmasking the effects of student engagement on first-year college grades and persistence. *Journal of Higher Education, 79,* 540–563. doi:10.1080/00221546.2008.11772116

Landorf, H., & Doscher, S. P. (2015). Defining global learning at Florida International University. *Diversity and Democracy, 18*, 24–25. Retrieved from the Association of American Colleges & Universities website: https://www.aacu.org/diversitydemocracy/2015/summer/landorf

Paper Airplanes. (2019). Our mission. Retrieved from https://www.paper-airplanes.org

Polona, S., & Iztok, P. (2018). *The concept of customer relationship management (CRM) in higher education.* Paper presented at the 27th International Scientific Conference on Economic and Social Development, Rome, Italy.

Rigo, G.-E., Pedron, C., Caldeira, M., & Silva de Araujo, C. C. (2016). CRM adoption in a higher education institution. *Journal of Information Systems and Technology Management, 13*, 45–60. doi:10.4301/S180717752016000100003

Seeman, E. D., & O'Hara, M. (2006). Customer relationship management in higher education: Using information systems to improve the student-school relationship. *Campus-Wide Information Systems, 23*, 24–34. doi:10.1108/10650740610639714

Tinto, V. (1997). Classrooms as communities: Exploring the educational character of student persistence. *Journal of Higher Education, 68*, 599–623. doi:10.1080/00221546.1997.11779003

Wyatt, L. G. (2011). Nontraditional student engagement: Increasing adult student success and retention. *Journal of Continuing Higher Education, 59*, 10–20. doi:10.1080/07377363.2011.544977

Yang, D., Baldwin, S., & Snelson, C. (2017). Persistence factors revealed: Students' reflections on completing a fully online program. *Distance Education, 38*, 23–36. doi:10.1080/01587919.2017.1299561

CHAPTER 15

Creatively Advising Online Learners:

Encouraging 21st-Century Students to Connect, Network, and Engage in Virtual Settings

Arielle Norment

GROWING NUMBERS OF colleges and universities are offering distance education, and online learners continue to fill virtual classrooms and communities. With this influx of online learners, researchers are now encouraging student affairs professionals, including academic advisors, to switch their focus from primarily supporting traditional on-campus students to also incorporating the support of online learners as well (Jenkins, 2018; Ohrablo, 2016; Redmond, Heffernan, Abawi, Brown, & Henderson, 2018).However, online learners, who have a different set of needs than traditional on-campus students, are still considered a new population for many academic advisors to work with in a supportive role, as many institutions are not recognizing a requirement to directly advise these students (Schroeder & Terras, 2015). Moreover, "many [advisors] ignore the unique characteristics of adult [online] learners and rarely address student groups independently"(Schroeder & Terras, 2015, p. 42). Therefore, there is a critical need to advance advising practices to meet these new learner demands, and of equal importance is academic advisors understanding how to effectively advise, support, and develop this growing population (Ohrablo, 2016).

This chapter focuses on how to enhance online learners' college experiences through the creative and effective use of various technology tools in the advising process. The use of these tools and resources is examined specifically for the virtual academic advisor. Best practices and strategies for how to cultivate relationships with students and retain students who learn at a distance, while guiding them through their academic journey, are also discussed.

Defining Academic Advising

Winston, Enders, and Miller (1982) defined *academic advising* as:

A developmental process which assists students in the clarification of their life/career goals and in the development of educational plans for the realization of these goals. It is a decision-making process by which students realize their maximum educational potential through communication and information exchanges; it is ongoing, multifaceted, and the responsibility of both student and advisor. The advisor serves as a facilitator of communication, a coordinator of learning experiences through course and career planning and academic progress review, and an agent of referral to other campus agencies as necessary. (para. 6)

Distance advising is defined as "a minimum set of core services relating to academic advising which assist distance learners in identifying and achieving their maximum educational potential" (Varney, 2009, para. 3). Academic advising highly benefits the success of students who learn at a distance. As a formal link between the higher education institution, the academic department, and the student (Jenkins, 2018; Vianden & Barlow, 2015), advising should be valued for all online learners.

High Touch From a Distance

Colleges and universities across the United States are increasing their online presence, with 15% of students completing their coursework completely online in 2016, and 17% of students taking at least one online or hybrid course in combination with in-person coursework (Redmond et al., 2018; Seaman, Allen, & Seaman, 2018). Similar to on-campus learners, online learners require and benefit greatly from *high touch* advising, where students are fully supported, provided personalized contact, encouraged, and made aware of support services/resources on a continuous basis (Bonk & Khoo, 2014; Ohrablo, 2016; Varney, 2009). However, many advisors fear or struggle with the thought of advising virtually. According to Sandeen and Barr (2006), "A student can enroll, participate in classes, conduct research, take examinations, use the library, and graduate through an online setting, without ever having to set foot on a traditional college campus" (p. 107). With this knowledge, student affairs professionals need to provide all student populations with the skills and resources to be academically successful in virtual settings while enrolled at their institutions. Specifically, redefining the role of advising for students in online settings is important, as this support is a critical component for the academic success of fully online learners (Jenkins, 2018). Designing an advising strategy that ensures success for each student from the point of enrollment to graduation is a challenging yet essential everyday responsibility.

Using Student Development Theory and Models to Support Online Learners

As a formal link between the institution, the academic department, and the student (Jenkins, 2018; Vianden & Barlow, 2015), distance advisors can use higher education theory and educational models to replicate face-to-face student-advisor relationships and services at a distance while also implementing innovative approaches to support the unique characteristics of distance learners (Bonk & Khoo, 2014; Ohrablo, 2016; Steele, 2005). For example, for on-campus in-person student advising, advisors take into consideration students' needs, educational preparedness, motivation levels, and even situational factors (e.g., family support, income, age, location, disabilities) to determine how to best support the learner.

For online student advising, advisors should take these same considerations into account prior to holding advising sessions, as well as learners' reasons for seeking online education. The reasons for deciding to take online courses vary from student to student and include flexibility and convenience in course offerings due to demanding work schedules, affordability of online courses, emotional well-being, learning preferences, interest in career advancement while working (real-time learning), decrease in commuting cost, or technical skill improvement opportunities, to name a few (Schroeder & Terras, 2015). The goals of advising, however, should remain the same for all students, while allowing adjustments or accommodations for students based on wherever they are (Ohrablo, 2016).

Inclusive Student Services Process Model

Floyd and Casey-Powell's (2004) inclusive student services process model was formulated from Miller and Prince's (1976) student development process model and includes five phases of student support services for both on-campus and online learners. These five phases include: (a) the learner intake phase (admissions and orientation), (b) the learner intervention phase (self-development and independent learning), (c) the learner support phase (academic advising and instructional support), (d) the learner transition phase (personal and professional transitions), and (e) the measurement phase (evaluation of success and feedback for improvement areas). One way to ensure student services are inclusive of all learners is for academic advisors to prepare themselves to support students at each of these phases.

As an example, academic advisors can highlight the first phase by collaborating with the admissions and recruitment departments to set up virtual information sessions or program open houses. This phase can also include student onboarding opportunities through virtual orientation sessions and initial telephone or video conference calls to welcome new students to the institution.

For the second phase, academic advisors can provide effective and efficient mentoring and guidance to each student in the advisor's caseload. This can include discussing and setting personal, professional, and educational goals with individual students and directing students to appropriate student support services provided by the campus in virtual settings.

The third phase can be accomplished through virtual advising office hours where students can speak with advisors one on one, plan out their individualized plans of study, and review academic strategies related to success in online classrooms. Additionally, academic advisors can lead departmental academic success workshops for online learners through live virtual sessions or prerecorded webinars.

In the fourth phase, academic advisors can guide students to make successful transitions to the workforce. Such career planning can be accomplished through virtual mock interviews or webinars with an institution's career services center. Lastly, academic advisors can measure online learners' success—the fifth phase—through confidential online suggestion boxes or feedback forms and yearly survey assessment tools that can be requested from students via e-mail or social media and then analyzed. Floyd and Casey-Powell's (2004) inclusive student services process model is a list of collaborative concepts where advising and multiple student affairs professionals work together to play a significant role in a student's academic success. However, this is just one example to follow. Another surrounds the theory of student involvement, which can also benefit an online learner's academic success.

Student Development Theory

According to Tinto (1975), "A person will tend to withdraw from college when [they] perceive that an alternative form of investment of time, energies, and resources will yield greater benefits, relative to costs, over time than will staying in college" (pp. 97–98). Therefore, to persist to graduation, students from all populations have to be confident the time and finances they are investing into a higher education degree are worthwhile. Online learners also need to see the benefit of their invested time and energy to remain motivated to complete their educational goals.

In his theory of student involvement, Astin (1984) discussed various areas of student engagement (an investment of one's time) and academic achievement related to student retention and success. Astin (1984) defined involvement as "the amount of physical and psychological energy that the student devotes to the academic experience" (p. 518). Astin described resource theory as multiple ingredients used to increase student learning, and, if adequate and effective, they will contribute to student learning and development. Academic advisors use multiple "ingredients" to promote student learning by encouraging students to actively engage with the campus community, even from afar. Academic advisors can help students see their educational investment (Tinto, 1975) as worthwhile through the use of these multiple ingredients.

One ingredient that can be developed by advisors for online learners is setting up an online space for students to communicate with one another and work together in virtual study group sessions. Students can also become more active or collaborative with one another through increased involvement in student groups and organizations via online spaces. For example, advisors can encourage the use of live streaming services to make events and activities on campus accessible to online learners. This can help advisors to promote the use of student support services virtually to online learners and increase the availability of additional student resources, including joining a student group or organization. Helping students to engage further with, commit to, or simply value their education and the virtual campus community can help advisors to apply Astin's (1984) resource theory to practice.

Technology and Innovative Tools

Checklists

How to use: Checklists are a way for distance advisors to create simple electronic checklists (reminders) for online learners.

Tools:

- Canva
  https://www.canva.com/create/checklists
- Checkli
  https://www.checkli.com
- Venngage
  https://venngage.com/features/checklist-maker

Clip art and graphics

How to use: Free clip art or royalty free images can be used when creating announcements, presentations, and banners.

Tools:

- Clker
  https://www.clker.com
- Flickr
  https://www.flickr.com
- Webestools
  http://www.webestools.com/banner-animated-maker-generator-gif-banners-free-online.html

Online conferencing systems

How to use: Online conferencing tools can be used to host virtual new student orientations, online welcome week events, virtual faculty/student meet and greets, and small group advising sessions.

Tools:

- AnyMeeting
  https://www.anymeeting.com
- Go-to-Meeting
  https://www.gotomeeting.com
- Skype
  https://www.skype.com
- Vialogues
  https://vialogues.com
- WebEx
  https://www.webex.com/video-conferencing
- Zoom
  https://zoom.us
- Institution learning management system (e.g., Blackboard, Brightspace, Canvas, Moodle, Webstudy)

Presentations
How to use: Presentation tools can be used to visually engage with distance learners.

Tools:
 	
• Adobe Photoshop
   https://www.adobe.com/products/photoshop.html
• Microsoft Publisher
   https://www.microsoft.com/publisher
• Sway
   https://sway.com

Podcasting
How to use: Podcasting tools can be used to create easy and convenient podcasts or voice recordings to provide announcements and reminders in a more creative format for online learners.

Tools:
 	
• Podbean
   https://www.podbean.com
• Vocaroo
   https://vocaroo.com

Scheduling
How to use: Virtual appointment scheduling systems allow online learners to schedule academic advising appointments on the go through mobile-friendly websites.

Tools:
 	
• Acuity Scheduling
   https://www.acuityscheduling.com
• Timetrade
   https://www.timetrade.com

Screencasts/videos
How to use: Free, interactive videos can be created when developing announcements, presentations, and banners.

Tools:
 	
• Jing
   https://jing.en.softonic.com
• Biteable
   https://biteable.com

Student networking
How to use: Student networking tools are excellent resources for academic advisors to promote and encourage virtual student study groups and networking among peers.

Tools:
 	
• CourseNetworking
   https://www.thecn.com
• Watch2gether
   https://www.watch2gether.com

Text reminders
How to use: Create a phone number (outside of your personal) to text reminders to students.
Tools:
• Google Voice *https://voice.google.com/u/0/signup*
• Remind *https://www.remind.com*
• TextNow *https://www.textnow.com/downloads*

Tutorials
How to use: Create tutorials with markup tools to communicate and share information with students.
Tools:
• Camtasia *https://www.techsmith.com/video-editor.html*
• ScreencastOmatic *https://screencast-o-matic.com*
• Snagit *https://www.techsmith.com/screen-capture.html*

Going Beyond the Transactional Relationship to High Touch

As an academic advisor, a timely, effective, and technologically advanced framework to use in support of online learners can benefit this everchanging student population (Underwood & Anderson, 2018), and "if utilized effectively, technology in advising contributes positively to the student experience, supporting goals toward increased retention and improving learners' academic success" (para. 1). Advisors may consider ways they could further support and engage students in fully online settings. Begin this process by considering what new innovative strategies can be adopted to raise the effectiveness and efficiency of student advising for online learners while also increasing student performance and success. Additionally, think about how a high-touch advising model for online learner advisees can be implemented creatively and effectively.

It is likely this will not be accomplished by simply using or introducing technology to online learners, as the use of technology alone does not directly lead to student success or career preparedness (Jenkins, 2018). However, by implementing traditional and new advising techniques through the creative use of technology tools, the advisor increases their chances of making a larger impact on their students' success. For example, as an academic advisor for fully online learners in previous professional roles, I had to think beyond the traditional open houses and congratulatory calls and e-mails to newly admitted students, as the traditional welcome weeks and campus-based orientations were typically out of reach for online and geographically dispersed populations. Instead, I had to consider how I could effectively use technology tools and which tools would be most beneficial to online learners.

Tips for Getting Started

Connecting with online learners takes a few simple steps to get started:

• **Define your role as a distance advisor.** You can become a more effective distance academic advisor if you understand the online learner population (i.e., student preferences and needs) and how such a role is defined.

• **Determine what it means to provide high-quality online learning experiences.** Online learners are still a fairly new (but growing) population of students. Online learners experience a different set of challenges than traditional students, and it takes time to determine specific online learner needs.

• **Gain department or administrative support.** Academic advisors have a higher chance of securing financial resources for the technology tools and services required to fully support online learners with a departmental commitment.

• **Replicate the face-to-face student-advisor relationships.** Determine how you can replicate in-person student support services for online learners through the effective use of technology tools.

• **Network with your peers.** Consider starting an advising committee that specifically highlights the needs of online learners to create a welcoming environment for idea sharing among academic advisors.

Leveraging Technology to Impact Academic Advising for Online Learners

An essential aspect of academic advising is informing students of the various support resources and student affairs services available to them. One way to increase online learner engagement outside of the classroom is to bring campus support services and events to students virtually. A few examples of the types of services and events traditionally offered on campus that can also be offered to online learners are provided next.

Virtual new student orientations. There is traditionally a new student orientation session held prior to the start of students' first term. This may or may not be associated with a week of "welcome"— congratulatory and informative events and activities to help new students get acquainted with the college or university. These orientations and welcome events help to transition students (and their families) to the institution successfully. Such events ease the nerves usually associated with the idea of starting something new or fresh (Robichaud, 2016; Taylor, Dunn, & Winn, 2015) by introducing incoming students to norms and expectations. These events may also provide a brief overview of the school and institution policies, and provide information related to pertinent points of contact and student resources, such as support services, financial aid, advising, registration, graduation and degree requirements, campus dining and residence life, security, disability services, and the bookstore. This week of events may even include resource fairs, student expos, luncheons, meet and greets with faculty and staff, and a host of social events for students to meet one another.

Online learners may miss out on these opportunities to meet new people; learn about campus resources, services, and policies; and feel like members of the campus community, even though these components of the campus are equally important to welcoming online learners. Similar to campus-based students, online learners should be fully supported from their first day as a student. To achieve this, orientation and welcome week can be replicated in a virtual setting with proper planning, administrative resources and support. For example, if your institution has purchased a video conferencing interface (e.g., Zoom, Skype, Adobe Connect, WebEx, or Go-to-Meeting), large events—such as virtual student expos, faculty meet and greets, and new student orientation—can be held by putting these tools to use. Such video conferencing systems allow the opportunity for online learners to connect with the campus. Specifically related to new student orientation, advisors can schedule a synchronous event to cover new student basics.

You may also consider including a review of available virtual student support resources, inviting your division/department dean to provide a welcome speech, and, through live synchronous formats, allowing students, faculty, and staff to communicate with each other using features, such as webcams and microphones. Additionally, students can feel more connected to the campus in a virtual orientation setting if school swag is mailed to online learners prior to the date of the virtual session. This allows online learners to show off their school pride online. Advisors can also encourage students to submit photos wearing a school T-shirt or holding a mug, for example, prior to orientation, and the advisor can create a slideshow to embed into the online orientation to further welcome students and strengthen students' institutional affiliation.

Features of most web conferencing options available to higher education institutions include phone conferencing, closed captioning, participant engagement features, mobile compatibility, audio/video interfacing for both event hosts and participants, whiteboard text editing, personalized profiles, file upload options, and the ability to break out into mini specialized "rooms" if an advisor would like online learners to gather by program, department, or specialty group. If the cost of these technology tools is not in the current institutional or departmental budget, some companies offer free versions available through Zoom and Skype. Also consider using your institution's learning management system (LMS) to host such events via Blackboard, Brightspace, Canvas, Moodle, Webstudy, or another system. All of the systems listed here, and many others, have live classroom or collaboration interface options for virtual events and collaborative sessions and may already be included in your institution's budget. The use of these online collaborative learning classrooms and web/video conferencing tools can help students feel engaged, connected, and part of the virtual campus community (Kretovics, 2003).

It is always recommended to save, record, and share all virtual events with online learners who may be unable to attend a live synchronous event so they can attend at their own convenience. No matter the platform or technology tool, do not forget to welcome and keep online learners engaged!

Community pages and online learner engagement. Community pages (or resource portals) provide a synchronized location for current online learners to network with their peers, stay up to date on program-specific announcements and policy changes, job and internship opportunities, webinar and orientation recordings, associated professional organization updates, and faculty and student highlights. This is in addition to general academic program information and reminders. The amount of information that can be shared in such a virtual setting is endless, with the exception of sharing personal or student-specific identifiable information, which should only be shared via secure student-advisor platforms to avoid inadvertently violating FERPA (Family Educational Rights and Privacy Act) guidelines. To create a community page for online learners, contact an instructional designer or member of the LMS instructional technology team.

Since these community pages (or resource portals) typically are housed in the institution's LMS for online learning, students will most likely visit the site regularly and have easy access to advisor communication and announcements. There often is also an option to send announcements immediately to a student's institutional e-mail account in addition to posting in the LMS. This is an important feature to have from an advisor's perspective as it may be difficult to ensure virtual learners are actively reading their e-mails, which is traditionally the main form of contact for distance learners. However, having announcements and updates housed in one synchronized location can make it easier for students to log in and have immediate access to pertinent information in the same place as where they access their courses.

Something else to consider: At times, by not having scheduled face-to-face interactions with online learners, distance advisors should be more creative in gaining and keeping a student's attention and interests when meeting with them. Some additional steps advisors could take include further engaging online learners through daily or weekly announcements within a community page and using various free technology tools to keep students connected. Some effective tools advisors have found to be impactful in virtual platforms are provided in this chapter. All of these tools are designed to be user friendly, accessible, and easy to share! They also allow advisors to be more creative with updates and reminders. Effective use of these tools can increase engagement and interaction with students and the material being communicated.

Online appointment schedulers. An online appointment scheduler allows students to schedule an advising appointment on the go through a mobile website. In the past, I have used Timetrade and Acuity Scheduling, which both require a fee but are highly effective resources for students that can easily be merged with Microsoft Outlook, Gmail, and other platforms. Schedulers also allow academic advisors to set their available advising hours and block off their calendar as necessary. When an appointment or meeting is added to the calendar, the scheduled time will automatically be removed as an available timeslot for an advising appointment. Then, when students use an advisor's personalized link to access their calendar, they can select an available time, provide their name and student ID number and the purpose for the advising session, and highlight any specific questions they have prior to the appointment, which will allow the advisor time to prepare accordingly.

An online scheduling tool can save the advisor and the student time when trying to organize time to speak. Additionally, students can select the method of contact with which they are most comfortable, whether they are local and want to meet in person, are at a distance and prefer to video chat, or want to schedule a telephone call. To provide online learners with the same quality resources and services as on-campus students, when scheduling appointments, it is important to view and treat each interaction the same. For example, when meeting with a student in person to discuss general registration details, would an advisor be completing administrative tasks in the background? Absolutely not! Communicating with online learners is not a simple administrative task, and the same support and attention should be provided for all students regardless of the form of contact. Keeping this in mind can be an easy way to enhance the online learner experience and be truly engaged with online learners during advising appointments.

Virtual small group advising sessions. Virtual small group advising sessions can be an excellent resource for students to ask academic-related questions that may be beneficial for other students within a virtual group setting. This is another opportunity for advisors to connect online learners with one another and build community. Some information advisors present virtually may pertain exclusively to students' academic major or cover popular advising topics, such as registering for classes, applying for related certification, declaring a minor, and preparing for graduation and degree clearing. One of the

Potential Challenges and Practical Solutions

When initially deciding to become more creative and technical in an advising space, many challenges may arise, such as the following:

Potential Challenge: Initial fears of the unknown.

> **Practical Solution:** There are many common myths not only associated with online learning itself but advising online learners. However, they are myths! There are many opportunities to connect and engage with online learners if you meet them where they are from a distance through the proper use of technology tools.

Potential Challenge: Lack of departmental support.

> **Practical Solution:** Establishing a substantial budget may be a challenge when selecting the technology tools you wish to begin implementing in your distance advising routine. Considering the use of free technology tools will be helpful when you lack additional funding, and these tools can be just as effective as paid resources.

Potential Challenge: Technical competency levels.

> **Practical Solution:** Scheduled training through your instructional technology division or with an instructional designer can help build your technological proficiency. There are also free tutorials and trainings available through many of the suggested technology tools websites provided in this chapter.

highlights of these sessions is they can be scheduled virtually using one the same virtual interface systems used for virtual new student orientation, including the institution's LMS or a free video conference resource such as Skype, Zoom, or even Facebook Live.

Virtual faculty/student meet and greets. Virtual meet and greets can be created to help students and faculty get to know one another in an online setting. One goal for this type of virtual event can be to increase engagement among students, faculty, and staff outside of their online classrooms. You can begin such an event by allowing faculty and staff to introduce themselves (using live video features), discuss their expertise/interest areas, and become more personable to students prior to opening the "virtual floor" to students. Students can then share details about themselves, their interests, and their area of study through synchronous experiences and possibly network with faculty who share similar interests.

Closing the Gap Between On-Campus Resources and Online Learners

Now that I have shared what can be done to increase engagement in virtual settings, what are the next steps? First, gain support from your administration and seek further training, as needed, on specific technology tools. Does the dean or division/department support efforts to expand advising resources to online learners? Do they understand the benefits? Are the unique characteristics of your distance learners understood, including when they are available (days/times) to take advantage of virtual resources and events, and can their preferences be accommodated? Is further training needed on using technological tools to support online learners? Is the department willing to support this training or professional development? Gaining administrative support for training and budget allocations will help get efforts to support online learners headed in the right direction.

Simply using technology tools does not lead to direct student success, nor do these tools increase retention rates or student satisfaction on their own. Advisors must become more experienced and skilled with these tools and welcome the use of technology to further engage online learners. These tools can complement an already existing advising model. This is just the beginning! As advisors become more accepting of using technology tools in creative and engaging ways to enhance the virtual college experience, new and innovative ideas will continue to be developed and implemented successfully. However, for now, begin to use the services and resources offered in this chapter to create a diverse, welcoming, and enriching campus environment for online learners.

Conclusion

By only having support services readily available to on-campus students, institutions risk lowering retention and student success rates among online learners, which can affect the institution's overall enrollment rates in the future. According to Finley and Chapman (2011), "Online students have much to offer" (para. 8). Unless advisors and other student affairs professionals provide these students with a high-quality online experience, they will be unable to reach their full academic potential (Finley & Chapman, 2011; Jenkins, 2018).

"Generally, adults take an interest in higher education when they have determined that there will be a return on their investment of time, money, and effort" (Fairchild, 2003, p. 11), and, unfortunately, lack of support decreases students' interest to persist and obtain a higher education degree (Fairchild, 2003; Jenkins, 2018). With developments in technology, higher education institutions have the opportunity to offer support to both on-campus and online learners. With this in mind, it is imperative student affairs professionals provide opportunities for all students to connect with the institution and receive support services on campus and at a distance (Kretovics, 2003). Let's connect and engage with all students!

? Questions for Reflection

- How can you clearly identify and understand the difference between traditional advising and distance advising?
- What are some effective high-touch advising techniques/strategies for online learners?
- How can you demonstrate awareness and understanding of the skills necessary to advise online learners from a distance?
- How can you demonstrate a depth of knowledge to enhance student success with online learners?
- What technology tools and resources are available to further connect and engage with online learners?

References

Astin, A. (1984). Student involvement: A developmental theory for higher education. *Journal of College Student Personnel, 25*, 297–308.

Bonk, C., & Khoo, E. (2014). *Adding some TEC-Variety: 100+ activities for motivating and retaining learners online*. Bloomington, IN: Open World Books.

Fairchild, E. (2003). Multiple roles of adult learners. In D. Kilgore & P. J. Rice (Eds.), *Meeting the special needs of adult students* (New Directions for Student Services, No. 102, pp. 11–16). San Francisco, CA: Jossey-Bass.

Finley, S., & Chapman, J. (2011). Actively including online students in the college experience. *NACADA Clearinghouse of Academic Advising Resources*. Retrieved from https://www.nacada.ksu.edu/resources/academic-advising-today/view-articles/actively-including-online-students-in-the-college-experience.aspx

Floyd, D., & Casey-Powell, D. (2004). New roles for student support services in distance learning. In B. L. Bower & K. P. Hardy (Eds.), *From distance education to e-learning: Lessons along the way* (New Directions for Community Colleges, No. 128, pp. 57–61). San Francisco, CA: Jossey-Bass. doi:10.1002/cc.175

Kretovics, M. (2003). The role of student affairs in distance education: Cyber-services or virtual communities. *Online Journal of Distance Learning Administration, 6*(3). Retrieved from http://www.westga.edu/~distance/ojdla/fall63/kretovics63.html

Jenkins, S. (2018). *Online learners: A study of their advising attitudes, experiences, and learning* (Doctoral dissertation). Retrieved from https://pdxscholar.library.pdx.edu/open_access_etds/4657

Miller, T. K., & Prince, J. S. (1976). *The future of student affairs: A guide to student development for tomorrow's higher education*. San Francisco, CA: Jossey-Bass.

Ohrablo, S. (2016). Advising online students: Replicating best practice of face-to-face advising. *NACADA Clearinghouse of Academic Advising Resources*. Retrieved from https://www.nacada.ksu.edu/resources/clearinghouse/view-articles/advising-online-students-replicating-best-practices-of-face-to-face-advising.aspx

Redmond, P., Heffernan, A., Abawi, L., Brown, A., & Henderson, R. (2018). An online engagement framework for higher education. *Online Learning, 22*, 183–204. doi:10.24059/olj.v22i1.1175

Robichaud, W. (2016). Orientation programs to increase retention in online community colleges. *Distance Learning Issue, 13*, 57–65. Retrieved from https://www.thefreelibrary.com/Orientation+programs+to+increase+retention+in+online+community...-a0464244296

Sandeen, A., & Barr, M. (2006). *Critical issues for student affairs: Challenges and opportunities*. San Francisco, CA: Jossey-Bass.

Schroeder, S., & Terras, K. (2015). Advising experiences and needs of online, cohort, and classroom adult learners. *NACADA Journal, 35*, 42–55. doi:10.12930/NACADA-13-044

Seaman, J. E., Allen, I., & Seaman, J. (2018). *Grade increase: Tracking distance education in the United States*. Retrieved from Online Learning Consortium website: https://onlinelearningconsortium.org/read/grade-increase-tracking-distance-education-united-states

Steele, G. (2005). Advising distance learners. *NACADA Clearinghouse of Academic Advising Resources*. Retrieved from http://www.nacada.ksu.edu/resources/clearinghouse/view-articles/advising-distance-learners.aspx

Taylor, J. M., Dunn, M., & Winn, S. K. (2015). Innovative orientation leads to improved success in online courses. *Online Learning, 19*(4). doi:10.24059/olj.v19i4.570

Tinto, V. (1975). Dropout from higher education: A theoretical synthesis of recent research. *Review of Educational Research, 45*, 89–125. doi:10.3102/00346543045001089

Underwood, Z. W., & Anderson, M. (2018, March). Technology and academic advising: A case for embracing change in academic advising. *Academic Advising Today, 41*(1). Retrieved from https://www.nacada.ksu.edu/resources/academic-advising-today/view-articles/technology-and-academic-advising-a-case-for-embracing-change-in-academic-advising.aspx

Varney, J. (2009). Strategies for success in distance advising. *NACADA Clearinghouse of Academic Advising Resources*. Retrieved from https://www.nacada.ksu.edu/resources/clearinghouse/view-articles/distance-advising-strategies.aspx

Vianden, J., & Barlow, J. (2015). Strengthen the bond: Relationships between academic advising quality and undergraduate student loyalty. *NACADA Journal, 35*, 15–27. doi:10.12930/NACADA-15-026

Winston, R. B., Jr., Enders, S. C., & Miller, T. K. (Eds.). (1982). Developmental approaches to academic advising. *New Directions for Student Services* (No. 17). San Francisco, CA: Jossey-Bass. doi:10.1002/ss.37119821701

CHAPTER 16

Creating Sense of Belonging Through Virtual Student Affairs Supports:
Tools and Strategies for Developing Social Presence

Annalisa Teixeira

VARIOUS FUNCTIONAL AREAS within student affairs focus on building a sense of belonging among students, both through staff-student and peer-to-peer connections (Maestas, Vaquera, & Zehr, 2007; Means & Pyne, 2017; Ribera, Miller, & Dumford, 2017; Spanierman et al., 2013; Strayhorn, 2012). With the increase of online degree programs and courses, such work must occur increasingly in virtual spaces. Sense of belonging is widely known in student affairs to have a positive impact on persistence (Davis, Hanzsek-Brill, Petzold, & Robinson, 2019; Hausmann, Schofield, & Woods, 2007; Maestas et al., 2007); yet, investigating how such belonging can be developed and supported in virtual spaces in student affairs is still developing. In comparison, community building in online teaching and learning has an established presence in the literature and continues to receive great attention (Aldosemani, Shepherd, Gashim, & Dousay, 2016; Dolan, Kain, Reilly, & Bansal, 2017; Oliphant & Branch-Mueller, 2016; Rubin & Fernandes, 2013), which can inform the practices of student affairs professionals.

The aim of this chapter is to translate research-based practices for cultivating a sense of community in online teaching to the work of virtual student affairs. First, the role sense of belonging plays in student affairs work to retain students through services, centers, and programs is discussed. Next, research-based principles that guide community creation and interaction in online academic teaching are explored. To illustrate how such principles might be relevant to student affairs work, different interactive tools and apps are highlighted and applied to examples of diverse, virtually delivered student affairs support to provide student affairs leaders and practitioners with tangible tools and strategies for virtual engagement and interaction.

Building Sense of Belonging to Increase Online Learner Retention

Particularly for online degree programs, there is a necessity to move student support services, centers, and programs that develop sense of belonging into virtual spaces. Picciano (2016) emphasized, "If a college expects to attract a wide audience or student base for fully online programs, then it must invest in a full gamut of academic, library, and support services" (p. 14). Furthermore, supporting students' sense of belonging in virtual spaces is poised to benefit all students, not just those in online degree programs, including students whose access to campus resources might be impacted by work schedules, family duties, commutes, and/or mobility concerns or disabilities.

Sense of belonging is a long-established construct shown to positively impact student persistence in college (Davis et al., 2019; Hausmann et al., 2007; Maestas et al., 2007). Hoffman, Richmond, Morrow, and Salomone (2002) defined sense of belonging as a "subjective sense of affiliation and identification with the university community" (p. 288). It is understood the more connected students might feel to an institution, the more likely they are to persist (Tinto, 1997), and sense of belonging can be fostered through student-student and staff-student interactions (Tinto, 2012). Dimensions of sense of belonging include valued involvement, or "the experience of being valued, needed, and accepted" (Hagerty, Lynch-Sauer, Patusky, Bouwsema, & Collier, 1992, p. 173), and fit, defined as the perception one's characteristics "articulate with or complement the system or environment" (p. 173). It is also important to recognize students from underrepresented and/or marginalized backgrounds can experience sense of belonging and isolation in distinct ways (Strayhorn, 2012; Vaccaro & Newman, 2016), warranting further exploration than is undertaken in this chapter.

Given sense of belonging can be fostered through both staff-student and student-student interactions, best practices for virtual student affairs engagement can be applied to both staff-student interactions, such as advising or academic coaching, as well as staff-facilitated group interaction (student-student) that might occur within a course shell in a learning management system (LMS), either as a seminar or used as an online community meeting space. Such student-student interactions might include orientation programming, seminars on study strategies or career readiness, or community development for student organizations or identity-based retention initiatives (e.g., student veterans, underrepresented minorities, or first-generation and/or low-income students). This chapter draws from best practices for virtual interaction stemming from research on online education and sense of community that is translated and aims to apply such practices to virtual student affairs work focusing on developing students' sense of belonging. To do so, the social presence element within the community of inquiry model (Garrison, 2007; Garrison, Anderson, & Archer, 2000), the sense of community construct (Rovai, 2001), and the virtual community development framework (Moore, Gathman, & Ducheneaut, 2009) are examined.

Student Affairs' Role in Developing Social Presence for Online Learners

Online and distance education researchers have long investigated what causes some online learners to persist and others to disengage (Angelino, Williams, & Natvig, 2007; Aragon & Johnson, 2008; Boston et al., 2009; Clay, Rowland, & Packard, 2008; Cochran, Campbell, Baker, & Leeds, 2014; Morris, Wu, & Finnegan, 2005; Simpson, 2003). An important construct explored in this literature is sense of community (Rovai, 2001), which is understood to be developed through interactivity between instructor and students. When social connection is not felt, learners can suffer from isolation and disconnectedness, which, in turn, can affect engagement and persistence in the course (Angelino et al., 2007). The community of inquiry model's element of social presence (Garrison et al., 2000) is used to examine interactivity between student affairs practitioners and online learners. Social presence has been shown to have a positive impact on sense of belonging for online learners, thereby decreasing distance between individuals (Zilka, Cohen, & Rahimi, 2018).

According to Garrison et al. (2000), social presence is "the ability of participants in the Community of Inquiry to project their personal characteristics into the community, thereby presenting themselves to the other participants as 'real people'" (p. 89). Such presence is developed when "instructors and students interact with each other in meaningful and consistent ways throughout an online course" (Shelton, Hung, & Lowenthal, 2017, p. 60) through the indicators of emotional expression, open communication, and group cohesion (Garrison et al., 2000). Each indicator is further explored in the following sections, along with innovative technology tools used to engage each area of social presence and that can be integrated into common LMSs, referred to as Learning Tools Interoperability (LTI). LTI, developed by the IMS Global Learning Consortium (2019), standardizes how web-based apps and tools, developed by vendors separate from the LMS, integrate with the LMS so users do not need to leave the LMS or use separate logins to use third-party learning tools. To this end, it is recommended the later referenced interactive tools and apps (see Technology and Innovative Tools sidebar) be integrated with an institution's LMS, if possible, so the LMS serves as the central meeting point from which these apps are accessed and used. To illustrate how such tools might play a role in virtual student affairs support, examples from various student affairs services, centers, and programs are referenced in this chapter.

Emotional Expression

This indicator refers to the "ability and confidence to express feelings related to the educational experience" (Garrison et al., 2000, pp. 99). Expressing emotions such as closeness and warmth can be challenging for distance engagement, particularly communication that is simply text based, potentially limiting important staff-student and student-student socioemotional support. To overcome such challenges, humor and self-disclosure (personal sharing) can help to close social distance.

To establish emotional expression and the trust needed for such personal sharing (Rovai, 2001), student affairs professionals might consider using digital storytelling tools and video conferencing tools. Digital storytelling tools like Flipgrid, Vimeo, VoiceThread, and YouTube allow users to share introductions, personal stories and identities, and feelings around their educational experience (Beins, 2016; Martin & Bolliger, 2018; Oliphant & Branch-Mueller, 2016). Adobe Connect, Big Blue Button, Go Pisces, Google Hangout, Skype, and Zoom are all video conferencing tools that can be used to facilitate emotional expression through the immediacy and intimacy of video and audio (Beins, 2016; Exter, Korkmaz, Harlin, & Bichelmeyer, 2009; Lowenthal, Dunlap, & Snelson, 2017; Steele, Robertson, & Mandernach, 2018). Such tools can be used for one-on-one support, staff-student support, and one-to-many support for facilitating discussion among a smaller or larger group of students. As evidence of impact, Renner-Potacco, Orellana, and Salazar (2017), in their study on the use of video conferencing in one-on-one and group tutoring, demonstrated increased social presence through the use of video, texting emoticons, and tutees' names.

Both digital storytelling and video conferencing tools could be used in transitional seminars and for smaller cohort-based support, such as identity-based retention initiatives and mentoring programs. One example might be a first-generation mentoring program in which juniors and seniors mentor first-year students. Digital storytelling activities could emphasize shared lived experiences, and the peer mentor could use video conferencing software to connect with mentees.

Open Communication

"Reciprocal and respectful exchanges" (Garrison et al., 2000, p. 100) define open communication. Acknowledgment of others' comments and contributions helps to establish a sense of community, such as giving compliments or expressing appreciation. Discussion forums can strengthen open communication given the opportunities to like and respond to others' posts in a visible way. Staff can help to strengthen open communication by responding to posts and praising students who respond to peer postings to model such reciprocal interaction. Most LMSs have an internal function for discussion forums that allows students to post text and images, but additional LTI tools (e.g., Piazza, VoiceThread) offer rich media options for posting and responding to posts, including audio responses, which can help layer emotional expression with open communication. The Canvas LMS offers video and audio posting and responses in its Discussion tool, as well as social media functions like the ability to "like" a post. An additional advantage would be to have students build out their profiles within the LMS to establish an identity as they post in forums, including having a photo, a bio, and even external links to social media accounts (Calhoun & Green, 2015).

Student affairs professionals can use discussion forums as student question and answer sessions or with a prompt that facilitates student-student sharing. With these uses, staff would monitor posting and be a participant, such as a career specialist managing a forum on acing interviews. Students could post questions on best practices for interview preparation, and they could share their experiences interviewing for career positions. In addition, discussion forums can be designed as a more casual, student-student interactive space, acting as a virtual "lounge" for miscellaneous postings and questions. Such a lounge could be created for a virtual student support center.

Beyond using discussion forums, text-based communication (computer-mediated chat) is an opportunity for open or reciprocal communication but with even greater immediacy since exchanges are in real time (synchronous, rather than forums, which are asynchronous). Examples of tools include Slack, Pronto, and Skype, with the LMS offering an internal tool, such as Canvas' Chat function. Chat rooms offer a space for students to connect with a staff coordinator and other students, such as a peer mentor and other mentees. Biology tutors could use a chat room to offer services, or a Slack channel could be established to communicate with students involved in student government or committees.

Group Cohesion

Group cohesion refers to "activities that build and sustain a sense of group commitment" (Garrison et al., 2000, p. 101). Such group cohesion allows for sharing personal meaning and contextualized and personalized dialogues. Wikis and other collaborative tools, as well as quiz games, can all be used to develop greater group cohesion in a transitional seminar or online community. Collaborative tools could be internal functions within the LMS, such as the Pages function in Canvas that can serve as a wiki, but additional apps include Campus Pack, Mahara, Wikispaces, Google Docs/Sites, Wordpress (collaborative tools), and Kahoot or Quizles (quiz games).

There are diverse ways student affairs professionals might use such cohesive tools with students. A disability center could manage a shared blog in its online community space as a platform for students who might want to blog or vlog (video blog) a day in the life of a differently abled student to connect with others and raise their visibility among peers. The staff of a community service center could manage a wiki page where students might highlight national organizations or non-profits for which they have volunteered, offering a summary of what they did and reviewing the experience for other students to consider. Peer writing specialists could use Google Docs to create resources to support their peers. Quiz games like Kahoot and Quizlet are not limited to academic support tools but can be used to educate students on student resources, school trivia, or financial aid knowledge.

A clear synergy exists among the three categories of social presence, with many of the tools and ideas for their application activating more than one indictor. The following section imagines how a suite of student affairs supports can be offered to students in a centralized, virtual student support center using an LMS and its functions, as well as a number of aforementioned LTI tools.

Technology and Innovative Tools

Emotional expression

Digital storytelling:
- Flipgrid
  https://flipgrid.com
- Vimeo
  https://vimeo.com
- VoiceThread
  https://voicethread.com
- YouTube
  https://www.youtube.com

Video conferencing:
- Adobe Connect
  https://www.adobe.com/products/adobeconnect/meetings.html
- BigBlueButton
  https://bigbluebutton.org
- Go Pisces
  https://www.gopisces.com
- Skype
  https://www.skype.com/en
- Zoom
  https://zoom.us

Open communication

Discussion forums:
- Piazza
  https://piazza.com
- VoiceThread
  https://voicethread.com

Computer-mediated chat:
- Pronto
  https://pronto.io
- Slack
  https://slack.com
- Skype
  https://www.skype.com/en

Group cohesion

Wikis and collaborative tools:
- Campus Pack
  https://campuspack.net
- Google Docs/Sites
  https://docs.google.com
- Mahara
  https://mahara.org
- Wikispaces
  https://www.wikispaces.com
- Wordpress
  https://wordpress.com

Learning games:
- Kahoot
  https://kahoot.com
- Quizlet
  https://quizlet.com

Imagining a Virtual Student Support Center

This section fleshes out a hypothetical example of a virtual student support center at a completely online, four-year institution that aims to engage hundreds or thousands of incoming and current students. For this example, the Canvas LMS is referenced. Note that with Canvas courses with an excess of 2,000 enrolled students, issues can occur with the gradebook, such as loading time and crashing. It is recommended the course manager or instructor disable the Grades function when enrolling more than 2,000 students.

Using the Learning Management System

The LMS is not only a central place to integrate diverse interactive technologies into one interface, but also it can serve as a virtual "center" housing a suite of services or as a "community meeting space" for programs. As mentioned, the Canvas LMS includes many international functions that support social presence, such as discussion forums (Discussions), a wiki function (Pages), a synchronous chat feature (Chat), video conferencing with a record option (Conferences), and an integration with Google Docs (Collaborations). Additionally, there is a calendar function with which virtual events (e.g., webinars and chat hours) can be organized, and further integration with LTIs like Piazza and VoiceThread are possible.

In face-to-face student affairs support, use of and access to student spaces might include a student swiping into a center, attending a workshop or program, or going to an appointment. In virtual student affairs work, use and access could mean entering a Canvas course shell and interacting synchronously and asynchronously with staff and peers. A "center" might show up as a course tile on a student's LMS dashboard alongside their academic courses. This would be an example of Aldosemani et al.'s (2016) recommendation "portals to the space should be housed within existing tools (e.g., learning management systems, websites, blogs, wikis) to facilitate access and encourage use" (p. 1026). Students could customize their LMS dashboard and add and subtract the student affairs services, centers, and programs relevant to their needs, goals, and identities. Virtually, these spaces could be centralized as they often are at brick-and-mortar colleges and universities. In the following sections, examples of services and supports a student support center delivers virtually to online learners are presented.

For this scenario, imagine students are invited through e-mail to "enroll" in the course that houses the "center," thus allowing them to access the space. The students might be provided with a technical document on how to best flesh out their profile in Canvas, a link to a screen capture video that gives them a "tour" of the virtual center, and tips for using the space. Examples of interactivity in this virtual student support center might include the activities summarized in Table 16.1, which are categorized according to asynchronous and synchronous deliveries and span the social presence indicators of emotional expression, open communication, and group cohesion.

Table 16.1. Imagining a Virtual Student Support Center With Asynchronous and Synchronous Interactivity

Asynchronous	Synchronous
• Every fall, the center offers sections of a first-year transitional course for college success. The course starts with introductions, and students use VoiceThread to vlog and record a short video introducing themselves. • Students can view a previously recorded webinar, Finding Your Community as an Online Student. • An online support group for student parents to interact in designated discussion forums. Staff post tips and resources periodically to help sustain engagement. • The discussion forum The Lounge is a designated informal space for miscellaneous student postings. • Students post in the Slack channel #studyjam to trade tips and strategies for succeeding in various online courses.	• Before the fall semester begins, students have the option to join a live webinar that gives them a real-time tour of the center's services and programs, including career services, financial aid, and tutoring. Students can type questions for the presenters in real time. • New students attend a virtual panel to hear about academic tips from soon-to-graduate seniors. • Students attend appointments with an academic coach or peer mentor using integrated video conferencing software. They are virtually "face-to-face" with staff and can hear their voice in real time. • Peer mentors for the center hold drop-in chat hours where students can join the chat room to get quick questions answered.

Tips for Getting Started

- **Orient yourself with the LMS.** If you are not already familiar with your institution's LMS, take time to learn how to navigate the system. Review the LTIs available that integrate with your campus-specific LMS.

- **Learn from others.** Seek out educational technology workshops and YouTube videos to learn more about how other practitioners are using the LTIs mentioned in this chapter to support interactivity and sense of belonging.

- **Collaborate with vendor and campus staff.** Get to know the support staff of your LMS vendor and your campus team of instructional designers to learn more about how to integrate LTIs into your course shell.

Establishing a Thriving Virtual Center

Thriving virtual spaces can be characterized by their ease of access, social density, and robust activities and structures that encourage social interaction (Moore et al., 2009). Repurposing the LMS should offer ease of access, but what remains is how to attract students to the virtual space. How might engagement be sustained to reach a social density of students that allows for authentic and frequent peer-peer interaction? Aldosemani et al. (2016) described best practices for the creation of thriving virtual spaces that are more informal meeting locations beyond the classroom:

1. Engage in a sophisticated needs analysis before designing an online, informal third space, including identifying goals, resources, and stakeholders.

2. Empathize with users/students to decide what resources and activities will bring consistent traffic to the space and what norms will guide interaction.

3. Consider that multiple development cycles may be needed to create a critical mass of users to successfully establish an online third space.

To create social density in an online community, Aldosemani et al. (2016) suggested first mandating or incentivizing participation, even though this is contrary to the informality that marks a third space. After a certain period of mandated or incentivized use, students hopefully would adopt the space as their own and opt in to visiting the space for social purposes with some regularity (group cohesion). For instance, students in a first-year transitional seminar could be required to enter the "center" and post in general discussion forums open to all students. Through their participation, these students might engage other students who are not enrolled in the seminar by responding to the nonenrolled students' posts so they feel acknowledged (open communication). Once engagement has reached a critical mass, new users invited to the space would hopefully stay and engage, as they would see an established, active community of peers who regularly share and express themselves through posting, chat, and video (emotional expression).

Student affairs professionals can help facilitate peer-to-peer interaction through praising engagement, like responding to a post themselves or complimenting a student's reply to a post (e.g., "It sounds like you two have a lot in common!"). Professionals can make themselves available for one-on-one support through distance advising. Given the best practices related to the power of image and voice for embodying intimacy and immediacy explored previously (Beins, 2016), consider prioritizing video conferencing software for distance advising to support the social presence indicator of open communication. High-touch advising and coaching that is intensive and ongoing has been shown to pattern positively with persistence (Bettinger & Baker, 2014), with a particular focus on academically vulnerable students (Jaggars & Karp, 2016). To close the distance gap with online learners, developmental advising and academic coaching that engages online learners around personal and academic goals should be emphasized (Gravel, 2012). If advising and coaching are both intensive and developmental, a lower touch model might include group advising or academic coaching using video conferencing or chat rooms.

Remaining Challenges

Like any number of opportunities technology might provide, challenges are present as well. As mentioned earlier, feelings of isolation and disconnectedness can be associated with virtual spaces, requiring student affairs professionals to use tools for interactivity with intention. The undertaking to build a virtual student support center in an LMS could be resource intensive. Picciano (2016) described providing services virtually might be an even more challenging undertaking than online academic instruction considering the number of student affairs staff who typically serve large populations of students.

Recognizing equity and inclusion, we must be mindful at each step that, in virtualizing services, centers, and programs, we make no assumptions about digital literacies, access to devices, Internet connectivity, and what constitutes universal design and Americans With Disabilities Act compliance. It might be argued students' digital

 Potential Challenges and Practical Solutions

Potential Challenge: The digital literacies of students will vary, and it is a common fallacy today's students are digital natives who have grown up with unfettered access to technology and the Internet. Students returning to school may not be a member of a digital native generation at all.

Practical Solution: Challenge assumptions about the digital literacies of students and be sure to create FAQs, offer technical/support documents, and hold user testing to support use and access among diverse students.

Potential Challenge: Adopting new tools that support virtual interactivity is an investment for both staff and student users.

Practical Solution: Consider using tools that might already be in use or at least already available to the student body to increase the likelihood of engagement and avoid a steeper learning curve. For instance, Gmail might be the student e-mail provider on your campus. Already integrated in Gmail is a chat function and Google Hangout for video conferencing.

literacy development is within the scope of the support student affairs professionals provide. Lastly, educating ourselves and engaging in dialogue with campus experts in universal design can help maximize access for students with differing abilities.

Conclusion

In this chapter, two bodies of literature—sense of belonging research from student affairs and sense of community research from online teaching and distance education—were connected and applied. Recognized in this literature is that the establishment of communities in and outside of the classroom—academic and cocurricular—is a high-impact practice for student engagement in higher education (Kuh, 2009).

Innovative technology tools that support the development of social presence were presented, focusing on the LTIs that communicate with various LMSs. The ways in which such LTIs and LMS functions could be applied to student affairs support were also illustrated. Further, a large-scale virtual student support center was offered as an example of how student affairs practitioners might package and deliver student affairs support within an LMS. Fortunately, LTI and LMS technologies should already be in place at universities and colleges with established resources and supports. Additionally, students should already be familiar with their campus' LMS; if not, engaging with student affairs professionals in the LMS can contribute to their digital literacy development, which can help them succeed in their online academic coursework.

The examples presented in this chapter may have affirmed the numerous ways institutions are virtualizing student affairs work already. In any case, it is clear there are many evidence-based, technology-driven practices student affairs professionals can adopt from research on the teaching of online academic courses. Doing so can help student affairs practitioners be more impactful in helping students feel connected, even in virtual spaces. After all, "distance is a pedagogical phenomenon—not a geographical one" (Dolan et al., 2017, p. 46).

? Questions for Reflection

- How have you established an online persona previously in your student affairs role? How have you successfully engaged with your students already in virtual spaces, formally and informally?

- If you work with peer staff, what roles could they play in your virtual spaces? What resources and perspectives could they offer?

- What services and programs would make up a virtual student support center for your institution? Which LTIs mentioned in this chapter would be most appropriate for the support your institution offers?

References

Aldosemani, T. I., Shepherd, C. E., Gashim, I., & Dousay, T. (2016). Developing third places to foster sense of community in online instruction. *British Journal of Educational Technology, 47,* 1020–1031. doi:10.1111/bjet.12315

Angelino, L. M., Williams, F. K., & Natvig, D. (2007). Strategies to engage online students and reduce attrition rates. *Journal of Educators Online, 4,* 1–14. doi:10.9743/JEO.2007.2.1

Aragon, S. R., & Johnson, E. S. (2008). Factors influencing completion and noncompletion of community college online courses. *American Journal of Distance Education, 22,* 146–158. doi:10.1080/08923640802239962

Beins, A. (2016). Small talk and chit chat: Using informal communication to build a learning community online. *Transformations: The Journal of Inclusive Scholarship and Pedagogy, 26,* 157–175. doi:10.1353/tnf.2016.0022

Bettinger, E. P., & Baker, R. B. (2014). The effects of student coaching: An evaluation of a randomized experiment in student advising. *Educational Evaluation and Policy Analysis, 36,* 3–19. doi:10.3102/0162373713500523

Boston, W., Díaz, S. R., Gibson, A. M., Ice, P., Richardson, J., & Swan, K. (2009). An exploration of the relationship between indicators of the community of inquiry framework and retention in online programs. *Journal of Asynchronous Learning Networks, 13,* 67–83. doi:10.24059/olj.v14i1.1636

Calhoun, D. W., & Green, L. S. (2015). Utilizing online learning communities in student affairs. In M. Benjamin (Ed.), *Learning communities from start to finish* (New Directions for Student Services, No. 149, pp. 55–66). San Francisco, CA: Jossey-Bass. doi:10.1002/ss.20117

Clay, M. N., Rowland, S., & Packard, A. (2008). Improving undergraduate online retention through gated advisement and redundant communication. *Journal of College Student Retention: Research, Theory & Practice, 10,* 93–102. doi:10.2190/CS.10.1.g

Cochran, J. D., Campbell, S. M., Baker, H. M., & Leeds, E. M. (2014). The role of student characteristics in predicting retention in online courses. *Research in Higher Education, 55,* 27–48. doi:10.1007/s11162-013-9305-8

Davis, G. M., Hanzsek-Brill, M. B., Petzold, M. C., & Robinson, D. H. (2019). Students' sense of belonging: The development of a predictive retention model. *Journal of the Scholarship of Teaching and Learning, 19,* 117–127. doi:10.14434/josotl.v19i1.26787

Dolan, J., Kain, K., Reilly, J., & Bansal, G. (2017). How do you build community and foster engagement in online courses? In R. A. R. Gurung & D. J. Voelker (Eds.), *Big picture pedagogy: Finding interdisciplinary solutions to common learning problems* (New Directions for Teaching and Learning, No. 151, pp. 45–60). San Francisco, CA: Jossey-Bass. doi:10.1002/tl.20248

Exter, M. E., Korkmaz, N., Harlin, N. M., & Bichelmeyer, B. A. (2009). Sense of community within a fully online program: Perspectives of graduate students. *Quarterly Review of Distance Education, 10,* 177–194. Retrieved from https://www.learntechlib.org/p/103634

Garrison, D. R. (2007). Online community of inquiry review: Social, cognitive, and teaching presence issues. *Journal of Asynchronous Learning Networks, 11,* 61–72. doi:10.24059/olj.v11i1.1737

Garrison, D. R., Anderson, T. & Archer, W. (2000). Critical inquiry in a text-based environment: Computer conferencing in higher education. *The Internet and Higher Education, 2,* 87–105. doi:10.1016/S1096-7516(00)00016-6

Gravel, C. A. (2012). Student-advisor interaction in undergraduate online degree programs: A factor in student retention. *NACADA Journal, 32,* 56–67. doi:10.12930/0271-9517-32.2.56

Hagerty, B. M. K., Lynch-Sauer, J., Patusky, K. L., Bouwsema, M., & Collier, P. (1992). Sense of belonging: A vital mental health concept. *Archives of Psychiatric Nursing, 5,* 172–177. doi:10.1016/0883-9417(92)90028-H

Hausmann, L. R. M., Schofield, J. W., & Woods, R. L. (2007). Sense of belonging as a predictor of intentions to persist among African American and White first-year college students. *Research in Higher Education, 48,* 803–839. doi:10.1007/s11162-007-9052-9

Hoffman, M., Richmond, J., Morrow, J., & Salomone, K. (2002). Investigating "sense of belonging" in first-year college students. *Journal of College Student Retention, 4,* 227–256. doi:10.2190/DRYC-CXQ9-JQ8V-HT4V

IMS Global Learning Consortium. (2019). LTI fundamentals FAQ. Retrieved from https://www.imsglobal.org/lti-fundamentals-faq

Jaggars, S. S., & Karp, M. M. (2016). Transforming the community college student experience through comprehensive, technology-mediated advising. In N. L. Maxwell & A. E. Person (Eds.), Comprehensive reform for student success (New Directions for Community Colleges, No. 176, pp. 53–62). San Francisco, CA: Jossey-Bass. doi:10.1002/cc.20222

Kuh, G. D. (2009). What student affairs professionals need to know about student engagement. *Journal of College Student Development, 50,* 683–706. doi:10.1353/csd.0.0099

Lowenthal, P. R, Dunlap, J. C., & Snelson, C. (2017). Live synchronous web meetings in asynchronous online courses: Reconceptualizing virtual office hours. *Online Learning Journal, 21,* 177–194. doi:10.24059/olj.v21i4.1285

Maestas, R., Vaquera, G. S., & Zehr, L. M. (2007). Factors impacting sense of belonging at a Hispanic-serving institution. *Journal of Hispanic Higher Education, 6,* 237–256. doi:10.1177/1538192707302801

Martin, F., & Bolliger, D. U. (2018). Engagement matters: Student perceptions on the importance of engagement strategies in the online learning environment. *Online Learning Journal, 22,* 205–222. doi:10.24059/olj.v22i1.1092

Means, D. R., & Pyne, K. B. (2017). Finding my way: Perceptions of institutional support and belonging in low-income, first-generation, first-year college students. *Journal of College Student Development, 58,* 907–924. doi:10.1353/csd.2017.0071

Moore, R. J., Gathman, E. C. H., & Ducheneaut, N. (2009). From 3D space to third place: The social life of small virtual spaces. *Human Organization, 68,* 230–240. doi:10.17730/humo.68.2.q673k16185u68v15

Morris, L. V., Wu, S.-S., & Finnegan, C. L. (2005). Predicting retention in online general education courses. *American Journal of Distance Education, 19,* 23–36. doi:10.1207/s15389286ajde1901_3

Oliphant, T., & Branch-Mueller, J. (2016). Developing a sense of community and the online student experience. *Education for Information, 32,* 307-321. doi:10.3233/EFI-160979

Picciano, A. G. (2016). *Online education policy and practice: The past, present, and future of the digital university.* New York, NY: Routledge.

Renner-Potacco, D., Orellana, A., & Salazar, A. (2017). Innovations in academic support: Factors influencing student adoption of synchronous videoconferencing for online support in high-risk STEM courses. *Quarterly Review of Distance Education, 18,* 1–17. Retrieved from https://www.infoagepub.com/products/Quarterly-Review-of-Distance-Education-18-3

Ribera, A. K., Miller, A. L., & Dumford, A. D. (2017). Sense of peer belonging and institutional acceptance in the first year: The role of high-impact practices. *Journal of College Student Development, 58,* 545–563. doi:10.1353/csd.2017.0042

Rovai, A. P. (2001). Building classroom community at a distance: A case study. *Educational Technology Research and Development, 49,* 33–48. doi:10.1007/BF02504946

Rubin, B., & Fernandes, R. (2013). Measuring the community in online classes. *Journal of Asynchronous Learning Network, 17,* 115–136. Retrieved from http://www.learntechlib.org/p/154172

Shelton, B. E., Hung, J.-L., & Lowenthal, P. R. (2017). Predicting student success by modeling student interaction in asynchronous online courses. *Distance Education, 38,* 59–69. doi:10.1080/01587919.2017.1299562

Simpson, O. (2003). *Student retention in online, open and distance learning.* London, England: Routledge.

Spanierman, L. B., Soble, J. R., Mayfield, J. B., Neville, H. A., Aber, M., Khuri, L., & De La Rosa, B. (2013). Living learning communities and students' sense of community and belonging. *Journal of Student Affairs Research and Practice, 50,* 308–325. doi:10.1515/jsarp-2013-0022

Steele, J. P., Robertson, S. N, & Mandernach, B. J. (2018). Beyond content: The value of instructor-student connections in the classroom. *Journal of the Scholarship of Teaching and Learning, 18*, 130–150. doi:10.14434/josotl.v18i4.23430

Strayhorn, T. L. (2012). *College students' sense of belonging: A key to educational success for all students.* New York, NY: Routledge.

Tinto, V. (1997). Colleges as communities: Exploring the educational character of student persistence. *Journal of Higher Education, 68*, 599–623. doi:10.1080/00221546.1997.11779003

Tinto, V. (2012). *Completing college: Rethinking institutional action.* Chicago, IL: University of Chicago Press.

Vaccaro, A., & Newman, B. M. (2016). Development of a sense of belonging for privileged and minoritized students: An emergent model. *Journal of College Student Development 57*, 925–942. doi:10.1353/csd.2016.0091

Zilka, G. C., Cohen, R., & Rahimi, I. D. (2018). Teacher presence and social presence in virtual and blended courses. *Journal of Information Technology Education: Research, 17*, 103–126. doi:10.28945/4061

THE AUTHORS

STEPHANIE SMITH BUDHAI is associate professor at Neumann University in the School of Education and Human Services. She has experience in a variety of student affairs functional areas, including multicultural affairs, career services, honors programming, civic engagement, residence life, counseling, and advising. She also has developed fully online graduate programs and has integrated student services into the online learner experience. Smith Budhai is author of several books and articles on online learning and technology, including *Best Practices in Engaging Online Learners Through Active and Experiential Learning Strategies* (Routledge, 2016). She received the 2017 award for Excellence in Teacher Education from the International Society for Technology in Education and is the treasurer of the Pennsylvania Association for Educational Communications and Technology. Smith Budhai holds an MEd in college student development from the University of Maryland, College Park, and a PhD in learning technologies from Drexel University.

KATHRYN P. ALESSANDRIA has been a professor of counselor education at West Chester University since 2003; prior to that she was a counselor at James Madison University. She is a past member-at-large of the American College Counseling Association (ACCA) and recipient of the 2013 ACCA College Counseling Advocacy Award and 2018 ACCA Professional Leadership Award. Alessandria has represented ACCA on the Higher Education Mental Health Alliance (HEMHA) since 2008, is a past HEMHA Chair (2012–2013), and served on the subcommittees for *College Counseling from a Distance* and a forthcoming guide on animals on campus.

COURTNEY BATTISTA BISH serves as vice president for student affairs and dean of students at the State University of New York (SUNY) at Canton. With nearly 20 years of progressive leadership in higher education, she provides leadership and vision to the college's Division of Student Affairs and has been instrumental in advocating for the needs of online learners. Battista Bish has served in various capacities throughout her career including college housing, Title IX, and student conduct. Her specialized interest in crisis response and management afforded her the opportunity to revitalize and chair the campus's Behavioral Intervention Team. She has presented at conferences throughout the Northeast on issues related to student life.

SHERRY A. BENTON is founder and chief science officer for TAO Connect, Inc. She is also Professor Emeritus in the Department of Psychology at the University of Florida. Benton has more than 25 years of clinical and research experience in counseling psychology. She has been president of the American Academy of Counseling Psychology and president of the Association of Counseling Center Training Agencies. The recipient of numerous professional awards, Benton is an American Psychological Association fellow and a diplomate in the American Academy of Counseling Psychology. Her publications have focused on college student mental health, stepped care models of service, substance use and prevention, and digital behavioral health services. Benton has delivered many presentations on adapting student affairs services to the digital world, artificial intelligence and behavioral health, telebehavioral health, and the future of psychotherapy.

CHRISTOPHER CORBETT serves as the director of counseling and student support services at SCAD, where he oversees mental health and accommodation services across the world wide SCAD campus. He has held several roles in collegiate mental health after completing postdoctoral work at the University of South Carolina. He is a past president of the American College Counseling Association and currently serves as chair-elect for the Higher Education Mental Health Alliance. As a clinical psychologist, he is an advocate for multidisciplinary approaches to clinical work and transformational work culture. He has presented on a host of topics related to college mental health and highly values collaborative relationships with his higher education peers.

ANITA CRAWLEY has served as an academic and career counselor at community colleges in Illinois and Maryland. She created and instructed various student and faculty development courses both on campus and online. Following a couple of stints directing distance learning programs, she moved to California where she consulted for the Online Education Initiative and is continuing her consulting work in the areas of online learning and student support. Crawley is the author of *Supporting Online Students: A Guide to Planning, Implementing, and Evaluating Services* (Jossey-Bass, 2012). She has also published chapters in *The Handbook of Student Affairs Administration* (Jossey-Bass, 2009, 2015) and served as co-editor for a special issue of the *Journal of Asynchronous Learning Networks* on innovative services for online learners.

MADELEINE D. FRANKFORD is a National Council on Family Relations certified family life educator and has worked closely with the University of North Alabama Office of Title IX to manage student campus climate survey data, organize Title IX programming, and facilitate Title IX/bystander intervention trainings. Frankford teaches students about the community responsibility approach to violence prevention and has become a masterful prevention educator, a tireless advocate, and a leader in the movement to end violence on the University of North Alabama campus and in the North Alabama community.

ANDREW M. GORETSKY serves as dean of students at Arcadia University. While at The George Washington University, Goretsky served as director for the GW Graduate, Distance, and Professional Student Experience, with responsibilities that involved engaging with online learners. His research focuses on student engagement and mobile technology.

MADISON L. HANSEN serves as academic integrity program director in the Office of the Dean of Students at Boise State University. In this position, she is a student conduct administrator and provides proactive education to students and faculty to help prevent incidents of academic misconduct and support the campus community in upholding academic integrity, engaging authentically with learning, and safeguarding the value of degrees. Hansen's prior experience in writing center consultation and administration, as well as teaching first-year writing, informs her approach to creating opportunities for accountability and the development of academic skills within student affairs.

ANDREW S. HERRIDGE is a PhD candidate in higher education research at Texas Tech University with a minor in women's and gender studies and a graduate certificate in e-learning and online teaching. He holds a BA in psychology and English from Florida State University and an MEd in college student affairs administration from the University of West Florida. His research interests include access and equity in higher education, LGBTQIA students and resources, institutional leadership and policy, and international higher education.

ANDREA N. HUNT is associate professor of sociology and director of the Mitchell-West Center for Social Inclusion at the University of

North Alabama. She is a violence prevention educator and delivers training on campus and in the community. Her teaching and research focuses on diverse families, race and ethnicity, gender, hip hop culture, and social justice.

LISA J. JAMES serves as associate director in the Texas Tech University (TTU) Ethics Center. In her role, James coordinates core programs, including the Southwest Regional Consortium for Academic Integrity; Global Ethics Day, an annual event partnering with Carnegie Council for Ethics in International Affairs; and TTU ethics workshops. She offers in-class presentations to undergraduate students and student organizations focusing on academic integrity and other ethical topics. Her areas of research interest are access and equity focusing on underrepresented student populations.

SUSAN R. KOMIVES is Professor Emerita in the student affairs graduate program at the University of Maryland. She is past president of ACPA–College Student Educators International and the Council for the Advancement of Standards in Higher Education and was the senior student affairs officer on two college campuses. She has published 12 books, including *Leadership for a Better World* (Jossey-Bass, 2009), *Handbook for Student Leadership Programs* (Jossey-Bass, 2011), and *Student Services: A Handbook for the Profession* (Jossey-Bass, 1996, 2003). She was on the team that developed *Learning Reconsidered* (ACPA & NASPA, 2004) and is editor of the *New Directions for Student Leadership* series. She was recognized by NASPA–Student Affairs Administrators in Higher Education with the 2019 John L. Blackburn Distinguished Pillar Award.

HILARY LANDORF is the founding executive director of the Office of Global Learning Initiatives and associate professor of international and intercultural education at Florida International University. She has written, consulted, and presented internationally on integrating global learning into higher education. Her most recent book is

Making Global Learning Universal: Promoting Inclusion and Success for All Students (Stylus, 2018).

NICOLE LONG is executive director for planning and strategy in the Division of Student Life at the University of Delaware. She has over 15 years of experience in higher education as a student affairs administrator and research analyst in institutional assessment and research offices. Long holds a BA in mathematics from DePauw University, an MEd in college student personnel from Ohio University, and a PhD in college student personnel administration and graduate certificate in measurement, statistics, and evaluation from the University of Maryland, College Park.

JON MCNAUGHTAN is an assistant professor at Texas Tech University where his research covers two critical junctures of higher education: the role and experience of college presidents, and the role of community colleges in enhancing the STEM pipeline. He hopes to answer questions on the role of community colleges in the production of STEM professionals and provide insight on how community colleges can better support students in these fields. McNaughtan holds a PhD with a focus on organizational behavior from the University of Michigan.

MOLLY A. MOTT is associate provost and dean of academic support services and instructional technologies at the State University of New York (SUNY) at Canton. With extensive experience in student and academic affairs, Mott has overseen the expansion of services for online learners and enhanced the university's reputation as a leader in supporting student success in both virtual and traditional environments. She has presented at state, regional, national, and international conferences on distance learning and leads efforts across the university system to promote student access and completion.

ARIELLE NORMENT is assistant dean of the business and technology division for the Community College of Philadelphia and an adjunct professor for Southern New Hampshire University. Having served as a student affairs professional for more than eight years, Normet has significant experience in student development, student support, recruitment, academic counseling, and academic advising. She holds a BS in child development and family relations from Indiana University of Pennsylvania and an MS in higher education administration with a concentration in student development and affairs from Drexel University.

MONICA OSBURN is executive director of the Counseling Center and Prevention Services at North Carolina State University. Prior to NC State, she was director of the Counseling Center at The University of North Carolina at Pembroke for 10 years. She is a past president of the American College Counseling Association and member of the Association for University and College Counseling Center Directors (AUCCCD), where she was most recently recognized as an AUCCCD Lifetime Achievement Award winner in 2018 and Director of the Year in 2017. As a licensed professional counselor, Osburn believes in a multidisciplinary approach to college counseling. She is an advocate for comprehensive counseling centers and has presented on a multitude of college counseling issues.

BONNIE PETERS is chief student services officer and director of student experience for the California Virtual Campus–Online Education Initiative. Prior to 2014, Peters spent 15 years at San Diego City College, where she counseled and taught students both on campus and online. Throughout her career, she has provided leadership in a variety of student services. In 2005, she developed the college's online counseling program, a first among community colleges, both regionally and nationally. She holds an MS in counseling and an MA in teaching and learning with technology. Her current professional endeavors include encouraging colleges and universities to intentionally provide support services as an integral part of distance education programs, primarily via a one-stop online student support center/hub.

JASMINE POSEY is a career advisor at the Georgia Institute of Technology. In this role she provides career guidance to students in the College of Computing. Posey has over five years of professional experience providing services within hospitals, schools, shelters, and universities. She holds a BS in psychology from Valdosta State University and an MS in clinical mental health counseling from Mercer University

L. BAHIA SIMONS–LANE is the executive director of the U.S. Japan Exchange and Teaching (JET) Programme Alumni Association, which furthers U.S.-Japan relations by supporting alumni of the JET Program. Simons-Lane's dissertation research focuses on the global perspective of undergraduates at Florida International University (FIU). Her past research has looked at the perspectives of Japanese students after study abroad in English-speaking countries, the history of the Comparative and International Education Society, and on global learning programs at FIU.

JEANNETTE SMITH is director of student activities and the College Activities Building at Evergreen State College. As a scholar-practitioner with 15 years of work experience in higher education, her research interests include policy, equity, financial aid, and student development. As a first-generation woman of color, Smith has a passion for supporting students of marginalized identities.

MATT SMITH is the homeless student stability program supervisor for the State of Washington, Office of Superintendent of Public Instruction. He previously served as director of the Center for Academic Support and Achievement and Multi-Ethnic and Cultural

Affairs at Tacoma Community College. His research interests include antiracist policy and practice to close equity gaps and the role of mentoring in college access and success.

KRISTIN SOWDEN is an associate director of career advising in the School of Arts and Sciences at the University of Pennsylvania. She is a proud first-generation college student and is completing her PhD in strategic leadership with a concentration in organizational science from James Madison University.

DEBORAH J. TAUB is a professor and chair of the Department of Student Affairs Administration at Binghamton University. She has over 20 years of experience as a faculty member in student affairs administration. Prior to coming to Binghamton University, she taught at Purdue University and the University of North Carolina at Greensboro. Taub is a member of the editorial board of the *Journal of Student Affairs Research and Practice* and was a directorate member of ACPA's Coalition for Women's Identities. She has been recognized frequently for her scholarship and teaching, including ACUHO-I's Research and Publication Award, NASPA's Robert H. Shaffer Award for Academic Excellence as a Graduate Faculty Member, ACPA Diamond Honoree, and ACPA's Annuit Coeptis Senior Professional Award.

ANNALISA TEIXEIRA serves as director of resident and fellow development at the University of California, Davis School of Medicine. She previously developed and coordinated success coaching and learning strategies at UC Davis, Division of Student Affairs. She holds a PhD in Spanish from UC Davis, with a background in second language acquisition, cognitive learning science, and educational technology.

MELISSA M. VITO serves as interim vice provost for academic innovation at The University of Texas at San Antonio, where she is helping to lead the development of online programs and digital fluency. She founded Melissa Vito Strategy Group, a consulting firm specializing in supporting colleges and universities in envisioning and implementing online programs. She also serves as a thought leader with Adobe and is a frequent speaker on a variety of student affairs topics, digital fluency, career-related issues, and online learning. The recipient of numerous professional awards, Vito retired from a distinguished career at the University of Arizona, where she held positions as senior vice president for student affairs and enrollment management and senior vice provost for academic initiatives and student success, as well as leading the strategy and development of online programs. She holds a bachelor's degree in journalism and English, and two master's degrees in higher education administration and counseling from the University of Arizona; and a doctorate in educational leadership from Northern Arizona University.

CHRISTIAN K. WUTHRICH serves as dean of students at Boise State University. In this role, he advocates for student needs, promotes accountability, works to encourage student engagement in the university, and serves as a resource for the campus community. Wuthrich's experience in higher education and the student affairs field includes serving as a fraternity and sorority affairs advisor, alcohol abuse and drug use prevention educator, student conduct administrator, and a faculty member in higher education administration.

J.L. WYATT earned her PhD in higher education leadership from Mercer University in 2014. She has served in various student affairs leadership roles such as director of career services and director of admissions processing to academic leadership roles such as assistant vice president of academic records. Wyatt currently serves as faculty at Southern New Hampshire University and Grand Canyon University. Her research interests include engaging online learners, higher education policy, and access and retention for underrepresented populations.

Index